Mrs Ba...
THE·DROVER
AND·OTHER·VERSES

The Ballad of THE·DROVER
AND·OTHER·VERSES

HENRY LAWSON

ANGUS & ROBERTSON PUBLISHERS

*Unit 4, Eden Park, 31 Waterloo Road,
North Ryde, NSW, Australia 2113, and
16 Golden Square, London W1R 4BN,
United Kingdom*

*This book is copyright.
Apart from any fair dealing for the
purposes of private study, research,
criticism or review, as permitted
under the Copyright Act, no part may
be reproduced by any process without
written permission. Inquiries should
be addressed to the publishers.*

*First published in Australia
by Angus & Robertson Publishers in 1918
as* Poetical Works of Henry Lawson
*Reprinted 1973, 1974, 1976, 1979, 1980
This edition 1988*

Copyright © *This selection and presentation
Angus & Robertson Publishers 1918*

*National Library of Australia
Cataloguing-in-publication data.*

*Lawson, Henry, 1867-1922.
    The ballad of the drover and other verses.*

    ISBN 0 207 15887 8.

    I. Title. II. Title: Poetical works of Henry Lawson.

A821'.2

*Printed in Australia
by Australian Print Group*

PREFACE

The death of Henry Lawson marked the close of the period in Australian literature which began with Henry Kendall. While living, Lawson had many imitators, but no peers; with his death we turned a page to which there can be no additions. He belonged to a past of struggle, pain, and triumph, when the country was in the making. Others will use those days to give their work background of colour and romance; but there can be none to walk where he walked, none to see with his eyes.

To say that Henry Lawson has now become a classic is to miss the real meaning of the man. The true student can never ignore his work, but his appeal is infinitely wider. With every decade that appeal must increase; for, reading Lawson, our children's children will hear the living voice of those who laid the foundations of all they prize and love.

About Henry Lawson the man, as distinct from the poet, a tradition will grow up which may leave the future wondering. All that is bizarre and grotesque, culled from the half-memories of those who knew him least, will make an embroidery of literary gossip which may envelop him in a mystery as interesting as it is unreal. Little things will be dragged from their hiding, big things warped from their setting, and made to subserve the meaner issues of some controversy about his doings and his ways. To this the memory of all great men is subject; too often the prophet's ragged robe is more interesting to slight minds than the message he spoke. But Lawson will outlive it all. When the last word of praise or dispraise is spoken, men will turn to his work and find the real man there, the brother-soul with the vision, the brother-heart with the passion of goodwill for his kind.

This edition of his poems brings them within easy reach of every Australian reader; and I think the man who has gone from us could seek no fairer memorial in the hearts of his people than the knowledge that his words are being read and re-read by those who with every reading love him more.

DAVID McKEE WRIGHT.

March 1925.

INTRODUCTION

When James Cook lifted the veil that so long had masked the *terra incognita* of the south, a fresh breeze of adventure blew across the souls of Englishmen. Here for conquest were virgin lands—lands with no history, no legend of achievement or shame—and needing for their conquest no sword, but only strong hearts and an enduring purpose. Men might have seen in their dreams a wider, sweeter England rising as by magic over far oceans, free of fettering old-world traditions, a source of light and leading to all. To claim that such a vision has been realized would be as yet too much; but the foundations have been laid. The wide spaces of the Australian continent are developing a race British in fibre and texture, yet unlike the peoples of Britain in every mere external. It is hard to discern the heights to which this race may attain in the brave days yet to be; but a nation in the making is always an object of supreme interest. Processes that in the days of the Heptarchy moulded Kent and Yorkshire are even now moulding Tasmania and Queensland. It was inevitable that such a race in the making, such a land in the shaping, should find its singer; and that, the singer found, his music should be different from that of all others.

Henry Lawson is the first articulate voice of the real Australia. Other singers in plenty the southern continent knows and has known—men and women following bravely in the broad pathway where Byron strode and Wordsworth loitered; but one alone has found the heart of the new land, its rugged strength, its impatience of old restraints, its hopes and fears and despairs, its irreverence and grim humour, and the tenderness and courage that underlie them all. Lawson is never exquisite as are our greater lyrists. The axe-marks show in his work everywhere. But he is sincere and strong and true; and the living beauty in that sincerity and strength and truth grips us more than any delicate craftsmanship. His laughter is as genuine as that of the wind and the sea; he weeps as Australians of the bush weep, with dry eyes and a hard curving mouth. He knows men and women—his men and women. In the world's loneliest places he has grasped hard hands alive with heroic meaning; in crowded cities, where the shames of older nations have overflowed into the new, he has felt the throb of emotions too fine for civilization's sordid setting. In Lawson, too, there is a splendid scorn—the scorn of the Things-that-Are—and always as he looks into the eyes of his world, seeking the best in the worst, his indignation blazes against the shams and the shows that have been brought across the seas to hold Liberty from her purpose. Lawson has lived his people's life, seen with their eyes, felt throb for throb with them in pain and joy; and he sets it all to a rugged music of his own that goes straight to the heart.

When in April 1915, Australians made the historic landing at Gaba Tepe, the unexpectant world saw young soldiers from a peaceful Commonwealth bearing themselves in the stress of war like veterans of the older fighting nations. The spectacle arrested and surprised. But Lawson had sung of these things more than twenty years before. Nothing that Australians did in Gallipoli, or later in the fields of France, was new or strange to those who remembered the bugle note of his early poems. With prophetic insight he had dreamed a people's dream—had felt in that soldier-heart of his early manhood the tremor of a coming tempest, though the world skies were then clear—and had foreknown with every fibre of his being the way in which men of the bush and the mountain and plain would respond to the battle-call.

What of the man who has done and felt these things? He lives his life in Australia still*—a life very close to ours, yet remote and lonely as that of genius is wont to be. London called to him, and he left us for a while, but came back more Australian than when he went away. You meet him in the street and are arrested by his eyes. Are there such eyes anywhere else under such a forehead? He has the softened speech of the deaf, but the eyes speak always more than the voice; and the grasp of his hand is brotherly. A sense of great sympathy and human kindliness is always about him. You will not talk much with Lawson, but you will not lightly forget your first meeting. A child will understand him better than a busy city man, for the child understands the eternal language of the heart written in the eye; and Australia, strong-thewed pioneer though she be, has enough of the child left in her to understand her son.

Henry Lawson was born in a tent on the Grenfell goldfield in 1867. His father was a Norse sailor who became a digger; his mother came of a Kentish family of gipsy blood and tradition. Henry spent his boyhood on old mining fields, and on a selection his father had taken up. Later, he came to Sydney and learned coach-painting, attended a night school, dabbled in hypnotism, and was caught in the wave of socialism. Very early his verses attracted attention. He was the voice of a new movement; the ringing, surging

* This was written in 1918.

rebellion of his song echoed the unrest of the eighties and nineties, years full of great labour strikes and the breaking up of old political parties. Then he wandered far into the interior of Australia—his fame growing all the while—saw and shared the rude strenuous life of his brothers in a dozen varieties of toil, crossed over to New Zealand, and added to the tang of the gum-leaves something of the salt of the great Southern ocean. He has lived the life that he sings, and seen the places of which he writes; there is not a word in all his work which is not instantly recognized by his readers as honest Australian. The drover, the stockman, the shearer, the rider far on the skyline, the girl waiting at the sliprails, the big bush funeral, the coach with flashing lamps passing at night along the ranges, the man to whom home is a bitter memory and his future a long despair, the troops marching to the beat of the drum, the coasting vessel struggling through blinding gales, the great grey plain, the wilderness of the Never-Never—in long procession the pictures pass, and every picture is a true one because Henry Lawson has been there to see with the eyes of his heart.

At twenty-one, Lawson was probably the most remarkable writer of verse in Australia. Some critics of those days thought his genius prematurely developed, and likely to flame up strongly and fade away swiftly. Lawson disappointed their predictions. He remained; he continued to write; he gathered grip and force as the years went by. His verses cover a wide range of years. Before he had reached his twenty-first birthday, Lawson, keenly alive to all the movements about him in Sydney, found one political faction discussing a closer imperialism of a rather mechanical pattern, while another cried for an equally machine-made socialism. He listened to the outpourings of oratory one night, and, remembering the growth of wealth and luxury on the one hand and the increasing squalor of the city slums on the other, went home and wrote "Faces in the Street"—a notable achievement that brought him immediate local fame. Seven years afterwards, still with the passionate hope of a purifying revolution in his heart, he saw "The Star of Australasia" rise through tumult and battle smoke, and foretold, in lines that surge and sweep, the storm that was to break down divisions between rich and poor and to call to life a great nationhood through a baptism of blood. At forty-eight he sang of "My Army, O My Army", the struggling "Vanguard" always suffering in the trenches of civilization that others might go on to victory. Never was the view of the final triumph obscured; but the means by which it might be attained seemed more clouded in doubt as the years went by. Then, when he had completed his full half-century of life, the poet's vision cleared. At fifty he wrote "England Yet", a song of pride in a greater nationality, wider and more embracing than the old Australia of his dreams. Here is natural progression of thought—a mind growing with the years, a hope enlarging with the great movements of the race.

In simpler and homelier themes the continual widening of his sympathy is equally marked. "The Drover's Sweetheart", with its sob of delight in the last stanza, was written at twenty-two. Ten years afterwards he penned the tenderest and most perfect of all his poems, "The Sliprails and the Spur". Dear old "Black Bonnet" —a picture as true as it is sweet in all years and all places—first tripped to church in his verse when he was forty-nine; at fifty, "Scots of the Riverina" showed that he had not lost his power of dealing with the tragedy that underlies life's commonplace. The reader may trace a similar growth of sympathy for the men and women whom civilization condemns, or who have come to be regarded as "down and out". He saw "Sweeney" with battered humorous face and empty bottle in 1891; "Past Carin'", with its completeness of heartbreak, was written in 1899; and the grim realism of "One-Hundred-and-Three", which must stand among Lawson's greatest efforts, appeared in 1908. Always there is growth, apparent from year to year and decade to decade. The verses vary greatly in merit and manner, but the thought and feeling behind them move on into wider places. Lawson fulfilled his first promise and did something more.

Of Lawson's place in literature it is idle to speak. Something of what Burns did for Scotland, something of what Kipling did for India, he has done for Australia; but he is not in the least like either Kipling or Burns. Judged as verse, his work has nearly always a certain crudity; judged by the higher standard of poetry, it is often greatest when the crudity is most apparent. In the coming chances and changes it is daring to predict immortality for any writer. The world is being remade in fire and pain; in that remaking every standard of achievement may be altered utterly from those to which we have been accustomed; but, if permanency is to be looked for anywhere, it is in vital, red-blooded work such as Lawson's—work that came so straight from the heart that it must always find a heart to respond to it. All Australia is there, painted with a big brush in the colours in which its people see it.

D. M. W.

September 1918.

CONTENTS

The Sliprails and the Spur 1	The Teams 49
The Star of Australasia 2	When the World was Wide 50
Faces in the Street 5	The Light on the Wreck 53
The Wander-Light 8	The Great Grey Plain 53
The Roaring Days 9	Scots of the Riverina 55
The Vagabond 11	Out Back 55
Since Then 14	The Drover's Sweetheart 57
Sweeney 16	The Southerly Buster 59
The Blue Mountains 17	Written Afterwards 60
Past Carin' 18	England Yet 61
Sydney-Side 20	Ballad of the Drover 62
Dan the Wreck 21	After All 64
Jack Dunn of Nevertire 23	Black Bonnet 65
Ports of the Open Sea 25	The Vanguard 68
Taking His Chance 27	My Army, O My Army! 68
To Jim 28	Rain in the Mountains 70
The Lights of Cobb & Co. 30	Talbragar 70
Middleton's Rouseabout 31	The Shakedown on the Floor . . 72
One-Hundred-And-Three 32	Peter Anderson & Co. 73
Bertha 36	The Song and the Sigh 77
On the Night Train 37	Trooper Campbell 77
The Shearing-Shed 38	The Route March 81
The Glass on the Bar 39	Ballad of the Elder Son 81
Reedy River 40	Knocked Up 85
A New John Bull 42	The Never-never Land 86
Ballad of the Rouseabout 43	The Jolly Dead March 87
Andy's Gone with Cattle 44	Kiss in the Ring 89
Bill 45	For'ard 90
Mallacoota Bar 47	To an Old Mate 92
When Your Pants Begin to Go . . 48	Says You 93

Andy's Return	94
Song of the Old Bullock-Driver	95
I'm a Rebel Too	97
Song of the Darling River	98
The Good Samaritan	99
To Hannah	102
Shearers	103
The Army of the Rear	104
New-chum Jackeroos	105
The Cambaroora Star	106
The Water-Lily	110
Tracks that Lie by India	111
New Life, New Love	112
May Night on the Mountains	112
The Captains	113
A Voice from the City	114
Cameron's Heart	115
Genoa	117
Eureka	118
Knocking Around	120
The Bush Fire	121
The Drunkard's Vision	123
Dons of Spain	124
The Cattle-dog's Death	125
Second Class Wait Here	126
The Outside Track	127
The Storm That is to Come	128
Men We Might Have Been	130
Booth's Drum	131
Mount Bukaroo	133
Bourke	134
Sticking to Bill	136
Drums of Battersea	137
The Wreck of the Derry Castle	139
Ruth	140
To My Cultured Critics	149
Pigeon Toes	150
The Battling Days	153
The Fire at Ross's Farm	154
The Shame of Going Back	157
Farewell to the Bushmen	158
Break O'Day	158
Cross-Roads	159
Men Who Come Behind	160
Riding Round the Lines	161
The Christ of the Never	162
A Prouder Man Than You	163
From the Bush	164
The Separation	165
Cherry-Tree Inn	166
Foreign Lands	166
Passing of Scotty	168
The Three Kings	169
Rovers	170
The Bush Girl	172
Marshall's Mate	173
The Old Jimmy Woodser	175
Waratah and Wattle	176
Australian Engineers	177
Eurunderee	178
Do You Think that I Do Not Know	179
The Ghost	180
The Last Review	181

The Old Bark School 184	When the Army Prays for Watty 236
Paroo River 185	After the War 237
Billy's Square Affair 187	As Good as New 240
The Boss-Over-the-Board 188	The King, The Queen and I .. 241
Robbie's Statue 189	The Shearer's Dream 242
Tambaroora Jim 191	Foreign Engineers 243
Rejected 192	The Free-Selector's Daughter.. 244
O'Hara, J.P. 193	The Shanty on the Rise 245
Bill and Jim Fall Out 196	Poets of the Tomb 247
Ballad of Mabel Clare 197	Grog-An'-Grumble Steeplechase 248
The Strangers' Friend 200	Hawkers 249
The Captain of the Push 202	Bursting of the Boom 250
Corny Bill................ 204	The Greenhand Rouseabout .. 251
Mary Called Him Mister 206	His Majesty's Garden Spade.. 253
Up the Country 207	Sign of the Old Black Eye 254
Days When We Went Swimming 208	Australian Bards and Bush Reviewers 256
Ripperty! Kye! Ahoo! 209	Song of the Back to Front 257
Rise Ye! Rise Ye! 211	Because of Her Father's Blood. 258
Song of Old Joe Swallow 212	When There's Trouble on Your Mind.................. 261
Here's Luck 214	My Literary Friend 262
With Dickens 215	Dogs of War 263
Professional Wanderers 221	But What's the Use 265
Saint Peter 222	Song of General Sick-and-Tiredness 266
A Word to Texas Jack 223	
Down the River 225	
The City Bushman 226	
Trouble on the Selection 229	
The Fourth Cook 230	
The Old Head Nurse 231	
Jack Cornstalk 235	
Write it Down for Me 236	

THE SLIPRAILS AND THE SPUR

The colours of the setting sun
   Withdrew across the Western land—
He raised the sliprails, one by one,
   And shot them home with trembling hand;
Her brown hands clung—her face grew pale—
   Ah! quivering chin and eyes that brim!—
One quick, fierce kiss across the rail,
   And, "Good-bye, Mary!" "Good-bye, Jim!"

Oh, he rides hard to race the pain
   Who rides from love, who rides from home;
But he rides slowly home again,
   Whose heart has learnt to love and roam.

A hand upon the horse's mane,
   And one foot in the stirrup set,
And, stooping back to kiss again,
   With "Good-bye, Mary! don't you fret!
When I come back"—he laughed for her—
   "We do not know how soon 'twill be;
I'll whistle as I round the spur—
   You let the sliprails down for me."

She gasped for sudden loss of hope,
   As, with a backward wave to her,
He cantered down the grassy slope
   And swiftly round the darkening spur.
Black-pencilled panels standing high,
   And darkness fading into stars,
And, blurring fast against the sky,
   A faint white form beside the bars.

And often at the set of sun,
   In winter bleak and summer brown,
She'd steal across the little run,
   And shyly let the sliprails down,
And listen there when darkness shut
   The nearer spur in silence deep,
And when they called her from the hut
   Steal home and cry herself to sleep.

And he rides hard to dull the pain
  Who rides from one that loves him best...
And he rides slowly back again,
  Whose restless heart must rove for rest.

THE STAR OF AUSTRALASIA

We boast no more of our bloodless flag that rose from a nation's slime;
Better a shred of a deep-dyed rag from the storms of the olden time.
From grander clouds in our peaceful skies than ever were there before
I tell you the Star of the South shall rise—in the lurid clouds of war.
It ever must be while blood is warm and the sons of men increase;
For ever the nations rose in storm, to rot in a deadly peace.
There'll come a point that we will not yield, no matter if right or wrong;
And man will fight on the battle-field while passion and pride are strong—
So long as he will not kiss the rod, and his stubborn spirit sours—
For the scorn of Nature and curse of God are heavy on peace like ours.

    .   .   .   .   .

There are boys out there by the western creeks, who hurry away from school
To climb the sides of the breezy peaks or dive in the shaded pool,
Who'll stick to their guns when the mountains quake to the tread of a mighty war,
And fight for Right or a Grand Mistake as men never fought before;
When the peaks are scarred and the sea-walls crack till the farthest hills vibrate,
And the world for a while goes rolling back in a storm of love and hate.

    .   .   .   .   .

There are boys today in the city slum and the home of wealth and pride
Who'll have one home when the storm is come, and fight for it side by side,

Who'll hold the cliffs against armoured hells that batter a coastal town,
Or grimly die in a hail of shells when the walls come crashing down.
And many a pink-white baby girl, the queen of her home today,
Will see the wings of the tempest whirl the mist of our dawn away—
Will live to shudder and stop her ears to the thud of the distant gun,
And know the sorrow that has no tears when a battle is lost and won—
As a mother or wife in the years to come will kneel, wide-eyed and white,
And pray to God in her darkened home for the "men in the fort tonight".

．　．　．　．　．　．　．

But, oh! if the cavalry charge again as they did when the world was wide,
'Twill be grand in the ranks of a thousand men in that glorious race to ride,
And strike for all that is true and strong, for all that is grand and brave,
And all that ever shall be, so long as man has a soul to save.
He must lift the saddle, and close his "wings", and shut his angels out,
And steel his heart for the end of things, who'd ride with a stockman scout,
When the race they ride on the battle-track, and the waning distance hums,
When the shelled sky shrieks, and the rifles crack like stockwhips amongst the gums—
And the straight is reached and the field is gapped and the hoof-torn sward grows red
With the blood of those who are handicapped with iron and steel and lead;
And the gaps are filled, though unseen by eyes, with the spirit and with the shades
Of the world-wide rebel dead who'll rise and rush with the Bush Brigades.

．　．　．　．　．

All creeds and trades will have soldiers there—give every class
    its due—
And there'll be many a clerk to spare for the pride of the jackeroo.
They'll fight for honour and fight for love, and a few will fight
    for gold,
For the devil below and for God above, as our fathers fought
    of old;
And some half-blind with exultant tears, and some stiff-lipped,
    stern-eyed,
For the pride of a thousand after-years and the old eternal pride,
The soul of the world they will feel and see in the chase and the
    grim retreat—
They'll know the glory of victory—and the grandeur of defeat.
The South will wake to a mighty change ere a hundred years
    are done
With arsenals west of the mountain range and every spur its gun.
And many a rickety son of a gun, on the tides of the future
    tossed,
Will tell how battles were really won that History says were lost,
Will trace the field with his pipe, and shirk the facts that are
    hard to explain,
As grey old mates of the diggings work the old ground over again—
How "This was our centre, and this a redoubt, and that was a
    scrub in the rear,
And this was the point where the Guards held out, and the
    enemy's lines were here."

    .   .   .   .   .   .

They'll tell the tales of the nights before and the tales of the ship
    and fort
Till the sons of Australia take to war as their fathers took to sport,
Till their breath comes deep and their eyes grow bright at the
    tales of our chivalry
And every boy will want to fight, nor care what the cause may be—
When the children run to the doors and cry: "Oh, mother, the
    troops are come!"
And every heart in the town leaps high at the first loud thud
    of the drum.
They'll know, apart from its mystic charm, what music is at last,
When, proud as a boy with a broken arm, the regiment marches
    past.
And the veriest wreck in the drink-fiend's clutch, no matter how
    low or mean,
Will feel, when he hears that march, a touch of the man that he
    might have been.

And fools, when the fiends of war are out and the city skies aflame,
Will have something better to talk about than an absent woman's shame,
Will have something nobler to do by far than jest at a friend's expense.
Or blacken a name in a public bar or over a backyard fence.
And this we learn from the libelled past, though its methods were somewhat rude—
A Nation's born where the shells fall fast, or its lease of life renewed.
We in part atone for the ghoulish strife and the crimes of the peace we boast,
And the better part of a people's life in the storm comes uppermost.

The selfsame spirit that drives a man to the depths of drink and crime
Will do the deeds in the heroes' van that live till the end of time.
The living death in the lonely bush, the greed of the selfish town,
And even the creed of the outlawed push is chivalry—upside down.
'Twill be while ever our blood is hot, while ever the world goes wrong,
The nations rise in a war, to rot in a peace that lasts too long.
And southern Nation and southern State, aroused from their dream of ease
Must sign in the Book of Eternal Fate their stormy histories.

1895

FACES IN THE STREET

They lie, the men who tell us, for reasons of their own,
That want is here a stranger, and that misery's unknown;
For where the nearest suburb and the city proper meet
My window-sill is level with the faces in the street—
   Drifting past, drifting past,
   To the beat of weary feet—
While I sorrow for the owners of those faces in the street.

And cause I have to sorrow, in a land so young and fair,
To see upon those faces stamped the marks of Want and Care;
I look in vain for traces of the fresh and fair and sweet
In sallow, sunken faces that are drifting through the street—
   Drifting on, drifting on,
   To the scrape of restless feet;
I can sorrow for the owners of the faces in the street.

In hours before the dawning dims the starlight in the sky
The wan and weary faces first begin to trickle by,
Increasing as the moments hurry on with morning feet,
Till like a pallid river flow the faces in the street—
        Flowing in, flowing in,
        To the beat of hurried feet—
Ah! I sorrow for the owners of those faces in the street.

The human river dwindles when 'tis past the hour of eight,
Its waves go flowing faster in the fear of being late;
But slowly drag the moments, whilst beneath the dust and heat
The city grinds the owners of the faces in the street—
        Grinding body, grinding soul,
        Yielding scarce enough to eat—
Oh! I sorrow for the owners of the faces in the street.

And then the only faces till the sun is sinking down
Are those of outside toilers and the idlers of the town,
Save here and there a face that seems a stranger in the street
Tells of the city's unemployed upon their weary beat—
        Drifting round, drifting round,
        To the tread of listless feet—
Ah! my heart aches for the owner of that sad face in the street.

And when the hours on lagging feet have slowly dragged away,
And sickly yellow gaslights rise to mock the going day,
Then, flowing past my window, like a tide in its retreat,
Again I see the pallid stream of faces in the street—
        Ebbing out, ebbing out,
        To the drag of tired feet,
While my heart is aching dumbly for the faces in the street.

And now all blurred and smirched with vice the day's sad end is seen,
For where the short "large hours" against the longer "small hours" lean,
With smiles that mock the wearer, and with words that half entreat,
Delilah pleads for custom at the corner of the street—
        Sinking down, sinking down,
        Battered wreck by tempests beat—
A dreadful, thankless trade is hers, that Woman of the Street.

But, ah! to dreader things than these our fair young city comes,
For in its heart are growing thick the filthy dens and slums,
Where human forms shall rot away in sties for swine unmeet
And ghostly faces shall be seen unfit for any street—
                Rotting out, rotting out,
                For the lack of air and meat—
In dens of vice and horror that are hidden from the street.

I wonder would the apathy of wealthy men endure
Were all their windows level with the faces of the Poor?
Ah! Mammon's slaves, your knees shall knock, your hearts in terror beat,
When God demands a reason for the sorrows of the street,
                The wrong things and the bad things
                And the sad things that we meet
In the filthy lane and alley, and the cruel, heartless street.

I left the dreadful corner where the steps are never still,
And sought another window overlooking gorge and hill;
But when the night came dreary with the driving rain and sleet,
They haunted me—the shadows of those faces in the street,
                Flitting by, flitting by,
                Flitting by with noiseless feet,
And with cheeks that scarce were paler than the real ones in the street.

Once I cried: "O God Almighty! if Thy might doth still endure,
Now show me in a vision for the wrongs of Earth a cure."
And, lo, with shops all shuttered I beheld a city's street,
And in the warning distance heard the tramp of many feet,
                Coming near, coming near,
                To a drum's dull distant beat—
'Twas Despair's conscripted army that was marching down the street!

Then, like a swollen river that has broken bank and wall,
The human flood came pouring with the red flags over all,
And kindled eyes all blazing bright with revolution's heat,
And flashing swords reflecting rigid faces in the street—
                Pouring on, pouring on,
                To a drum's loud threatening beat,
And the war-hymns and the cheering of the people in the street.

And so it must be while the world goes rolling round its course,
The warning pen shall write in vain, the warning voice grow hoarse,
For not until a city feels Red Revolution's feet
Shall its sad people miss awhile the terrors of the street—
        The dreadful, everlasting strife
        For scarcely clothes and meat
In that pent track of living death—the city's cruel street.

THE WANDER-LIGHT

Oh, my ways are strange ways and new ways and old ways,
  And deep ways and steep ways and high ways and low;
I'm at home and at ease on a track that I know not
  And restless and lost on a road that I know.

      Then they heard the tent-poles clatter,
        And the fly in twain was torn—
      'Twas the soiled rag of a tatter
        Of the tent where I was born.
      Does it matter? Which is stranger—
        Brick or stone or calico?—
      There was One born in a manger
        Nineteen hundred years ago.

For my beds were camp beds and tramp beds and damp beds,
And my beds were dry beds on drought-stricken ground,
Hard beds and soft beds, and wide beds and narrow—
For my beds were strange beds the wide world round.

      And the old hag seemed to ponder
        With her grey head nodding slow—
      "He will dream, and he will wander
        Where but few would think to go.
      He will flee the haunts of tailors,
        He will cross the ocean wide,
      For his fathers they were sailors—
        All on his good father's side."

I rest not, 'tis best not, the world is a wide one—
And, caged for a moment, I pace to and fro;
I see things and dree things and plan while I'm sleeping,
I wander for ever and dream as I go.

  And the old hag she was troubled
   As she bent above the bed;
  "He will dream things and he'll see things
   To come true when he is dead.
  He will see things all too plainly,
   And his fellows will deride,
  For his mothers they were gipsies—
   All on his good mother's side."

And my dreams are strange dreams, are day dreams, are grey dreams,
And my dreams are wild dreams, and old dreams and new;
They haunt me and daunt me with fears of the morrow—
My brothers they doubt me—but my dreams come true.

THE ROARING DAYS

  The night too quickly passes
   And we are growing old,
  So let us fill our glasses
   And toast the Days of Gold;
  When finds of wondrous treasure
   Set all the South ablaze,
  And you and I were faithful mates
   All through the Roaring Days!

  Then stately ships came sailing
   From every harbour's mouth,
  And sought the Land of Promise
   That beaconed in the South;
  Then southward streamed their streamers
   And swelled their canvas full
  To speed the wildest dreamers
   E'er borne in vessel's hull.

  Their shining Eldorado
   Beneath the southern skies
  Was day and night for ever
   Before their eager eyes.
  The brooding bush, awakened,
   Was stirred in wild unrest,
  And all the year a human stream
   Went pouring to the West.

The rough bush roads re-echoed
　　The bar-room's noisy din,
When troops of stalwart horsemen
　　Dismounted at the inn.
And oft the hearty greetings
　　And hearty clasp of hands
Would tell of sudden meetings
　　Of friends from other lands.

And when the cheery camp-fire
　　Explored the bush with gleams,
The camping-grounds were crowded
　　With caravans of teams;
Then home the jests were driven,
　　And good old songs were sung,
And choruses were given
　　The strength of heart and lung.

Oft when the camps were dreaming,
　　And fires began to pale,
Through rugged ranges gleaming
　　Swept on the Royal Mail.
Behind six foaming horses,
　　And lit by flashing lamps,
Old Cobb and Co., in royal state,
　　Went dashing past the camps.

Oh, who would paint a goldfield,
　　And paint the picture right,
As old Adventure saw it
　　In early morning's light?
The yellow mounds of mullock
　　With spots of red and white,
The scattered quartz that glistened
　　Like diamonds in light;

The azure line of ridges,
　　The bush of darkest green,
The little homes of calico
　　That dotted all the scene.
The flat straw hats, with ribands.
　　That old engravings show—
The dress that still reminds us
　　Of sailors, long ago.

I hear the fall of timber
   From distant flats and fells,
The pealing of the anvils
   As clear as little bells,
The rattle of the cradle,
   The clack of windlass-boles,
The flutter of the crimson flags
   Above the golden holes.

Ah, then their hearts were bolder,
   And if Dame Fortune frowned
Their swags they'd lightly shoulder
   And tramp to other ground.
Oh, they were lion-hearted
   Who gave our country birth!
Stout sons, of stoutest fathers born,
   From all the lands on earth!

Those golden days are vanished,
   And altered is the scene;
The diggings are deserted,
   The camping-grounds are green;
The flaunting flag of progress
   Is in the West unfurled,
The mighty Bush with iron rails
   Is tethered to the world.

THE VAGABOND

WHITE handkerchiefs wave from the short black pier
   As we glide to the grand old sea—
But the song of my heart is for none to hear
   If none of them waves for me.
A careless roaming life is mine,
   Ever by field or flood—
For not far back in my father's line
   Was a dash of the Gipsy blood.

Flax and tussock and fern,
   Gum and mulga and sand,
Reef and palm—but my fancies turn
   Ever away from land;

Strange wild cities in ancient state,
  Range and river and tree,
Snow and ice. But my star of fate
  Is ever across the sea.

A god-like ride on a thundering sea
  When all but the stars are blind—
A desperate race from Eternity
  With a gale-and-a-half behind.
A jovial spree in the cabin at night,
  A song on the rolling deck,
A lark ashore with the ships in sight,
  Till—a wreck goes down with a wreck.

A smoke and a yarn on the deck by day,
  When life is a waking dream,
And care and trouble so far away
  That out of your life they seem.
A roving spirit in sympathy,
  Who has travelled the whole world o'er—
My heart forgets, in a week at sea,
  The trouble of years on shore.

A rolling stone—'tis a saw for slaves—
  Philosophy false as old—
Wear out or break 'neath the feet of knaves,
  Or rot in your bed of mould!
But I'd rather trust to the darkest skies
  And the wildest seas that roar,
Or die, where the stars of Nations rise,
  In the stormy clouds of war.

Cleave to your country, home and friends,
  Die in the sordid strife—
You can count your friends on your finger ends
  In the critical hours of life.
Sacrifice all for the family's sake,
  Bow to their selfish rule!
Slave till your big soft heart they break—
  The heart of the "family fool".

I've never a love that can sting my pride,
  Nor a friend to prove untrue;
For I leave my love ere the turning tide,
  And my friends are all too new.

The curse of the Powers on a peace like ours,
    With its greed and its treachery—
A stranger's hand, and a stranger-land,
    And the rest of the world for me!

But why be bitter? The world is cold
    To one with a frozen heart;
New friends are often so like the old,
    They seem of the Past a part—
As a better part of the past appears,
    When enemies, parted long,
Are come together in kinder years,
    With their better nature strong.

I had a friend, ere my first ship sailed,
    A friend I never deserved—
For the selfish strain in my blood prevailed
    As soon as my turn was served.
And the memory haunts my heart with shame—
    Or, rather, the pride that's there;
In different guises, but soul the same,
    I meet him everywhere.

I had a chum. When the times were tight
    We starved in Australian scrubs;
We froze together in parks at night,
    And laughed together in pubs.
And I often hear a laugh like his
    From a sense of humour keen,
And catch a glimpse in a passing phiz
    Of his broad, good-humoured grin.

And I had a love—'twas a love to prize—
    But I never went back again . . .
I have seen the light of her kind grey eyes
    In many a face since then.

    .   .   .   .   .

The sailors say 'twill be rough tonight,
    As they fasten the hatches down;
The south is black, and the bar is white,
    And the drifting smoke is brown.

The gold has gone from the western haze,
    The sea-birds circle and swarm—
But we shall have plenty of sunny days,
    And little enough of storm.

The hill is hiding the short black pier,
    As the last white signal's seen;
The points run in, and the houses veer,
    And the great bluff stands between.
So darkness swallows each far white speck
    On many a wharf and quay;
The night comes down on a restless deck,—
    Grim cliffs—and—The Open Sea!

SINCE THEN

I met Jack Ellis in town today—
    Jack Ellis—my old mate, Jack.
Ten years ago, from the Castlereagh,
We carried our swags together away
    To the Never-Again, Out Back.

But times have altered since those old days,
    And the times have changed the men.
Ah, well! there's little to blame or praise—
Jack Ellis and I have tramped long ways
    On different tracks since then.

His hat was battered, his coat was green,
    The toes of his boots were through,
But the pride was his! It was I felt mean—
I wished that my collar was not so clean,
    Nor the clothes I wore so new.

He saw me first, and he knew 'twas I—
    The holiday swell he met.
Why have we no faith in each other? Ah, why?—
He made as though he would pass me by,
    For he thought that I might forget.

He ought to have known me better than that,
   By the tracks we tramped far out—
The sweltering scrub and the blazing flat,
When the heat came down through each old felt hat
   In the hell-born western drought.

. . . . . .

He took my hand in a distant way
   (I thought how we parted last),
And we seemed like men who have nought to say
And who meet—"Good-day," and who part—
     "Good-day,"
   Who never have shared the past.

I asked him in for a drink with me—
   Jack Ellis—my old mate, Jack—
But his manner no longer was careless and free,
He followed, but not with the grin that he
   Wore always in days Out Back.

I tried to live in the past once more—
   Or the present and past combine,
But the days between I could not ignore—
I couldn't but notice the clothes he wore,
   And he couldn't but notice mine.

He placed his glass on the polished bar,
   And he wouldn't fill up again;
For he is prouder than most men are—
Jack Ellis and I have tramped too far
   On different tracks since then.

He said that he had a mate to meet,
   And "I'll see you again", said he,
Then he hurried away through the crowded street,
And the rattle of 'buses and scrape of feet
   Seemed suddenly loud to me.

SWEENEY

It was somewhere in September, and the sun was going down,
When I came, in search of copy, to a Darling-River town;
"Come-and-Have-a-Drink" we'll call it—'tis a fitting name, I think—
And 'twas raining, for a wonder, up at Come-and-Have-a-Drink.

Underneath the pub veranda I was resting on a bunk
When a stranger rose before me, and he said that he was drunk;
He apologized for speaking; there was no offence, he swore;
But he somehow seemed to fancy that he'd seen my face before.

"No erfence," he said. I told him that he needn't mention it,
For I might have met him somewhere; I had travelled round a bit,
And I knew a lot of fellows in the Bush and in the streets—
But a fellow can't remember all the fellows that he meets.

Very old and thin and dirty were the garments that he wore,
Just a shirt and pair of trousers, and a boot, and nothing more;
He was wringing-wet and really in a sad and sinful plight,
And his hat was in his left hand, and a bottle in his right.

He agreed: You can't remember all the chaps you chance to meet,
And he said his name was Sweeney—people lived in Sussex-street.
He was camping in a stable, but he swore that he was right,
"Only for the blanky horses walkin' over him all night."

He'd apparently been fighting, for his face was black-and-blue,
And he looked as though the horses had been treading on him, too,
But an honest, genial twinkle in the eye that wasn't hurt
Seemed to hint of something better, spite of drink and rags and dirt.

It appeared that he mistook me for a long-lost mate of his—
One of whom I was the image, both in figure and in phiz—
(He'd have had a letter from him if the chap was livin' still,
For they'd carried swags together from the Gulf to Broken Hill).

Sweeney yarned awhile, and hinted that his folks were doing well,
And he told me that his father kept the Southern Cross Hotel;
And I wondered if his absence was regarded as a loss
When he left the elder Sweeney—landlord of the Southern Cross.

He was born in Parramatta, and he said, with humour grim,
That he'd like to see the city ere the liquor finished him,
But he couldn't raise the money. He was damned if he could think
What the Government was doing. Here he offered me a drink.

I declined—*'twas* self-denial—and I lectured him on booze,
Using all the hackneyed arguments that preachers mostly use;
Things I'd heard in temperance lectures (I was young and rather
	green),
And I ended by referring to the man he might have been.

Then a wise expression struggled with the bruises on his face,
Though his argument had scarcely any bearing on the case:
"What's the good o' keepin' sober? Fellers rise and fellers fall;
What I might have been and wasn't doesn't trouble me at all."

But he couldn't stay to argue, for his beer was nearly gone.
He was glad, he said, to meet me, and he'd see me later on,
But he guessed he'd have to go and get his bottle filled again;
And he gave a lurch and vanished in the darkness and the rain.

. . . .

And of afternoons in cities, when the rain is on the land,
Visions come to me of Sweeney with his bottle in his hand,
With the stormy night behind him, and the pub veranda-post—
And I wonder why he haunts me more than any other ghost.

I suppose he's tramping somewhere where the bushmen carry swags,
Dragging round the western stations with his empty tucker-bags;
And I fancy that of evenings, when the track is growing dim,
What he "might have been and wasn't" comes along and troubles
	him.

THE BLUE MOUNTAINS

ABOVE the ashes straight and tall,
   Through ferns with moisture dripping,
I climb beneath the sandstone wall,
   My feet on mosses slipping.

Like ramparts round the valley's edge
   The tinted cliffs are standing,
With many a broken wall and ledge,
   And many a rocky landing.

And round about their rugged feet
  Deep ferny dells are hidden
In shadowed depths, whence dust and heat
  Are banished and forbidden.

The stream that, crooning to itself,
  Comes down a tireless rover,
Flows calmly to the rocky shelf,
  And there leaps bravely over.

Now pouring down, now lost in spray
  When mountain breezes sally,
The water strikes the rock midway,
  And leaps into the valley.

    .   .   .   .   .

Now in the west the colours change,
  The blue with crimson blending;
Behind the far Dividing Range
  The sun is fast descending.

And mellowed day comes o'er the place,
  And softens ragged edges;
The rising moon's great placid face
  Looks gravely o'er the ledges.

PAST CARIN'

Now up and down the sidling brown
  The great black crows are flyin',
And down below the spur, I know,
  Another milker's dyin';
The crops have withered from the ground,
  The tank's clay bed is glarin',
But from my heart no tear nor sound,
  For I have got past carin'—
      Past worryin' or carin'—
      Past feelin' aught or carin';
      But from my heart no tear nor sound,
      For I have got past carin'.

Through Death and Trouble, turn about,
    Through hopeless desolation,
Through flood and fever, fire and drought,
    And slavery and starvation;
Through childbirth, sickness, hurt, and blight,
    And nervousness an' scarin',
Through bein' left alone at night,
    I've come to be past carin'.
        Past botherin' or carin',
        Past feelin' and past carin';
        Through city cheats and neighbours' spite,
        I've come to be past carin'.

Our first child took, in days like these,
    A cruel week in dyin',
All day upon her father's knees,
    Or on my poor breast lyin';
The tears we shed—the prayers we said
    Were awful, wild—despairin'!
I've pulled three through and buried two
    Since then—and I'm past carin'.
        I've grown to be past carin',
        Past lookin' up or carin';
        I've pulled three through and buried two
        Since then, and I'm past carin'.

'Twas ten years first, then came the worst,
    All for a barren clearin'.
I thought, I thought my heart would burst
    When first my man went shearin';
He's drovin' in the great North-west,
    I don't know how he's farin';
And I, the one that loved him best,
    Have grown to be past carin'.
        I've grown to be past carin',
        Past waitin' and past wearin':
        The girl that waited long ago
        Has lived to be past carin'.

My eyes are dry, I cannot cry,
    I've got no heart for breakin',
But where it was, in days gone by,
    A dull and empty achin'.

My last boy ran away from me—
I know my temper's wearin'—
But now I only wish to be
Beyond all signs of carin'.
Past wearyin' or carin',
Past feelin' and despairin';
And now I only wish to be
Beyond all signs of carin'.

SYDNEY-SIDE

Where's the steward?—Bar-room steward! Berth? Oh, any berth will do—
I have left a three-pound billet just to come along with you.
Brighter shines the Star of Rovers on a world that's growing wide,
But I think I'd give a kingdom for a glimpse of Sydney-side.

Run of rocky shelves at sunrise, with their base on ocean's bed;
Homes of Coogee, homes of Bondi, and the light-house on South Head;
For in loneliness and hardship—and with just a touch of pride—
Has my heart been taught to whisper, "You belong to Sydney-side."

Oh, there never dawned a morning, in the long and lonely days,
But I thought I saw the ferries streaming out across the bays—
And as fresh and fair in fancy did the picture rise again
As the sunrise flushed the city from Woollahra to Balmain;

With the sunny water frothing round the liners black and red,
And the coastal schooners working by the loom of Bradley's Head,
With the whistles and the sirens that re-echo far and wide—
All the life and light and beauty that belong to Sydney-side.

And the dreary cloud-line never veiled the end of one day more,
But the City set in jewels rose before me from "The Shore".
Round the sea-world shine the beacons of a thousand ports o' call,
But the harbour-lights of Sydney are the grandest of them all.

Toiling out beyond Coolgardie—heart and back and spirit broke,
Where the Rover's star gleams redly in the desert by the soak—
"But," says one mate to the other, "brace your lip and do not fret;
We will laugh on trams and 'buses—Sydney's in the same place yet."

Working in the South in winter, to the waist in dripping fern,
Where the local spirit hungers for each "saxpence" that you earn—
We can stand it for a season, for our world is growing wide,
And they all are friends and strangers who belong to Sydney-side.

"T'other-siders! T'other-siders!" Yet we wake the dusty dead.
For 'twas we that sent the backward province fifty years ahead;
We it is that trim Australia—making narrow country wide—
Yet we're always T'other-siders till we sail for Sydney-side.

DAN THE WRECK

TALL, and stout, and solid-looking,
    Yet a wreck;
None would think Death's finger's hooking
    Him from deck.
Cause of half the fun that's started—
    Hard-case Dan—
Isn't like a broken-hearted,
    Ruined man.

Walking-coat from tail to throat is
    Frayed and greened—
Like a man whose other coat is
    Being cleaned;
Gone for ever round the edging
    Past repair—
Waistcoat pockets frayed with dredging
    After "sprats" no longer there.

Wearing summer boots in June, or
    Slippers worn and old—
Like a man whose other shoon are
    Getting soled.
Pants? They're far from being recent—
    But, perhaps, I'd better not—
Says they are the only decent
    Pair he's got.

And his hat, I am afraid is
    Troubling him—
Past all lifting to the ladies
    By the brim.

But, although he'd hardly strike a
　　Girl, would Dan,
Yet he wears his wreckage like a
　　Gentleman.

Once—no matter how the rest dressed—
　　Up or down—
Once, they say, he was the best-dressed
　　Man in town.
Must have been before I knew him—
　　Now you'd scarcely care to meet
And be noticed talking to him
　　In the street.

Drink the cause and dissipation,
　　That is clear—
Maybe friend or kind relation
　　Cause of beer,
And the talking fool, who never
　　Reads or thinks,
Says, from hearsay: "Yes, he's clever;
　　But, you know, he drinks."

Where he lives, or how, or wherefore,
　　No one knows;
Lost his real friends, and therefore
　　Lost his foes.
Had, no doubt, his own romances—
　　Met his fate;
Tortured, doubtless, by the chances
　　And the luck that comes too late.

Now and then his boots are polished,
　　Collar clean,
And the worst grease-stains abolished
　　With ammonia or benzine:
Hints of some attempt to shove him
　　From the taps,
Or of someone left to love him—
　　Sister, p'r'aps.

After all, he is a grafter,
　　Earns his cheer—
Keeps the room in roars of laughter
　　When he gets outside a beer.

Yarns that would fall flat from others
   He can tell;
How he spent his stuff, my brothers,
   You know well.

Manner puts a man in mind of
   Old club balls and evening dress,
Ugly with a handsome kind of
   Ugliness.
One of those we'd say of, grimly,
   At the morgue—or mean hotel
Where they hold the inquests dimly:
   "He looked well!"

. . . . . .

I may be, so goes the rumour,
   Bad as Dan;
But I have not got the humour
   Of the man;
Nor the sight—well, deem it blindness,
   As the general public do—
And the love of human kindness,
   Or the grit to see it through.

JACK DUNN OF NEVERTIRE

It chanced upon the very day we'd got the shearing done,
A buggy brought a stranger to the West-o'-Sunday Run;
He had a round and jolly face, and sleek he was and stout—
He drove right up between the huts and called the super out.
We chaps were smoking after tea, and heard the swell inquire
For one as travelled by the name of "Dunn of Nevertire".
      Jack Dunn of Nevertire,
      Old Dunn of Nevertire;
There wasn't one of us but knew Jack Dunn of Nevertire.

"Jack Dunn of Nevertire," he said; "I was a mate of his;
And now it's twenty years since I set eyes upon his phiz.
There is no whiter man than Jack—no straighter south the line,
There is no hand in all the land I'd sooner grip in mine;

To help a mate in trouble Jack would go through flood and fire.
Great Scott! and don't you know the name of Dunn of Nevertire?
                Big Dunn of Nevertire,
                Long Jack from Nevertire;
He stuck to me through thick and thin, Jack Dunn of Nevertire.

"I did a wild and foolish thing while Jack and I were mates,
And I disgraced my guv'nor's name, an' wished to try the States.
My lamps were turned to Yankee-land, for I'd some people there.
And I was 'right' when someone sent the money for my fare;
I thought 'twas Dad, until I took the trouble to inquire
And found the man who sent the stuff was Dunn of Nevertire,
                Jack Dunn of Nevertire,
                Soft Dunn of Nevertire;
He'd won some money on a race—Jack Dunn of Nevertire.

"Now I've returned, by Liverpool, a swell of Yankee brand;
I reckon, guess, and kalkilate to wake my native land;
There is no better land, I swear, in all the wide world round—
I smelt the bush a month before we touched King George's Sound
And now I've come to settle down, the top of my desire
Is just to meet a mate o' mine called 'Dunn of Nevertire'.
                Was raised at Nevertire—
                The town of Nevertire;
He humped his bluey by the name of 'Dunn of Nevertire'.

"I've heard he's poor, and if he is, a proud old fool is he;
But, spite of that, I'll find a way to fix the old gumtree.
I've bought a station in the North—the best that could be had;
I want a man to pick the stock—I want a super bad;
I want no bully-brute to boss—no crawling, sneaking liar—
My station super's name shall be 'Jack Dunn of Nevertire!'
                Straight Dunn of Nevertire,
              Proud Jack from Nevertire;
I guess he's known up Queensland way—Jack Dunn of Nevertire."

The super said, while to his face a strange expression came:
"I *think* I've seen the man you want, I *think* I know the name;
Had he a jolly kind of face, a free and careless way,
Grey eyes that always seemed to smile, and hair just turning grey—

Clean-shaved, except a light moustache, long-limbed, an' tough as
   wire?"
"THAT'S HIM! THAT'S DUNN!" the stranger roared, "Jack Dunn of
   Nevertire!"
                      John Dunn of Nevertire,
                      Jack D. from Nevertire,
They said I'd find him here, the cuss!—Jack Dunn of Nevertire.

"I'd know his walk," the stranger cried, "though sobered, I'll allow."
"I doubt it much," the boss replied, "he don't walk that way now."
"Perhaps he don't!" the stranger said, "if years were hard on Jack;
But, if he were a mile away, I swear I'd know his back."
"I doubt it much," the super said, and sadly puffed his briar,
"I guess he wears a pair of wings—Jack Dunn of Nevertire;
                      Jack Dunn of Nevertire,
                      Brave Dunn of Nevertire,
He caught a fever nursing me, Jack Dunn of Nevertire."

We took the stranger round to where a gum-tree stood alone,
And in the grass beside the trunk he saw a granite stone;
The names of Dunn and Nevertire were plainly written there—
"I'm all broke up," the stranger said, in sorrow and despair,
"I guess he has a wider run, the man that I require;
He's got a river-frontage now, Jack Dunn of Nevertire;
                      Straight Dunn of Nevertire,
                      White Jack from Nevertire,
I guess Saint Peter knew the name of 'Dunn of Nevertire'."

PORTS OF THE OPEN SEA

    DOWN here, where the ships loom large in
        The gloom when the sea-storms veer,
    Down here on the south-west margin
        Of the western hemisphere,
    Where the might of a world-wide ocean
        Round the youngest land rolls free—
    Storm-bound from the World's commotion
        Lie the Ports of the Open Sea.

By the bluff where the grey sand reaches
    To the kerb of the spray-swept street,
By the sweep of the black sand beaches
    From the main-road travellers' feet,
By the heights, like a work Titanic,
    Begun ere the gods' work ceased,
By a bluff-lined coast volcanic
    Lie the Ports of the wild South-east.

By the steeps of the snow-capped ranges,
    By the scarped and terraced hills—
Far away from the swift life-changes,
    From the wear of the strife that kills—
Where the land in the spring seems younger
    Than a land of the Earth might be—
Oh! the hearts of the rovers hunger
    For the Ports of the Open Sea.

But the captains watch and harken
    For a sign of the South Sea's wrath—
Let the face of the South-east darken,
    And they turn to the ocean path.
Ay, the sea-boats dare not linger,
    Whatever the cargo be,
When the South-east lifts a finger
    By the Ports of the Open Sea.

Down South by the bleak Bluff faring,
    Or North where the Three Kings wait,
The storms of the South-east daring,
    They race through the foam-tossed strait.
Astern, where a white-winged roamer
    Found death in the tempest's roar,
The wash of the foam-flaked comber
    Runs green to the black-ribbed shore.

For the South-east lands are dread lands
    To the sailor high in the shrouds,
Where the low clouds loom like headlands,
    And the black bluffs blur like clouds.
When the breakers rage to windward
    And the lights are masked a-lee,
And the sunken rocks run inward
    To a Port of the Open Sea.

But oh! for the South-east weather—
    The sweep of the three-days' gale—
When far through the flax and heather
    The spindrift drives like hail.
Glory to man's creations
    That drive where the gale grows gruff,
When the homes of the sea-coast stations
    Flash white from the darkening bluff!

When the swell of the South-east rouses
    The wrath of the Maori sprite,
And the brown folk flee their houses
    To crouch in the flax by night,
And wait as they long have waited—
    In fear as the brown folk be—
The wave of destruction fated
    For the Ports of the Open Sea.

. . . . . .

Grey cloud to the mountain bases,
    Wild boughs in their rush and sweep,
The rounded hills in their places
    With tussocks like flying sheep;
The storm-bird alone and soaring
    O'er grasses and fern and tree;
And the beaches of boulder roaring
    The Hymn of the Open Sea.

TAKING HIS CHANCE

THEY stood by the door of the Inn on the Rise;
May Carney looked up in the bushranger's eyes:
"Oh! why did you come?—it was mad of you, Jack;
You know that the troopers are out on your track."
A laugh and a shake of his obstinate head—
"I wanted a dance, and I'll chance it," he said.

Some twenty-odd Bushmen had come to the ball,
But Jack from his youth had been known to them all,
And bushmen are soft where a woman is fair,
So the love of May Carney protected him there.
Through all the short evening—it seems like romance—
She danced with a bushranger taking his chance.

'Twas midnight—the dancers stood suddenly still,
For hoof-beats were heard on the side of the hill!
Ben Duggan, the drover, along the hillside
Came riding as only a bushman can ride.
He sprang from his horse, to the dancers he sped—
"The troopers are down in the gully!" he said.

Quite close to the shanty the troopers were seen.
"Clear out and ride hard for the ranges, Jack Dean!
Be quick!" said May Carney—her hand on her heart—
"We'll bluff them awhile, and 'twill give you a start."
He lingered a moment—to kiss her, of course—
Then ran to the trees where he'd hobbled his horse.

She ran to the gate, and the troopers were there—
The jingle of hobbles came faint on the air—
Then loudly she screamed: it was only to drown
The treacherous clatter of sliprails let down.
But troopers are sharp, and she saw at a glance
That someone was taking a desperate chance.

They chased, and they shouted, "Surrender, Jack Dean!"
They called him three times in the name of the Queen.
Then came from the darkness the clicking of locks;
The crack of a rifle was heard in the rocks!
A shriek, and a shout, and a rush of pale men—
And there lay the bushranger, chancing it then.

The sergeant dismounted and knelt on the sod—
"Your bushranging's over—make peace, Jack, with God!"
The dying man laughed—not a word he replied,
But turned to the girl who knelt down by his side.
He gazed in her eyes as she lifted his head:
"Just kiss me—my girl—and—I'll—chance it," he said.

TO JIM

I GAZE upon my son once more
  With eyes and heart that tire,
As solemnly he stands before
  The screen drawn round the fire;

With hands behind clasped hand in hand,
  Now loosely and now fast—
Just as his fathers used to stand
  For generations past.

A fair and slight and childish form,
  With big brown thoughtful eyes—
God help him, for a life of storm
  And stress before him lies.
A wanderer and a gipsy wild,
  I've learnt the world, and know,
For I was such another child—
  Ah, many years ago!

But in those dreamy eyes of him
  There is no hint of doubt—
I wish that you could tell me, Jim,
  The things you dream about.
You are a child of field and flood,
  For with the Gipsy strain
A strong Norwegian sailor's blood
  Runs red through every vein.

Dream on, my son, that all is true
  And things not what they seem—
'Twill be a bitter day when you
  Are wakened from your dream.
Be true, and slander never stings,
  Be straight, and all may frown—
You'll have the strength to grapple things
  That dragged your father down.

These lines I write with bitter tears
  And failing heart and hand,
But you will read in after years,
  And you will understand;
You'll hear the slander of the crowd,
  They'll whisper tales of shame;
But days will come when you'll be proud
  To bear your father's name.

THE LIGHTS OF COBB AND CO.

FIRE lighted; on the table a meal for sleepy men;
A lantern in the stable; a jingle now and then;
The mail-coach looming darkly by light of moon and star;
The growl of sleepy voices; a candle in the bar;
A stumble in the passage of folk with wits abroad;
A swear-word from a bedroom—the shout of "All aboard!"
"Tchk tchk! Git-up!" "Hold fast, there!" and down the range we go;
Five hundred miles of scattered camps will watch for Cobb and Co.

Old coaching towns already decaying for their sins;
Uncounted "Half-Way Houses", and scores of "Ten-Mile Inns";
The riders from the stations by lonely granite peaks;
The black-boy for the shepherds on sheep and cattle creeks;
The roaring camps of Gulgong, and many a "Digger's Rest";
The diggers on the Lachlan; the huts of Farthest West;
Some twenty thousand exiles who sailed for weal or woe—
The bravest hearts of twenty lands will wait for Cobb and Co.

The morning star has vanished, the frost and fog are gone,
In one of those grand mornings which but on mountains dawn;
A flask of friendly whisky—each other's hopes we share—
And throw our top-coats open to drink the mountain air.
The roads are rare to travel, and life seems all complete;
The grind of wheels on gravel, the trot of horses' feet,
The trot, trot, trot and canter, as down the spur we go—
The green sweeps to horizons blue that call for Cobb and Co.

We take a bright girl actress through western dusts and damps,
To bear the home-world message, and sing for sinful camps,
To stir our hearts and break them, wild hearts that hope and ache—
(Ah! when she thinks again of these her own must nearly break!)
Five miles this side the gold-field, a loud, triumphant shout:
Five hundred cheering diggers have snatched the horses out:
With "Auld Lang Syne" in chorus, through roaring camps they go
That cheer for her, and cheer for Home, and cheer for Cobb and Co.

Three lamps above the ridges and gorges dark and deep,
A flash on sandstone cuttings where sheer the sidlings sweep,
A flash on shrouded waggons, on water ghastly white;
Weird bush and scattered remnants of "rushes in the night";

Across the swollen river a flash beyond the ford:
Ride hard to warn the driver! He's drunk or mad, good Lord!
But on the bank to westward a broad and cheerful glow—
New camps extend across the plains new routes for Cobb and Co.

Swift scramble up the sidling where teams climb inch by inch;
Pause, bird-like, on the summit—then breakneck down the pinch;
By clear, ridge-country rivers, and gaps where tracks run high,
Where waits the lonely horseman, cut clear against the sky;
Past haunted half-way houses—where convicts made the bricks—
Scrub-yards and new bark shanties, we dash with five and six;
Through stringy-bark and blue-gum, and box and pine we go—
A hundred miles shall see tonight the lights of Cobb and Co.!

MIDDLETON'S ROUSEABOUT

    Tall and freckled and sandy,
      Face of a country lout;
    This was the picture of Andy,
      Middleton's Rouseabout.

    Type of a coming nation
      In the land of cattle and sheep;
    Worked on Middleton's station,
      Pound a week and his keep;

    On Middleton's wide dominions
      Plied the stockwhip and shears;
    Hadn't any opinions,
      Hadn't any "idears".

    Swiftly the years went over,
      Liquor and drought prevailed;
    Middleton went as a drover
      After his station had failed.

    Type of a careless nation,
      Men who are soon played out,
    Middleton was:—and his station
      Was bought by the Rouseabout.

Flourishing beard and sandy,
  Tall and solid and stout;
This is the picture of Andy,
  Middleton's Rouseabout.

Now on his own dominions
  Works with his overseers;
Hasn't any opinions,
  Hasn't any idears.

ONE-HUNDRED-AND-THREE

With the frame of a man and the face of a boy, and a manner strangely wild,
And the great, wide, wondering, innocent eyes of a silent-suffering child;
With his hideous dress and his heavy boots, he drags to Eternity—
And the Warder says, in a softened tone: "Catch step, One-Hundred-and-Three."

'Tis a ghastly parody of drill—or a travesty of work—
But One-Hundred-and-Three he catches step with a start, a shuffle and jerk.
He is silenced and starved and "drilled" in gaol—and a waster's son was he:
His sins were written before he was born—(Keep step! One-Hundred-and-Three.)

They 'shut a man in the four-by-eight, with a six-inch slit for air,
Twenty-three hours of the twenty-four, to brood on his virtues there.
The dead stone walls and the iron door close in like iron bands
On eyes that had followed the distant haze out there on the Level Lands.

Bread and water and hominy, and a scrag of meat and a spud,
A Bible and thin flat Book of Rules, to cool a strong man's blood;
They take the spoon from the cell at night—and a stranger would think it odd;
But a man might sharpen it on the floor, and go to his own Great God.

One-Hundred-and-Three, it is hard to believe that you saddled your
    horse at dawn,
And strolled through the bush with a girl at eve, or lolled with her
    on the lawn.
There were picnic parties in sunny bays, and ships on the shining
    sea;
There were foreign ports in the glorious days—(Hold up, One-
    Hundred-and-Three!)

A man came out at exercise time from one of the cells today:
'Twas the ghastly spectre of one I knew, and I thought he was
    far away;
We dared not speak, but he signed "Farewell—fare—well," and
    I knew by this
And the number stamped on his clothes (not sewn) that a heavy
    sentence was his.

Where five men do the work of a boy, with warders *not* to see—
It is sad and bad and uselessly mad, it is ugly as it can be,
From the flower-beds shaped to fit the gaol, in circle and line
    absurd,
To the gilded weathercock on the church, agape like a strangled
    bird—

Agape like a strangled bird in the sun, and I wonder what he
    can see—
The Fleet come in, and the Fleet go out? (Hold up, One-Hundred-
    and-Three!)
The glorious sea, and the bays and Bush, and the distant mountains
    blue—
(Keep step, keep step, One-Hundred-and-Three, for my heart is
    halting too).

The great, round church with its volume of sound, where we dare
    not turn our eyes—
They take us there from our separate hells to sing of Paradise;
The High Church service swells and swells where the tinted Christs
    look down—
It is easy to see who is weary and faint and weareth the thorny
    crown.

Though every creed hath its Certain Hope, yet here, in hopeless
    doubt,
Despairing prisoners faint in church, and the warders carry them out.

There are swift-made signs that are not to God as they march us hellward then;
It is hard to believe that we knelt as boys to "For ever and ever, Amen".

They double-lock at four o'clock; the warders leave their keys,
And the Governor strolls with a friend at eve through his stone conservatories;
Their window-slits are like idiot mouths, with square stone chins adrop,
And the weatherstains for the dribble, and the dead flat foreheads atop.

Rules, regulations—Red Tape and rules; all and alike they bind:
Under separate treatment place the deaf; in the dark cell shut the blind!
And somewhere down in his sandstone tomb, with never a word to save,
One-Hundred-and-Three is keeping step, as he'll keep it to his grave.

The press is printing its smug, smug lies, and paying its shameful debt—
It speaks of the comforts that prisoners have, and "holidays" prisoners get.
The visitors come with their smug, smug smiles through the gaol on a working day,
And the public hears with its large, large ears what "Authorities" have to say.

They lay their fingers on well-hosed walls, and they tread on the polished floors;
They peep in the generous, shining cans with their Ration Number Four.
And the visitors go with their smug, smug smiles; and the reporters' work is done;
Stand up! my men, who have done your time on Ration Number One!

He shall be buried alive without meat, for a day and a night unheard,
If he speak a word to his fellow-corpse—who died for want of a word.

He shall be punished, and he shall be starved, and he shall in
 darkness rot.
He shall be murdered, body and soul—and God saith: "Thou shalt
 not."

I've seen the remand-yard men go forth by the subway out of the
 yard—
And I've seen them come in with a foolish grin and a sentence
 of Three Years Hard.
They send a half-starved man to the Court, where the hearts of
 men they carve—
Then feed him up in the hospital to give him the strength to starve.

You get the gaol-dust into your throat, your skin goes the dead
 gaol-white;
You get the gaol-whine in your voice and in every letter you write.
And into your eyes comes the bright gaol-light—not the glare
 of the world's distraught,
Not the hunted look, nor the guilty look, but the awful look
 of the Caught.

The brute is a brute, and a kind man's kind, and the strong heart
 does not fail—
A crawler's a crawler everywhere, but a man is a man in gaol;
For the kindness of man to man is great when penned in a sand-
 stone pen—
The public call us the "criminal class", but the warders call us
 "the men".

We crave for sunlight, we crave for meat, we crave for the Might-
 have-Been,
But the cruellest thing in the walls of a gaol is the craving for
 nicotine.
Yet the spirit of Christ is in every place where the soul of a man
 can dwell—
It comes like tobacco in prison, or like news to the separate cell.

The champagne lady comes home from the course in charge of
 the criminal swell—
They carry her in from the motor-car to the lift in the Grand
 Hotel;
But armed with the savage Habituals Act they are waiting for
 you and me—
And drunkards in judgment on drunkards sit (Keep step, One-
 Hundred-and-Three!).

The clever scoundrels are all outside, and the moneyless mugs in
    gaol—
Men do twelve months for a mad wife's lies or Life for a strumpet's
    tale.
If the people knew what the warders know, and felt as the prisoners
    feel—
If the people knew, they would storm their gaols as they stormed
    the old Bastille.

Warders and prisoners, all alike, in a dead rot, dry and slow—
The author must not write for his own, and the tailor must not
    sew.
The billet-bound officers dare not speak, and discharged men dare
    not tell,
Though many and many an innocent man must brood in this barren
    hell.

Ay! clang the spoon on the iron floor, and shove in the bread
    with your toe,
And shut with a bang the iron door, and clank the bolt—just so;
But One-Hundred-and-Three is near the End when the clonking
    gaol-bell sounds—
He cannot swallow the milk they send when the doctor has gone
    his rounds.

. . . . . .

They have smuggled him out to the hospital, with no one to tell
    the tale,
But it's little that doctor or nurses can do for the patient from
    Starvinghurst Gaol.
The blanket and screen are ready to draw. . . . There are footsteps
    light and free—
And the angels are whispering over his bed: "Keep step—One-
    Hundred-and-Three."

BERTHA

Wide, solemn eyes that question me,
  Wee hand that pats my head—
Where only two have stroked before,
  And both of them are dead.

"Ah, poo-ah Daddy mine," she says,
  With wondrous sympathy—
Oh, baby girl, you don't know how
  You break the heart in me!

Let friends and kinsfolk work their worst,
  Let all say what they will,
Your baby arms go round my neck—
  I'm your own Daddy still!
And you kiss me and I kiss you,
  Fresh kisses, frank and free—
Ah, baby girl, you don't know how
  You break the heart in me!

When I was good I dreamed that when
  The snow showed in my hair
A household angel in her teens
  Would flit about my chair,
To comfort me as I grew old;
  But that shall never be—
Ah, baby girl, you don't know how
  You break the heart in me!

But one shall love me while I live,
  And soothe my troubled head,
And never brook an unkind word
  Of me when I am dead.
Her eyes shall light to hear my name
  Howe'er disgraced it be—
Ah, baby girl, you don't know how
  You help the heart in me!

ON THE NIGHT TRAIN

Have you seen the Bush by moonlight, from the train, go running by,
Here a patch of glassy water, there a glimpse of mystic sky?
Have you heard the still voice calling, yet so warm, and yet so cold:
'I'm the Mother-Bush that bore you! Come to me when you are old?"

Did you see the Bush below you sweeping darkly to the range,
All unchanged and all unchanging, yet so very old and strange!
Did you hear the Bush a-calling, when your heart was young
    and bold:
"I'm the Mother-Bush that nursed you! Come to me when you
    are old?"

Through the long, vociferous cutting as the night train swiftly sped,
Did you hear the grey Bush calling from the pine-ridge overhead:
"You have seen the seas and cities; all seems done, and all seems
    told;
I'm the Mother-Bush that loves you! Come to me, now you are old?"

THE SHEARING-SHED

"THE ladies are coming," the super says
  To the shearers sweltering there,
And "the ladies" means in the shearing-shed:
  "Don't cut 'em too bad. Don't swear."
The ghost of a pause in the shed's rough heart,
  And lower is bowed each head;
Then nothing is heard save a whispered word
  And the roar of the shearing-shed.

The tall, shy rouser has lost his wits;
  His limbs are all astray;
He leaves a fleece on the shearing-board
  And his broom in the shearer's way.
There's a curse in store for that jackeroo
  As down by the wall he slants—
But the ringer bends with his legs askew
  And wishes he'd "patched them pants".

They are girls from the city. Our hearts rebel
  As we squint at their dainty feet,
While they gush and say in a girly way
  That "the dear little lambs" are "sweet".
And Bill the Ringer, who'd scorn the use
  Of a childish word like damn,
Would give a pound that his tongue were loose
  As he tackles a lively lamb.

Swift thought of home in the coastal towns—
    Or rivers and waving grass—
And a weight on our hearts that we cannot define
    That comes as the ladies pass;
But the rouser ventures a nervous dig
    With his thumb in the next man's back;
And Bogan says to his pen-mate: "Twig
    The style of that last un, Jack."

Jack Moonlight gives her a careless glance—
    Then catches his breath with pain;
His strong hand shakes, and the sunbeams dance
    As he bends to his work again.
But he's well disguised in a bristling beard,
    Bronzed skin, and his shearer's dress;
And whatever he knew or hoped or feared
    Was hard for his mates to guess.

Jack Moonlight, wiping his broad, white brow,
    Explains, with a doleful smile,
"A stitch in the side," and "I'm all right now"—
    But he leans on the beam awhile,
And gazes out in the blazing noon
    On the clearing, brown and bare ....
She had come and gone—like a breath of June
    In December's heat and glare.

THE GLASS ON THE BAR

THREE bushmen one morning rode up to an inn,
And one of them called for the drinks with a grin;
They'd only returned from a trip to the North,
And, eager to greet them, the landlord came forth.
He absently poured out a glass of Three Star,
And set down that drink with the rest on the bar.

"There, that is for Harry," he said, "and it's queer,
'Tis the very same glass that he drank from last year;
His name's on the glass, you can read it like print,
He scratched it himself with an old bit of flint;
I remember his drink—it was always Three Star"—
And the landlord looked out through the door of the bar.

He looked at the horses, and counted but three:
"You were always together—where's Harry?" cried he.
Oh, sadly they looked at the glass as they said,
"You may put it away, for our old mate is dead;"
But one, gazing out o'er the ridges afar,
Said, "We owe him a shout—leave the glass on the bar."

They thought of the far-away grave on the plain,
They thought of the comrade who came not again,
They lifted their glasses, and sadly they said:
"We drink to the name of the mate who is dead."
And the sunlight streamed in, and a light like a star
Seemed to glow in the depth of the glass on the bar.

And still in that shanty a tumbler is seen,
It stands by the clock, always polished and clean;
And often the strangers will read as they pass
The name of a bushman engraved on the glass;
And though on the shelf but a dozen there are,
That glass never stands with the rest on the bar.

REEDY RIVER

TEN miles down Reedy River
　　A pool of water lies,
And all the year it mirrors
　　The changes in the skies.
Within that pool's broad bosom
　　Is room for all the stars;
Its bed of sand has drifted
　　O'er countless rocky bars.

Around the lower edges
　　There waves a bed of reeds,
Where water-rats are hidden
　　And where the wild-duck breeds;
And grassy slopes rise gently
　　To ridges long and low,
Where groves of wattle flourish
　　And native bluebells grow.

Beneath the granite ridges
    The eye may just discern
Where Rocky Creek emerges
    From deep green banks of fern;
And standing tall between them,
    The drooping sheoaks cool
The hard, blue-tinted waters
    Before they reach the pool.

Ten miles down Reedy River
    One Sunday afternoon,
I rode with Mary Campbell
    To that broad, bright lagoon;
We left our horses grazing
    Till shadows climbed the peak,
And strolled beneath the sheoaks
    On the banks of Rocky Creek.

Then home along the river
    That night we rode a race,
And the moonlight lent a glory
    To Mary Campbell's face;
I pleaded for my future
    All through that moonlight ride,
Until our weary horses
    Drew closer side by side.

Ten miles from Ryan's Crossing
    And five below the peak,
I built a little homestead
    On the banks of Rocky Creek;
I cleared the land and fenced it
    And ploughed the rich red loam;
And my first crop was golden
    When I brought Mary home.

   .   .   .   .   .   .

Now still down Reedy River
    The grassy sheoaks sigh;
The waterholes still mirror
    The pictures in the sky;
The golden sand is drifting
    Across the rocky bars;
And over all for ever
    Go sun and moon and stars.

But of the hut I builded
 There are no traces now,
And many rains have levelled
 The furrows of my plough.
The glad bright days have vanished;
 For sombre branches wave
Their wattle-blossom golden
 Above my Mary's grave.

A NEW JOHN BULL

A tall, slight, English gentleman
 With an eyeglass in his eye;
He mostly says "Good-bai" to you,
 When he means to say "Good-bye";
He shakes hands like a ladies' man,
 For all the world to see—
They know, in Corners of the World,
 No ladies' man is he.

A tall, slight English gentleman
 Who hates to soil his hands;
He takes his mother's drawing-room
 To most outlandish lands,
And when through hells we dream not of
 His battery prevails,
Removes the grime of gunpowder
 And polishes his nails.

He's what our blokes in Egypt call
 "A decent sort o' cove".
And if the Pyramids should fall
 He'd merely say "Bai Jove!"
And if the stones should block his path
 For one too boring day,
He'd call on Sergeant Whatsisname
 To clear those things away!

This quiet English gentleman
 Frequents the Empire's rim,
Where sweating sons of ebony
 Would go to hell for him.

And if he chances to get winged,
    Or smashed up rather worse,
He's quite apologetic to
    The doctor and the nurse.

A silent English gentleman—
    Though sometimes he says "Haw".
But should a monkey in its cage
    Appeal to British Law

For justice on some bullying ape,
    He'd listen most polite,
And do his very best to set
    The monkey's grievance right.

A thoroughbred whose ancestry
    Goes back to ages dim,
No labourer on his wide estates
    Need fear to speak to him.

Although he never showed a sign
    Of aught save sympathy,
He was the only gentleman
    That shamed the lout in me.

BALLAD OF THE ROUSEABOUT

A ROUSEABOUT of rouseabouts, from any land—or none—
I bear a nickname of the Bush, and I'm—a woman's son;
I came from where I camped last night, and at the day-dawn glow
I'll rub the darkness from my eyes, roll up my swag, and go.

Some take the track for bitter pride, some for no pride at all—
(But to us all the world is wide when driven to the wall)
Some take the track for gain in life, some take the track for loss—
And some of us take up the swag as Christ took up the Cross.

Some take the track for faith in men—some take the track for doubt—
Some flee a squalid home to work their own salvation out.
Some dared not see a mother's tears nor meet a father's face—
Born of good Christian families some leap, headlong, from Grace.

Oh, we are men who fought and rose, or fell from many grades;
Some born to lie, and some to pray, we're men of many trades;
We're men whose fathers were and are of high and low degree—
The sea was open to us, and we sailed across the sea.

We're haunted by the Past at times—and this is very bad,
Because we drink till horrors come, lest, sober, we go mad.
We judge not and we are not judged—'tis our philosophy;
There's something wrong with every ship that sails upon the sea.

From shearing-shed to shearing-shed we tramp to make a cheque—
Jack Cornstalk and the Ne'er-do-well, the Tar-boy and the Wreck.
We know the tucker tracks that feed—or leave one in the lurch—
The "Burgoo" (Presbyterian) track—the "Murphy" (Roman Church).

I've humped my swag to Bawley Plain, and farther out and on;
I've boiled my billy by the Gulf, and boiled it by the Swan;
I've thirsted in dry lignum swamps, and thirsted on the sand,
And eked the fire with camel dung in Never-Never Land.

I've tramped and camped, and "shore" and drunk with many mates
    Out Back—
And every one to me is Jack because the first was Jack—
A lifer sneaked from gaol at home (the straightest mate I met)—
A ratty Russian Nihilist—a British Baronet!

A rouseabout of rouseabouts, above—beneath regard,
I know how soft is this old world, and I have learnt how hard—
I learned what college had to teach, and in the school of men
By camp-fires I have learned, or, say, unlearned it all again.

We hold him true who's true to one however false he be
(There's something wrong with every ship that lies beside the quay);
We lend and borrow, laugh and joke, and when the past is drowned
We sit upon our swags and smoke and watch the world go round.

ANDY'S GONE WITH CATTLE

    Our Andy's gone with cattle now—
      Our hearts are out of order—
    With drought he's gone to battle now
      Across the Queensland border.

He's left us in dejection now;
    Our thoughts with him are roving;
It's dull on this selection now,
    Since Andy went a-droving.

Who now shall wear the cheerful face
    In times when things are slackest?
And who shall whistle round the place
    When Fortune frowns her blackest?

Oh, who shall cheek the squatter now
    When he comes round us snarling?
His tongue is growing hotter now
    Since Andy crossed the Darling.

Oh, may the showers in torrents fall,
    And all the tanks run over;
And may the grass grow green and tall
    In pathways of the drover;

And may good angels send the rain
    On desert stretches sandy;
And when the summer comes again
    God grant 'twill bring us Andy.

BILL

He shall live to the end of this mad old world as he's lived since the world began;
He never has done any good for himself, but was good to every man.
He never has done any good for himself, and I'm sure that he never will;
He drinks, and he swears, and he fights at times, and his name is mostly Bill.

He carried a freezing mate to his cave, and nursed him, for all I know,
When Europe was mainly a sheet of ice, thousands of years ago.
He has stuck to many a mate since then, he is with us everywhere still—
He loves and gambles when he is young, and the girls stick up for Bill.

He has rowed to a wreck, when the lifeboat failed, with Jim in
    a crazy boat;
He has given his lifebelt many a time, and sunk that another
    might float.
He has "stood 'em off" while others escaped, when the niggers
    rushed from the hill,
And rescue parties that came too late have found what was left of
    Bill.

He has thirsted on deserts that others might drink, he has given
    lest others should lack,
He has staggered half-blinded through fire or drought with a sick
    man on his back.
He is first to the rescue in tunnel or shaft, from Bulli to Broken
    Hill,
When the water breaks in or the fire breaks out, a leader of men
    is Bill!

He wears no Humane Society's badge for the fearful deaths he
    braved;
He seems ashamed of the good he did, and ashamed of the lives
    he saved.
If you chance to know of a noble deed he has done, you had
    best keep still;
If you chance to know of a kindly act, you musn't let on to Bill.

He is fierce at a wrong, he is firm in right, he is kind to the weak
    and mild;
He will slave all day and sit up all night by the side of a
    neighbour's child.
For a woman in trouble he'd lay down his life, nor think as
    another man will;
He's a man all through, and no other man's wife has ever been
    worse for Bill.

He is good for the noblest sacrifice, he can do what few men can;
He will break his heart that the girl he loves may marry a better
    man.
There's many a mother and wife tonight whose heart and eyes
    will fill
When she thinks of the days of the long-ago when she well might
    have stuck to Bill.

Maybe he's in trouble or hard up now, and travelling far for work,
Or fighting a dead past down tonight in a lone camp west of Bourke.
When he's happy and flush, take your sorrow to him and borrow
    as much as you will;
But when he's in trouble or stony-broke, you never will hear
    from Bill.

And when, because of its million sins, this earth is cracked like
    a shell,
He will stand by a mate at the Judgment Seat and comfort him
    down in—Well,—
I haven't much sentiment left to waste, but let cynics sneer as
    they will,
Perhaps God will fix up the world again for the sake of the likes
    of Bill.

MALLACOOTA BAR

We tried to get over the Bar today,
    Today on the morning tide:
But whether I go, or whether I stay
    Let Fate and the Bar decide;
But my Love—New Love—with your eyes of grey
    The weary world is wide!

We kedged her in and we poled her back
    In time from the ebbing tide,
For the sky was grey, and the rocks were black,
    And the rollers broke outside.
And it's oh, my Love, but the lines are slack,
    And the weary world is wide.

We'd try to get over the Bar tonight,
    Tonight on the higher tide;
But the moon is dull that last night was bright
    And the world is dark outside.
Oh, Love—New Love!—why your face so white,
    And the weary world so wide?

We tried to get over the Bar today,
    Tomorrow we'll try again—
Oh, Love! New Love of the grey eyes, say,
    Is the strife of man in vain?

The glass might lie, and the needle stray,
　　But the path of love is plain!

When over the Bar, there is no return
　　In the time of the autumn gales—
But whether the sea or the bush it be,
　　The heart of a man prevails—
Oh, Love! New Love, will you watch the sea
　　Where your Bushman sailor sails?

WHEN YOUR PANTS BEGIN TO GO

When you wear a cloudy collar and a shirt that isn't white,
And you cannot sleep for thinking how you'll reach tomorrow night,
You may be a man of sorrow, and on speaking terms with Care,
But as yet you're unacquainted with the Demon of Despair;
For I rather think that nothing heaps the trouble on your mind
Like the knowledge that your trousers badly need a patch behind.

I have noticed when misfortune strikes the hero of the play
That his clothes are worn and tattered in a most unlikely way;
And the gods applaud and cheer him while he whines and loafs
　　around,
But they never seem to notice that his pants are mostly sound;
Yet, of course, he cannot help it, for our mirth would mock his care
If the ceiling of his trousers showed the patches of repair.

You are none the less a hero if you elevate your chin
When you feel the pavement wearing through the leather, sock
　　and skin;
You are rather more heroic than are ordinary folk
If you scorn to fish for pity under cover of a joke;
You will face the doubtful glances of the people that you know;
But—of course, you're bound to face them when your pants begin
　　to go.

If, when flush, you took your pleasure, failed to make a god
　　of Pelf—
Some will say that for your troubles you can only thank yourself;
Some will swear you'll die a beggar, but you only laugh at that
While your garments hang together and you wear a decent hat;

You may laugh at their predictions while your soles are wearing
    through—
But a man's an awful coward when his pants are going too!

Though the present and the future may be anything but bright,
It is best to tell the fellows that you're getting on all right.
And a man prefers to say it—'tis a manly lie to tell,
For the folks may be persuaded that you're doing very well;
But it's hard to be a hero, and it's hard to wear a grin,
When your most important garment is in places very thin.

Get some sympathy and comfort from the chum who knows you
    best,
Then your sorrows won't run over in the presence of the rest;
There's a chum that you can go to when you feel inclined to whine,
He'll declare your coat is tidy, and he'll say: "Just look at mine!"
Though you may be patched all over he will say it doesn't show,
And he'll swear it can't be noticed when your pants begin to go.

Brother mine, and of misfortune! times are hard, but do not fret,
Keep your courage up and struggle, and we'll laugh at these things
    yet.
Though there is no corn in Egypt, surely Africa has some—
Keep your smile in working order for the better days to come!
We shall often laugh together at the hard times that we know,
And get measured by the tailor when our pants begin to go.

THE TEAMS

A CLOUD of dust on the long, white road,
    And the teams go creeping on
Inch by inch with the weary load;
And by the power of the green-hide goad
    The distant goal is won.

With eyes half-shut to the blinding dust,
    And necks to the yokes bent low,
The beasts are pulling as bullocks must;
And the shining tires might almost rust
    While the spokes are turning slow.

With face half-hid by a broad-brimmed hat,
    That shades from the heat's white waves,
And shouldered whip, with its green-hide plait,
The driver plods with a gait like that
    Of his weary, patient slaves.

He wipes his brow, for the day is hot,
    And spits to the left with spite;
He shouts at Bally, and flicks at Scot,
And raises dust from the back of Spot,
    And spits to the dusty right.

He'll sometimes pause as a thing of form
    In front of a settler's door,
And ask for a drink, and remark "It's warm",
Or say "There's signs of a thunderstorm";
    But he seldom utters more.

The rains are heavy on roads like these
    And, fronting his lonely home,
For days together the settler sees
The waggons bogged to the axletrees,
    Or ploughing the sodden loam.

And then, when the roads are at their worst,
    The bushman's children hear
The cruel blows of the whips reversed
While bullocks pull as their hearts would burst,
    And bellow with pain and fear.

And thus—with glimpses of home and rest—
    Are the long, long journeys done;
And thus—'tis a thankless life at the best!—
Is Distance fought in the mighty West,
    And the lonely battle won.

WHEN THE WORLD WAS WIDE

THE world is narrow and ways are short, and our lives are dull and slow,
For little is new where the crowds resort, and less where the wanderers go;

Greater or smaller, the same old things we see by the dull roadside—
And tired of all is the spirit that sings of the days when the world was wide.

When the North was hale in the march of Time, and the South and the West were new,
And the gorgeous East was a pantomime, as it seemed in our boyhood's view;
When Spain was first on the waves of change, and proud in the ranks of pride,
And all was wonderful, new and strange in the days when the world was wide.

Then a man could fight if his heart were bold, and win if his faith were true—
Were it love, or honour, or power, or gold, or all that our hearts pursue;
Could live to the world for the family name, or die for the family pride,
Could flee from sorrow and wrong and shame in the days when the world was wide.

They roved away in the ships that sailed ere science controlled the main,
When the strong, brave heart of a man prevailed as 'twill never prevail again;
They knew not whither, nor much they cared—let Fate or the winds decide—
The worst of the Great Unknown they dared in the days when the world was wide.

They raised new stars on the silent sea that filled their hearts with awe;
They came to many a strange countree and marvellous sights they saw.
The villagers gaped at the tales they told, and old eyes glistened with pride—
When barbarous cities were paved with gold in the days when the world was wide.

'Twas honest metal and honest wood, in the days of the Outward Bound,
When men were gallant and ships were good—roaming the wide world round.
The gods could envy a leader then when "Follow me, lads!" he cried—
They faced each other and fought like men in the days when the world was wide!

The good ship bound for the Southern Seas when the beacon was Ballarat,
With a "Ship ahoy!" on the freshening breeze, "Where bound?" and "What ship's that?"—
The emigrant train to New Mexico—the rush to the Lachlan-side—
Ah! faint is the echo of Westward Ho! from the days when the world was wide.

South, East, and West in advance of Time—and far in advance of Thought—
Brave men they were with a faith sublime—and is it for this they fought?
And is it for this damned life we praise the god-like spirit that died
At Eureka Stockade in the Roaring Days with the days when the world was wide?

. . . . .

With its dull, brown days of a-shilling-an-hour the dreary year drags round:
Is this the result of Old England's power?—the bourne of the Outward Bound?
Is this the sequel of Westward Ho!—of the days of Whate'er Betide?
The heart of the rebel makes answer "No! We'll fight till the world grows wide!"

The world shall yet be a wider world—for the tokens are manifest;
East and North shall the wrongs be hurled that followed us South and West.
The march of Freedom is North by the Dawn! Follow, whate'er betide!
Sons of the Exiles, march! March on! March till the world grows wide!

THE LIGHT ON THE WRECK

Out there by the rocks, at the end of the bank,
In the mouth of the river the *Wanderer* sank.
She is resting between the blue water and green,
And only her masts and her funnel are seen;
And you see, as day fades to its last crimson fleck,
On her foremost a lantern—a light on a wreck.

'Tis a light on a wreck, warning ships to beware
Of the drowned iron hull of the *Wanderer* there;
And the ships that come in and go out in the night
Keep a careful look out for the *Wanderer's* light.
There are rules for the harbour and rules for the wave;
But all captains stand clear of a ship in her grave.

And the stories of strong lives that ended in wrecks
Might be likened to lights over derelict decks;
Like the light where, in sight of the streets of the town,
In the mouth of the channel the *Wanderer* went down.
Keep a watch from the desk, as they watch from the deck;
Keep a watch from your home for the light on the wreck.

But the lights on the wrecks since creation began
Have been shining in vain for the vagabond clan.
They will never take warning, they will not beware;
They have for their watchwords, "What matter?" "What care?"
They steer without compass, and sail without check,
Till they drift to their grave 'neath a light on a wreck.

THE GREAT GREY PLAIN

Out West, where the stars are brightest,
    Where the scorching north wind blows,
The bones of the dead gleam whitest
    And the sun on a desert glows—
Yet within the selfish kingdom
    Where man starves man for gain,
Where white men tramp for existence—
    Wide lies the Great Grey Plain.

No break in its awful horizon,
    No blur in the dazzling haze,
Save where by the bordering timber
    The fierce, white heat-waves blaze,
And out where the tank-heap rises
    Or looms when the long days wane,
Till it seems like a distant mountain
    Low down on the Great Grey Plain.

From the camp, while the rich man's dreaming,
    Come the "traveller" and his mate,
In the ghastly daybreak seeming
    Like a swagman's ghost out late;
And the horseman blurs in the distance,
    While still the stars remain,
A low, faint dust-cloud haunting
    His track on the Great Grey Plain.

And all day long from before them
    The mirage smokes away—
The daylight ghost of an ocean
    Creeps close behind all day
With an evil, snake-like motion,
    Like the waves of a madman's brain:
'Tis a phantom *not* like water
    Out there on the Great Grey Plain.

There's a run on the Western limit
    Where a man lives like a beast;
And a shanty in the mulga
    That stretches to the East;
And the hopeless men who carry
    Their swags and tramp in pain—
The footman must not tarry
    Out there on the Great Grey Plain.

Out West, where the stars are brightest,
    Where the scorching north wind blows,
And the bones of the dead seem whitest,
    And the sun on a desert glows—
Out Back in the hungry distance
    That brave hearts dare in vain—
Where swagmen tramp for existence—
    There lies the Great Grey Plain.

SCOTS OF THE RIVERINA

The boy cleared out to the city from his home at the harvest time—
They were Scots of the Riverina, and to run from home was a crime.
The old man burned his letters, the first and last he burned,
And he scratched his name from the Bible when the old wife's back
 was turned.

A year went past, and another. There were calls from the firing-line;
They heard the boy had enlisted, but the old man made no sign.
His name must never be mentioned on the farm by Gundagai—
They were Scots of the Riverina with ever the kirk hard by.

The boy came home on his "final", and the township's bonfire
 burned.
His mother's arms were about him; but the old man's back was
 turned.
The daughters begged for pardon till the old man raised his hand—
A Scot of the Riverina who was hard to understand.

The boy was killed in Flanders, where the best and bravest die.
There were tears at the Grahame homestead, and grief in Gundagai;
But the old man ploughed at daybreak and the old man ploughed
 till the mirk—
There were furrows of pain in the orchard while his household
 went to the kirk.

The hurricane lamp in the rafters dimly and dimly burned,
And the old man died at the table when the old wife's back was
 turned.
Face down on his bare arms folded he sank with his wild grey hair
Outspread o'er the open Bible and a name rewritten there.

OUT BACK

The old year went, and the new returned, in the withering weeks
 of drought;
The cheque was spent that the shearer earned, and the sheds were
 all cut out;

The publican's words were short and few, and the publican's looks
    were black—
And the time had come, as the shearer knew, to carry his swag
    Out Back.

*For time means tucker, and tramp you must, where the scrubs and
    plains are wide,
With seldom a track that a man can trust, or a mountain peak to
    guide;
All day long in the dust and heat—when summer is on the track—
With stinted stomachs and blistered feet, they carry their swags
    Out Back.*

He tramped away from the shanty there, when the days were long
    and hot,
With never a soul to know or care if he died on the track or not.
The poor of the city have friends in woe, no matter how much they
    lack,
But only God and the swagman know how a poor man fares Out
    Back.

He begged his way on the parched Paroo and the Warrego tracks
    once more,
And lived like a dog, as the swagmen do, till the Western stations
    shore;
But men were many, and sheds were full, for work in the town was
    slack—
The traveller never got hands in wool, though he tramped for a
    year Out Back.

In stifling noons when his back was wrung by its load, and the air
    seemed dead,
And the water warmed in the bag that hung to his aching arm like
    lead.
Or in times of flood, when plains were seas and the scrubs were cold
    and black,
He ploughed in mud to his trembling knees, and paid for his sins
    Out Back.

And dirty and careless and old he wore, as his lamp of hope grew
    dim,
He tramped for years, till the swag he bore seemed part of himself
    to him.

As a bullock drags in the sandy ruts, he followed the dreary track,
With never a thought but to reach the huts when the sun went
    down Out Back.

It chanced one day when the north wind blew in his face like a
    furnace-breath,
He left the track for a tank he knew—'twas a shorter cut to death;
For the bed of the tank was hard and dry, and crossed with many a
    crack,
And, oh! it's a terrible thing to die of thirst in the scrub Out Back.

A drover came, but the fringe of law was eastward many a mile:
He never reported the thing he saw, for it was not worth his while.
The tanks are full, and the grass is high in the mulga off the track,
Where the bleaching bones of a white man lie by his mouldering
    swag Out Back.

For time means tucker, and tramp they must, where the plains and
    scrubs are wide,
With seldom a track that a man can trust, or a mountain peak to
    guide;
All day long in the flies and heat the men of the outside track,
With stinted stomachs and blistered feet, must carry their swags
    Out Back.

THE DROVER'S SWEETHEART

An hour before the sun goes down
    Behind the ragged boughs,
I go across the little run
    To bring the dusty cows;
And once I used to sit and rest
    Beneath the fading dome,
For there was one that I loved best
    Who'd bring the cattle home.

Our yard is fixed with double bails;
    Round one the grass is green,
The Bush is growing through the rails,
    The spike is rusted in;

It was from there his freckled face
   Would turn and smile at me;
For he'd milk seven in the race
   While I was milking three.

He kissed me twice and once again
   And rode across the hill;
The pint-pots and the hobble-chain
   I hear them jingling still . . .
About the hut the sunlight fails,
   The fire shines through the cracks—
I climb the broken stockyard rails
   And watch the bridle-tracks.

And he is coming back again—
   He wrote from Evatt's Rock;
A flood was in the Darling then
   And foot-rot in the flock.
The sheep were falling thick and fast
   A hundred miles from town,
And when he reached the line at last
   He trucked the remnant down.

And so he'll have to stand the cost;
   His luck was always bad,
Instead of making more, he lost
   The money that he had;
And how he'll manage, Heaven knows
   (My eyes are getting dim)
He says—he says—he don't—suppose
   I'll want—to—marry—him.

As if I wouldn't take his hand
   Without a golden glove—
Oh! Jack, you men won't understand
   How much a girl can love.
I long to see his face once more—
   Jack's dog! thank God, it's Jack!—
(I never thought I'd faint before)
   He's coming—up—the track.

THE SOUTHERLY BUSTER

There's a wind that blows out of the South in the drought,
    And we pray for the touch of his breath
When siroccos come forth from the Nor'-West and North,
    Or in dead calms of fever and death.
With eyes glad and dim we should sing him a hymn,
    For depression and death are his foes;
Oh, it gives us new life for the bread-winning strife
    When the glorious Old Southerly blows.

Old Southerly Buster! your forces you muster
    Where seldom a wind bloweth twice,
And your white-caps have hint of the snow-caps, and glint of
    The far-away barriers of ice.
No wind the wide sea on can sing such a paean
    Or do the great work that you do;
Our Own Wind and Only, from seas wild and lonely—
    Old Southerly Buster!—To you!

The yachts cut away at the close of the day
    From the breakers commencing to comb,
For a few he may swamp in the health-giving romp
    With the friendly Old Southerly home.
Oh, softly he plays through the city's hot ways
    To the beds where they're calling "Come, quick!"
He is gentle and mild round the feverish child,
    And he cools the hot brow of the sick.

'Tis a glorious mission, Old Sydney's Physician!—
    Broom, Bucket, and Cloth of the East!
'Tis a breeze and a sprayer that answers our prayer,
    And it's free to the greatest and least.
The red-lamp's a warning to drought and its scorning—
    A sign to the city at large—
Hence, Headache and Worry! Despondency, hurry!
    Old Southerly Buster's in charge!

Old Southerly Buster! your forces you muster
    Where seldom a wind bloweth twice,
And your white-caps have hint of the snow-caps and glint of
    The far-away barriers of ice.

No wind the wide sea on can sing such a paean,
  Or do the great work that you do;
Our Own Wind and Only, from seas wild and lonely—
  Old Southerly Buster!—To you!

WRITTEN AFTERWARDS

(To J. Le Gay Brereton)

So the days of my riding are over,
  The days of my tramping are done—
I'm about as content as a rover
  Will ever be under the sun;
I write, after reading your letter—
  My mind with old memories rife—
And I feel in a mood that had better
  Not meet the true eyes of the wife.

You must never admit a suggestion
  That old things are good to recall;
You must never consider the question:
  "Was I happier then, after all?"
You must banish the old hope and sorrow
  That make the sad pleasures of life;
You must live for Today and Tomorrow
  If you want to be just to the wife.

I have changed since the first day I kissed her,
  Which is due—Heaven bless her!—to her;
I'm respected and trusted—I'm "Mister",
  Addressed by the children as "Sir".
I feel the respect without feigning,
  And you'd laugh the great laugh of your life
If you only saw me entertaining
  An old lady friend of the wife.

By the way, when you're writing, remember
  You never went drinking with me,
And forget our Last Nights of December,
  Lest our several accounts disagree.

And, for my sake, old man, you had better
    Avoid the old language of strife,
For the technical terms of your letter
    Will be misconstrued by the wife.

Never hint of the girls appertaining
    To the past, when you're writing again,
For they take such a lot of explaining—
    And you know how I hate to explain.
There are some things, we know to our sorrow,
    That cut to the heart like a knife,
And your past is Today and Tomorrow
    If you want to be true to the wife.

No doubt you are dreaming as I did
    And going the careless old pace,
But my future grows dull and decided,
    And the world narrows down to the Place.
Let it be. If my reason's resented,
    You may do worse, old man, in your life;
Let me dream, too, that I am contented—
    For the sake of a true little wife.

ENGLAND YET

She's England yet! The nations never knew her;
    Or, if they knew, were ready to forget.
She made new worlds that paid no homage to her,
    Because she called for none as for a debt.
The bullying Power that deemed all nations craven,
    And thought her star of destiny had set,
Was sure that she would seek a coward's haven—
    And tempted her, and found her England yet!

We learn our England, and we soon forget,
To learn again that she is England yet.

They watched Britannia ever looking forward,
    But could not see the things her children saw.
They watched in Southern seas her boats pull shoreward,
    But only marked the eyeglass, heard the "Haw!"

In tents, and bungalows, and outpost stations,
   Thin white men ruled for her, unseen, unheard,
Ten millions of strange races and far nations
   Were ready to obey her at a word.

We learn our England, and in peace forget,
To learn in storm that she is England yet.

She's England yet; and men shall doubt no longer;
   And mourn no longer for what she has been.
She'll be a greater England and a stronger—
   A better England than the world has seen.
Our own, who reck not of a king's regalia,
   Tinsel of crowns, and courts that fume and fret,
Are fighting for her—fighting for Australia—
   And blasphemously hail her "England Yet!"

She's England yet, with little to regret—
Ay, more than ever, she'll be England yet!

1917

BALLAD OF THE DROVER

Across the stony ridges,
   Across the rolling plain,
Young Harry Dale, the drover,
   Comes riding home again.
And well his stock-horse bears him,
   And light of heart is he,
And stoutly his old packhorse
   Is trotting by his knee.

Up Queensland way with cattle
   He's travelled regions vast,
And many months have vanished
   Since home-folks saw him last.
He hums a song of someone
   He hopes to marry soon;
And hobble-chains and camp-ware
   Keep jingling to the tune.

Beyond the hazy dado
  Against the lower skies
And yon blue line of ranges
  The station homestead lies.
And thitherward the drover
  Jogs through the lazy noon,
While hobble-chains and camp-ware
  Are jingling to a tune.

An hour has filled the heavens
  With storm-clouds inky black;
At times the lightning trickles
  Around the drover's track;
But Harry pushes onward,
  His horses' strength he tries,
In hope to reach the river
  Before the flood shall rise.

The thunder, pealing o'er him,
  Goes rumbling down the plain;
And sweet on thirsty pastures
  Beats fast the plashing rain;
Then every creek and gully
  Sends forth its tribute flood—
The river runs a banker,
  All stained with yellow mud.

Now Harry speaks to Rover,
  The best dog on the plains,
And to his hardy horses,
  And strokes their shaggy manes.
"We've breasted bigger rivers
  When floods were at their height,
Nor shall this gutter stop us
  From getting home tonight!"

The thunder growls a warning
  The blue, forked lightnings gleam;
The drover turns his horses
  To swim the fatal stream.
But, oh! the flood runs stronger
  Than e'er it ran before;
The saddle-horse is failing,
  And only half-way o'er!

When flashes next the lightning,
    The flood's grey breast is blank;
A cattle-dog and packhorse
    Are struggling up the bank.
But in the lonely homestead
    The girl shall wait in vain—
He'll never pass the stations
    In charge of stock again.

The faithful dog a moment
    Lies panting on the bank,
Then plunges through the current
    To where his master sank.
And round and round in circles
    He fights with failing strength,
Till, gripped by wilder waters,
    He fails and sinks at length.

Across the flooded lowlands
    And slopes of sodden loam
The packhorse struggles bravely
    To take dumb tidings home;
And mud-stained, wet, and weary,
    He goes by rock and tree,
With clanging chains and tinware
    All sounding eerily.

AFTER ALL

The brooding ghosts of Australian night have gone from the bush and town;
My spirit revives in the morning breeze, though it died when the sun went down;
The river is high and the stream is strong, and the grass is green and tall,
And I fain would think that this world of ours is a good world after all.

The light of passion in dreamy eyes, and a page of truth well read,
The glorious thrill, in a heart grown cold, of the spirit I thought was dead,

A song that goes to a comrade's heart, and a tear of pride let fall—
And my soul is strong! and the world to me is a grand world after all!

Let our enemies go by their old dull tracks, and theirs be the fault or shame
(The man is bitter against the world who has only himself to blame);
Let the darkest side of the past be dark, and only the good recall;
For I must believe that the world, my dear, is a kind world after all.

It well may be that I saw too plain, or it may be I was blind;
But I'll keep my face to the dawning light, though the devil may stand behind!
Though the devil may stand behind my back, shall I see his shadow fall?
I'll read in the light of the morning stars—a good world after all.

Rest, for your eyes are weary, girl—you have driven the worst away—
The ghost of the man that I might have been is gone from my heart today;
We'll live for life and the best it brings till our twilight shadows fall;
My heart grows brave, and the world, my girl, is a good world after all.

BLACK BONNET

A DAY of seeming innocence,
   A glorious sun and sky,
And, just above my picket fence,
   Black Bonnet passing by.
In knitted gloves and quaint old dress,
   Without a spot or smirch,
Her worn face lit with peacefulness,
   Old Granny goes to church.

Her hair is richly white, like milk,
   That long ago was fair—
And glossy still the old black silk
   She keeps for "chapel wear";

Her bonnet, of a bygone style
   That long has passed away,
She must have kept a weary while
   Just as it is today.

The parasol of days gone by—
   Old days that seemed the best—
The hymn and prayer books carried high
   Against her warm, thin breast;
As she had clasped—come smiles come tears
   Come hardship, ay, and worse—
On market days, through faded years,
   The slender household purse.

Although the road is rough and steep,
   She takes it with a will,
For, since she hushed her first to sleep
   Her way has been uphill.
Instinctively I bare my head
   (A sinful one, alas!)
Whene'er I see, by church bells led,
   Brave Old Black Bonnet pass.

For she has known the cold and heat
   And dangers of the Track:
Has fought bush-fires to save the wheat
   And little home Out Back.
By barren creeks the Bushman loves,
   In stockyard, hut, and pen,
The withered hands in those old gloves
   Have done the work of men.

    .   .   .   .   .

They called it "Service" long ago,
   When Granny yet was young,
And in the chapel, sweet and low,
   As girls her daughters sung.
And when in church she bends her head
   (But not as others do)
She sees her loved ones, and her dead,
   And hears their voices too.

Fair as the Saxons in her youth,
  Not forward, and not shy;
And strong in healthy life and truth
  As after years went by;
She often laughed with sinners vain,
  Yet passed from faith to sight—
God gave her beauty back again
  The more her hair grew white.

She came out in the Early Days
  (Green seas, and blue—and grey)—
The village fair, and English ways,
  Seemed worlds and worlds away.
She fought the haunting loneliness
  Where brooding gum-trees stood;
And won through sickness and distress
  As Englishwomen could.

. . . . . .

By verdant swath and ivied wall
  The congregation's seen—
White nothings where the shadows fall,
  Black blots against the green.
The dull, suburban people meet
  And buzz in little groups,
While down the white steps to the street
  A quaint old figure stoops.

And then along my picket fence
  Where staring wallflowers grow—
World-wise Old Age, and Common-sense!—
  Black Bonnet, nodding slow.
But not alone; for on each side
  A little dot attends
In snowy frock and sash of pride,
  And these are Granny's friends.

To them her mind is clear and bright,
  Her old ideas are new;
They know her "real talk" is right,
  Her "fairy talk" is true.
And they converse as grown-ups may,
  When all the news is told;
The one so wisely young today,
  The two so wisely old.

At home, with dinner waiting there,
    She smooths her hair and face,
And puts her bonnet by with care
    And dons a cap of lace.
The table minds its p's and q's
    Lest one perchance be hit
By some rare dart, which is a part
    Of her old-fashioned wit.

   .   .   .   .   .

Her son and son's wife are asleep;
    She puts her apron on—
The quiet house is hers to keep,
    With all the youngsters gone.
There's scarce a sound of dish on dish
    Or cup slipped into cup,
When, left alone, as is her wish,
    Black Bonnet "washes up".

THE VANGUARD

They say, in all kindness, I'm out of the hunt—
Too old and too deaf to be sent to the Front.
A scribbler of stories, a maker of songs,
To the fireside and armchair my valour belongs.
*Yet in hopeless campaigns and in bitterest strife
I have been at the Front all the days of my life.*

Oh, your girl feels a princess, your people are proud,
As you march down the street to the cheers of the crowd;
And the Nation's behind you and cloudless your sky;
And you come back to Honour, or gloriously die;
*But for each thing that brightens, and each thing that cheers,
I have starved in the trenches these forty long years.*

MY ARMY, O MY ARMY!

My army, O my army! The time I dreamed of comes!
I want to see your colours; I long to hear your drums!
I heard them in my boyhood when all men's hearts seemed cold;
I heard them through the Years of Life—and now I'm growing old!
My army, O my army! The signs are manifold!

My army, O my army! My army and my Queen!
I sang your Southern battle-songs when I was seventeen!
They echoed down the Ages, they came from far and near;
They came to me from Paris, they came to me from Here!—
They came while I was marching with the Army of the Rear.

My Queen's dark eyes were flashing (oh, she was younger then!)
My Queen's Red Cap was redder than the reddest blood of men!
My Queen marched like an Amazon, with anger manifest—
Her wild hair darkly matted from a knife-gash in her breast
(For blood will flow where milk will not—her sisters knew the rest).

My legions ne'er were listed, they had no need to be;
My army ne'er was trained to arms—'twas trained to misery!
It took long years to mould it, but war could never drown
The shuffling of my army's feet at drill in Hunger Town—
A little child was murdered, and so Tyranny went down.

My army kept no order, my army kept no time;
My army dug no trenches, yet died in dust and slime;
Its troops were fiercely ignorant, as to the manner born;
Its clothes were rags and tatters—patched rags, the patches torn—
Ah me! It wore a uniform that I have often worn.

The faces of my army were ghastly as the dead;
My army's cause was Hunger, my Army's cry was "Bread!"
It called on God and Mary and Christ of Nazareth;
It cried to kings and courtesans that fainted at its breath—
Its women beat their poor, flat breasts where babes had starved to
    death.

. . . . . .

My army! O my army—I hear the sound of drums
Above the roar of battle—and, lo, my army comes!
Nor creed of man may stay it—nor war, nor nations' law
The pikes go through the firing-lines as pitchforks go through
    straw—
Like pitchforks through the litter—while empires stand in awe.

RAIN IN THE MOUNTAINS

The valley's full of misty clouds,
   Its tinted beauty drowning,
Tree-tops are veiled in fleecy shrouds,
   And mountain fronts are frowning.

The mist is hanging like a pall
   Above the granite ledges,
And many a silvery waterfall
   Leaps o'er the valley's edges.

The sky is of a leaden grey,
   Save where the north looks surly,
The driven daylight speeds away,
   And night comes o'er us early.

Dear Love, the rain will pass full soon,
   Far sooner than my sorrow,
But in a golden afternoon
   The sun may set tomorrow.

TALBRAGAR

Jack Denver died on Talbragar when Christmas Eve began,
And there was sorrow round the place, for Denver was a man;
Jack Denver's wife bowed down her head—her daughter's grief was wild,
And big Ben Duggan by the bed stood sobbing like a child.
But big Ben Duggan saddled up, and galloped fast and far,
To raise the biggest funeral yet seen on Talbragar.
        By station home
        And shearing shed
        Ben Duggan cried, "Jack Denver's dead!
        Roll up at Talbragar!"

He borrowed horses here and there, and rode all Christmas Eve,
And scarcely paused a moment's time the mournful news to leave;
He rode by lonely huts and farms until the day was done,
And then he turned his horse's head and made for Ross's Run.
No bushman in a single day had ridden half so far
Since Johnson brought the doctor to his wife at Talbragar.

        By digger's camps
        Ben Duggan sped—
        At each he cried, "Jack Denver's dead!
        Roll up at Talbragar!"

That night he passed the humpies of the splitters on the ridge,
And roused the bullock-drivers camped at Belinfante's Bridge;
And as he climbed the ridge again the moon shone on the rise—
Did moonbeams glisten in the mist of tears that filled his eyes?
He dashed the rebel drops away—for blinding things they are—
But 'twas his best and truest friend who died on Talbragar.
        At Blackman's Run
        Before the dawn,
        Ben Duggan cried, "Jack Denver's gone!
        Roll up at Talbragar!"

At all the shanties round the place they heard his horse's tramp,
He took the track to Wilson's Luck, and told the digger's camp,
But in the gorge by Deadman's Gap the mountain shades were black,
And there a newly-fallen tree was lying on the track;
He saw too late—and then he heard the swift hoof's sudden jar,
And big Ben Duggan ne'er again rode home to Talbragar.
        "The wretch is drunk,
        And Denver's dead—
        A burning shame!" the people said
        Next day at Talbragar.

For thirty miles round Talbragar the boys rolled up in strength,
And Denver had a funeral a good long mile in length;
Round Denver's grave that Christmas Day rough Bushmen's eyes were dim—
The Western Bushmen knew the way to bury dead like him;
But some returning homeward found, by light of moon and star,
Ben Duggan lying in the rocks, five miles from Talbragar.
        And far and wide
        When Duggan died,
        The bushmen of the western side
        Rode in to Talbragar.

THE SHAKEDOWN ON THE FLOOR

Set me back for twenty summers,
    For I'm tired of cities now—
Set my feet in red-soil furrows
    And my hands upon the plough,
With the two Black Brothers trudging
    On the home stretch through the loam,
While along the grassy sidling
    Come the cattle grazing home.

And I finish ploughing early,
    And I hurry home to tea—
There's my black suit on the stretcher,
    And a clean white shirt for me;
There's a dance at Rocky Rises,
    And, when they can dance no more,
For a certain favoured party
    There's a shakedown on the floor.

You remember Mary Carey,
    Bushmen's favourite at The Rise?
With her sweet small freckled features,
    Red-gold hair, and kind grey eyes;
Sister, daughter, to her mother,
    Mother, sister, to the rest—
And of all my friends and kindred
    Mary Carey loved me best.

Far too shy, because she loved me,
    To be dancing oft with me;
(What cared I, because she loved me,
    If the world were there to see?)
But we lingered by the sliprails
    While the rest were riding home,
Ere the hour before the dawning
    Dimmed the great star-clustered dome.

Small brown hands that spread the mattress,
    While the old folk winked to see
How she'd find an extra pillow
    And an extra sheet for me.

For a moment shyly smiling,
    She would grant me one kiss more—
Slip away and leave me happy
    By the shakedown on the floor.

Rock me hard in steerage cabins,
    Rock me soft in first saloons,
Lay me on the sandhill lonely
    Under waning Western moons;
But wherever night may find me—
    Till I rest for evermore—
I shall dream that I am happy
    In the shakedown on the floor.

PETER ANDERSON AND CO.

He had offices in Sydney, not so many years ago,
And his shingle bore the legend "Peter Anderson and Co.",
But his real name was Careless, as the fellows understood—
And his relatives decided that he wasn't any good.
'Twas their gentle tongues that blasted any "character" he had—
He was fond of beer and leisure—and the Co. was just as bad.
It was limited in number to a unit, was the Co.—
'Twas a bosom chum of Peter, and his Christian name was Joe.

'Tis a class of men belonging to these soul-forsaken years;
Third-rate canvassers, collectors, journalists and auctioneers.
They are never very shabby, they are never very spruce—
Going cheerfully and carelessly and smoothly to the deuce.
Some are wanderers by profession, turning up and gone as soon,
Travelling second-class, or steerage (when it's cheap they go saloon);
Free from all the "ists" and "isms", undisturbed by faith or doubt—
Lazy, purposeless, and useless—knocking round and hanging out.

They will take what they can come by, they will give what they can give,
God alone knows how they manage—God alone knows how they live!
They are nearly always hard-up, but are cheerful all the while—
Men whose energy and trousers wear out sooner than their smile!

They, no doubt, like us, are haunted by the boresome "if" or
 "might",
But their ghosts are ghosts of daylight—they are men who live
 at night!

Peter met you always smiling, always seemed to know you well,
Always gay and glad to see you, always had a joke to tell;
He could laugh when all was gloomy, he could grin when all
 was blue,
Sing a comic song and act it, and appreciate one, too.
Only cynical in cases where his own self was the jest,
And the humour of his good yarns made atonement for the rest.
Seldom serious—doing business just as 'twere a friendly game—
Cards or billiards—nothing graver. And the Co. was much the same.

They tried everything and nothing 'twixt the shovel and the press,
And were more or less successful in their ventures—mostly less.
Once they ran a country paper (till the plant was seized for debt)
And the local sinners chuckle over dingy copies yet.
Now and then they'd take an office, as they called it—make a dash
Into business life as "Agents"—something not requiring cash.
(You can always furnish cheaply, when your cash or credit fails,
With a packing-case, a hammer, and a pound of two-inch nails—
And, maybe, a drop of varnish, and sienna, too, for tints,
And a scrap or two of oilcloth and a yard or two of chintz.)

The office was their haven, for they lived there when hard-up—
A "daily" for a tablecloth—a jam tin for a cup;
If, perchance, the landlord's bailiff happened round in times like
 these
Just to seize the office-fittings—well, there wasn't much to seize.
They would leave him in possession. But at times when things
 grew hot
They would shoot the moon, and open where the landlord knew
 them not.
And when morning brought the bailiff there'd be nothing to be
 seen
Save a piece of bevelled cedar where the tenant's plate had been;
There would be no sign of Peter—there would be no sign of Joe—
But another portal boasted "Peter Anderson and Co."

And when times were locomotive, billiard-rooms and private bars—
Spicy parties at the cafe—long cab-drives beneath the stars;
Private picnics down the Harbour—shady campings-outs, you know—
No one would have dreamed 'twere Peter—no one would have thought 'twas Joe!
Free-and-easies in their "diggings", when the funds began to fail,
Bosom chums, cigars, tobacco, and a case of English ale—
Gloriously drunk and happy, till they heard the roosters crow—
And the landlady and neighbours made complaints about the Co.
But that life! it might be likened to a reckless drinking-song,
For it couldn't last for ever, and it never lasted long.

. . . .

Debt-collecting ruined Peter—people talked him round too oft
For his heart was soft as butter (and the Co.'s was just as soft);
He would cheer the haggard missus, and he'd tell her not to fret,
And he'd ask the worried debtor round with him to have a wet;
He would ask him round the corner, and it seemed to him and her
After each of Peter's visits, things were brighter than they were.
But, of course, it wasn't business—only Peter's careless way;
And perhaps it pays in heaven, but on earth it doesn't pay.
They got harder up than ever, and, to make it worse, the Co.
Went more often round the corner than was good for him to go.
"I might live," he said to Peter, "but I haven't got the nerve;
I am going, Peter, going—going, going—no reserve.
Eat and drink and love they tell us, for tomorrow we may die,
Buy experience—and we bought it—we're experienced, you and I."

Then, he made a weary movement with his hand across his brow—
"The death of such philosophy's the death I'm dying now.
Pull yourself together, Peter; 'tis the dying wish of Joe
That the business world shall honour Peter Anderson and Co.
Find again and follow up the old ambitions that you had—
See if you can raise a drink, old man, I'm feelin' mighty bad;
Hot and sweetened, nip o' butter—squeeze o' lemon, Pete," he sighed.
And, while Peter went to fetch it, Joseph went to sleep, and died
With a smile—anticipation, maybe, of the peace to come,
Or a joke to try on Peter—or, perhaps, it was the rum.

. . . .

Peter staggered, gripped the table, swerved as some old drunkard
    swerves;
At a gulp he drank the toddy, just to brace his shattered nerves.
It was awful, more than awful, but he had no time to think—
All is nothing! Nothing matters! Fill your glasses—dead man's drink.

   .   .   .   .   .   .

Peter mourned his buried comrade, feeling beaten and bereft,
Paid the undertaker cash, and then got drunk on what was left.
Then he shed some tears, half-maudlin, on the grave where lay
    the Co.,
And he drifted to a township where the city failures go.
There, though haunted by the man he was, the wreck he yet
    might be,
Or by the man he might have been, or by spectres of the three,
And the dying words of Joseph, ringing through his own despair,
Peter pulled himself together, and he started business there.

In a town of wrecks and failures they appreciated him—
Men who might have been, who had been, but who were not
    in the swim;
They would ask him who the Co. was—that queer company he
    kept—
And he'd always answer vaguely—he would say his partner slept;
That he had a sleeping partner—jesting while his spirit broke—
And they grinned above their glasses, for they took it for a joke.
He would shout while he had money, he would joke while he
    had breath—
No one seemed to care, or notice, how he drank himself to death;
Till at last there came a morning when his smile was seen no
    more—
He was gone from out the office, and his shingle from the door;
And a boundary-rider jogging out across the neighbouring run
Was attracted by a something that was blazing in the sun;
And he found that it was Peter, lying peacefully at rest,
With a bottle close beside him and the shingle on his breast.
Well, they analysed the liquor, and the doctor said that he
Had mixed his drink with something good for setting spirits free.
But "He's gone to look for Joseph", that was what the townsfolk said,
So a jury viewed him sadly, and they found—that he was dead.

THE SONG AND THE SIGH

The creek went down with a broken song,
  'Neath the sheoaks high;
The waters carried the tune along,
  And the oaks a sigh.

The song and the sigh went winding by,
  Went winding down;
Circling the foot of the mountain high
  And the hillside brown.

They were hushed in the swamp of the Dead
      Man's Crime,
  Where the curlews cried;
But they reached the river the selfsame time,
  And there they died.

And the creek of life goes winding on,
  Wandering by;
And bears for ever, its course upon,
  A song and a sigh.

TROOPER CAMPBELL

One day old Trooper Campbell
  Rode out to Blackman's Run;
His cap-peak and his sabre
  Were glancing in the sun.
'Twas New Year's Eve, and slowly
  Across the ridges low
The sad Old Year was drifting
  To where the old years go.

The trooper's mind was reading
  The love-page of his life—
His love for Mary Wylie
  Ere she was Blackman's wife;
He sorrowed for the sorrows
  Of the heart a rival won,
For he knew that there was trouble
      Out there on Blackman's Run.

The sapling shades had lengthened,
    The summer day was late,
When Blackman met the trooper
    Beyond the homestead gate;
And, if the hand of trouble
    Can leave a lasting trace,
The lines of care had come to stay
    On poor old Blackman's face.

"Not good day, Trooper Campbell,
    It's a bad, bad day for me—
You are of all the men on earth
    The one I wished to see.
The great black clouds of trouble
    Above our homestead hang;
That wild and reckless boy of mine
    Has joined M'Durmer's gang.

"Oh! save him, save him, Campbell,
    I beg in friendship's name!
For if they take and hang him,
    The wife would die of shame.
Could Mary and her sisters
    Hold up their heads again,
And face a woman's malice,
    Or claim the love of men?

"And if he does a murder
    We all were better dead.
Don't take him living, Trooper,
    If a price be on his head;
But shoot him! shoot him, Campbell,
    When you meet him face to face,
And save him from the gallows—
    And us from that disgrace."

"Now, Tom," cried Trooper Campbell,
    "You know your words are wild.
Wild though he is and reckless,
    Yet still he is your child;
Bear up and face your trouble,
    Yes, meet it like a man,
And tell the wife and daughters
    I'll save him if I can."

    .   .   .   .   .

The sad Australian sunset
  Had faded from the west;
But night brought darker shadows
  To hearts that could not rest;
And Blackman's wife sat rocking
  And moaning in her chair.
"Oh, the disgrace, disgrace," she moaned;
  "It's more than I can bear.

"In hardship and in trouble
  I struggled year by year
To make my children better
  Than other children here.
And if my son's a felon
  How can I show my face?
I cannot bear disgrace; my God,
  I cannot bear disgrace!

"Ah, God in Heaven pardon!
  I'm selfish in my woe—
My boy is better-hearted
  Than many that I know.
I'll face whatever happens,
  And, till his mother's dead,
My foolish child shall find a place
  To lay his outlawed head."

    . . . . .

Sore-hearted, Trooper Campbell
  Rode out from Blackman's Run,
Nor noticed aught about him
  Till thirteen miles were done;
When, close beside a cutting,
  He heard the click of locks,
And saw the rifle-muzzles
  Trained on him from the rocks.

But suddenly a youth rode out,
  And, close by Campbell's side:
"Don't fire! don't fire, in Heaven's name!
  It's Campbell, boys!" he cried.
Then one by one in silence
  The levelled rifles fell,
For who'd shoot Trooper Campbell
  Of those who knew him well?

On, bravely sat old Campbell,
   No sign of fear showed he.
He slowly drew his carbine;
   It rested by his knee.
The outlaws' guns were lifted,
   But none the silence broke,
Till steadfastly and firmly
   Old Trooper Campbell spoke,

"The boy that you would ruin
   Goes home with me, my men;
Or some of us shall never
   Ride through the Gap again.
You all know Trooper Campbell,
   And have you ever heard
That bluff or lead could turn him
   Or make him break his word?

"That reckless lad is playing
   A heartless villain's part;
He knows that he is breaking
   His poor old mother's heart.
He's going straight to ruin;
   But 'tis not that alone,
He'll bring dishonour to a name
   That I'd be proud to own.

"I speak to you, M'Durmer—
   If your heart's not granite quite,
And if you'd seen the trouble
   At Blackman's home tonight,
You'd help me now, M'Durmer—
   I speak as man to man—
I swore to save the foolish lad—
   I'll save him if I can."

"Oh, take him!" said M'Durmer,
   "He's got a horse to ride. . . ."
The youngster thought a moment,
   Then rode to Campbell's side. . . .
"Good-bye!" young Blackman shouted,
   As up the range they sped.
"Luck for the New Year, Campbell,"
   Was all M'Durmer said.

Then fast along the ridges
   Two horsemen rode a race,
The moonlight lent a glory
   To Trooper Campbell's face.
And ere the new year's dawning
   They reached the homestead gate—
"I found him," said the Trooper,
   "And not, thank God, too late!"

THE ROUTE MARCH

Did you hear the children singing, O my brothers?
Did you hear the children singing as our troops went
     marching past?
     In the sunshine and the rain,
      As they'll never sing again—
Hear the little schoolgirls singing as our troops went
     swinging past?

Did you hear the children singing, O my brothers?
Did you hear the children singing for the first man and
     the last?
     As they marched away and vanished
      To a tune we thought was banished—
Did you hear the children singing for the future and
     the past?

Shall we hear the children singing, O my brothers?
Shall we hear the children singing in the sunshine
   or the rain?
     There'll be sobs beneath the ringing
     Of the cheers, and 'neath the singing
There'll be tears of orphan children when Our Boys
   come back again!

BALLAD OF THE ELDER SON

A son of elder sons am I
   Whose boyhood days were cramped and scant;
Who lived the old domestic lie
   And breathed the old familiar cant.

Come, elder brothers mine, and bring
   Dull loads of care that you have won,
And gather round me while I sing
   The ballad of the elder son.

The elder son on barren soil,
   Where life is crude and lands are new,
Must share the father's hardest toil,
   And see the father's troubles through.
With no child-thoughts to match his own,
   No game to play, no race to run,
The youth his father might have known
   Is seldom for the elder son.

    .   .   .   .

A certain squatter had two sons
   Up Canaan way some years ago.
The graft was hard on those old runs,
   The sun was hot, and life was slow.
The younger brother coolly claimed
   The portion that he hadn't earned,
And sought the "life" for which untamed
   And high young spirits always yearned.

A year or so he knocked about,
   And spent his cheques on girls and wine,
But, getting stony in the drought,
   He took a job at herding swine;
And though he was a hog to swig,
   And fool with girls till all was blue—
'Twas rather rough to mind the pig
   And have to eat its tucker too.

Then, coming to himself, he said—
   He reckoned shrewdly, though dead beat—
"The rousers in my father's shed
   Have got more grub than they can eat;
I've been a fool, but such is fate—
   I guess I'll talk the guv'nor round:
'I've acted cronk,' I'll tell him straight;
   (He's had his time, too, I'll be bound).

"I'll tell him straight I've had my fling,
    I'll tell him 'I've been on the beer,
But put me on at anything,
    I'll graft with any bounder here.'"
He rolled his swag and struck for home,
    (By this time he was pretty slim),
And, when the old man saw him come—
    Well, you know how he welcomed him

They've brought the best robe in the house,
    The ring, and killed the fatted calf,
And now they hold a grand carouse,
    And eat and drink and dance and laugh:
While from the field the elder son—
    Whose character is not admired—
Comes plodding home when work is done,
    Extremely hot and very tired.

He asked the meaning of the sound
    Of such unwonted revelry,
They said his brother had been "found"
    (He'd found himself, it seems to me);
'Twas natural the elder son
    Should take the thing a little hard
And brood on what was past and done
    While standing, pensive, in the yard.

Now, he was hungry and knocked out
    And would, if they had let him be,
Have rested and cooled down, no doubt,
    And hugged his brother after tea
And welcomed him, and hugged his dad,
    And filled the wine-cup to the brim—
But, just when he was feeling bad,
    The old man came and tackled him.

He well might say with bitter tears
    While music swelled and flowed the wine—
"Lo, I have served thee many years
    Nor caused thee one grey hair of thine.
Whate'er thou bad'st me do I did
    And for my brother made amends;
Thou never gavest me a kid
    For merry-making with my friends."

(He was no heavy clod and glum
   Who could not trespass, sing or dance—
He could be merry with a chum,
   It seemed, if he had half a chance;
Perhaps, if further light we seek,
   He knew—and herein lay the sting—
His brother would clear out next week
   And promptly pop the robe and ring.)

The father said, "The wandering one,
   The lost is found, this son of mine,
But thou art always with me, son—
   Thou knowest all I have is thine."
(It seemed the best robe and the ring,
   The love and fatted calf were not;
But this was just a little thing
   The old man in his joy forgot.)

"And all I have"—the paltry bribe
   That he might slave contented yet,
While envied by his selfish tribe
   The birthright he might never get:
The worked-out farm and endless graft,
   The mortgaged home, the barren run—
The heavy, hopeless overdraft—
   The portion of the elder son.

Sometimes the Eldest takes the track
   When things at home have got too bad—
He comes not crawling, canting back
   To seek the blind side of his dad.
He always finds a knife and fork
   And meat between on which to dine,
And, though he sometimes deals in pork,
   He never eats his meals with swine.

The happy home, the overdraft,
   His birthright and his prospects gay,
And his share, likewise, of the graft,
   He leaves the rest to grab. And they—
Who'd always do the thing by halves,
   If anything for him was done—
Should kill a score of fatted calves
   To welcome home the eldest son.

KNOCKED UP

I'm lyin' on the barren ground that's baked and cracked with
    drought,
And dunno if my legs or back or heart is most wore out;
I've got no spirits left to rise and smooth me achin' brow—
I'm too knocked up to light a fire and bile the billy now.

Oh it's trampin', trampin', tra-a-mpin', in flies an' dust an' heat,
Or it's trampin', trampin', tra-a-mpin' through mud and slush 'n sleet;
It's tramp an' tramp for tucker—one everlastin' strife,
An' wearin' out yer boots an' heart in the wastin' of yer life.

They whine o' lost an' wasted lives in idleness and crime—
I've wasted mine for twenty years, and grafted all the time—
And never drunk the stuff I earned, nor gambled when I shore—
But somehow when you're on the track yer life seems wasted more.

A long dry stretch of thirty miles I've tramped this broilin' day,
All for the off-chance of a job a hundred miles away;
There's twenty hungry beggars wild for any job this year,
An' fifty might be at the shed while I am lyin' here.

The sinews in my legs seem drawn, red-hot—'n that's the truth;
I seem to weigh a ton, and ache like one tremendous tooth;
I'm stung between my shoulder-blades—my blessed back seems
    broke;
I'm too knocked out to eat a bite—I'm too knocked up to smoke.

The blessed rain is comin' too—there's oceans in the sky,
An' I suppose I must get up and rig the blasted fly;
The heat is bad, the water's bad, the flies a crimson curse,
The grub is bad, mosquitoes damned—but rheumatism's worse.

I wonder why poor blokes like me will stick so fast to breath,
Though Shakespeare says it is the fear of somethin' after death;
But though Eternity be cursed with God's almighty curse—
What ever that same somethin' is I swear it can't be worse.

For it's trampin', trampin', tra-a-mpin' through hell across the plain,
And it's trampin' trampin' tra-a-mpin' through slush 'n mud 'n rain—
A livin' worse than any dog—without a home 'n wife,
A-wearin' out yer heart 'n soul in the wastin' of yer life.

THE NEVER-NEVER LAND

By homestead, hut, and shearing-shed,
  By railroad, coach, and track—
By lonely graves where rest our dead,
  Up Country and Out Back;
To where beneath the clustered stars
  The dreamy plains expand—
My home lies wide a thousand miles
  In the Never-Never Land.

It lies beyond the farming belt,
  Wide wastes of scrub and plain,
A blazing desert in the drought,
  A lake-land after rain;
To the skyline sweeps the waving grass,
  Or whirls the scorching sand—
A phantom land, a mystic realm!
  The Never-Never Land.

Where lone Mount Desolation lies,
  Mounts Dreadful and Despair,
'Tis lost beneath the rainless skies
  In hopeless deserts there;
It spreads nor'-west by No-Man's-Land—
  Where clouds are seldom seen—
To where the cattle-stations lie
  Three hundred miles between.

The drovers of the Great Stock Routes
  The strange Gulf Country know,
Where, travelling for the northern grass
  The big lean bullocks go;
And camped by night where plains lie wide
  Like some old ocean's bed,
The stockmen in the starlight ride
  Round fifteen hundred head.

And west of named and numbered days
  The shearers walk and ride,
Jack Cornstalk and the Ne'er-do-well
  And Greybeard side by side;

They veil their eyes from moon and stars,
    And slumber on the sand—
Sad memories sleep as years go round
    In Never-Never Land.

O rebels to society!
    The Outcasts of the West—
O hopeless eyes that smile for me,
    And broken hearts that jest!
The pluck to face a thousand miles,
    The grit to see it through!
The Communism perfected
    Till man to man is True!

The Arab to the desert sand,
    The Finn to fens and snow,
The "Flax-stick" dreams of Maoriland,
    While seasons come and go.
Whatever stars may glow or burn
    O'er lands of East and West,
The wandering heart of man will turn
    To one it loves the best.

Lest in the city I forget
    True mateship, after all,
My water-bag and billy yet
    Are hanging on the wall.
And I, to save my soul, again
    Would tramp to sunsets grand
With sad-eyed mates across the plain
    In the Never-Never Land.

THE JOLLY DEAD MARCH

If I ever be worthy   famous—
    Which I'm sadly beginning to doubt—
When the angel whose place 'tis to name us
    Shall say to my spirit, "Pass out!"
I wish for no snivelling about me
    (My work was the work of the land)
But I hope that my country will shout me
    The price of a decent brass band.

Oh, let it strike up "Annie Laurie",
  And let it burst out with "Lang Syne"—
Twin voices of sadness and glory
  That have ever been likings of mine.
And give the French war-hymn deep-throated
  With "The Star-Spangled Banner" between,
But let the last mile be devoted
  To "Britannia" and "Wearing the Green".

Thump! thump! of the drums and "Te-ri-rit",
  Thump! thump! of the drum—'twill be grand,
Though only in dream or in spirit
  To ride or flit after that band!
While myself and my mourners go straying
  And strolling and drifting along,
With the cornets in front of us playing
  The tune of an old battle-song!

I ask for no "turn-out" to bear me;
  I ask not for railings or slabs,
And spare me, my country, oh, spare me
  The hearse and the long string of cabs!
And if, in the end—more's the pity—
  There's fame more than money to spare,
A vanman I know in the city
  Will cart me "This side up with care".

And my spirit will join the procession—
  Will pause, so to speak, on the brink—
Nor feel the least shade of depression
  When the mourners drop out for a drink;
It may be a hot day in December,
  Or a cold day in June it may be,
And a drink will but help them remember
  The good points the world missed in me.

"Unhook the West Port" for an orphan,
  An old digger chorus revive—
If you don't hear a whoop from the coffin,
  I am *not* being buried alive.
But I'll go with a spirit less bitter
  Than mine on this earth's ever been,
And, perhaps, to save trouble, Saint Peter
  Will pass me, two comrades between.

Thump! thump! of the drums we inherit—
    War-drums of my dreams—oh, it's grand!
Be this the reward of all merit
    To ride or march after a band!
As we, the World-Battlers, go straying
    And loving and laughing along—
With Hope in the lead of us playing
    The tune of a life-battle song!

Then let them strike up "Annie Laurie",
    And let 'em burst out with "Lang Syne",
Twin voices of sadness and glory
    That have ever been likings of mine.
Let them swell the French war-hymn deep-throated
    (And I'll not buck at "God Save the Queen")
But let the last mile be devoted
    To "Britannia" and "Wearing the Green".

KISS IN THE RING

I've not seen a picnic for many a day,
My heart has grown callous, my head has grown grey;
But old faded letters their memories bring,
And I'm thinking tonight about Kiss in the Ring.
        Kiss in the Ring,
        Kiss in the Ring—
Oh, it makes me remember old Kiss in the Ring!

We drove down the gullies, we drove down the creek,
We drove round the sidlings, we drove round the Peak,
In carts and in buggies the Bush girls to bring
To laugh with us there in sweet Kiss in the Ring.
        Kiss in the Ring,
        Kiss in the Ring—
I remember the days of sweet Kiss in the Ring.

And now I think sadly of years in their flight . . .
At the turn by the sliprails I kissed her good night.
She is under the turf, but old memories cling—
Do the angels dance with her to Kiss in the Ring?
        Kiss in the Ring,
        Sweet Kiss in the Ring—
Do the angels dance with her to Kiss in the Ring?

FOR'ARD

It is stuffy in the steerage where the second-classers sleep,
For there's near a hundred for'ard, and they're stowed away like sheep—
They are trav'lers for the most part in a straight 'n' honest path;
But their linen's rather scanty, an' there isn't any bath—
Stowed away like ewes and wethers that is shore 'n' marked 'n' draft;
But the shearers of the shearers always seem to travel aft—
      In the cushioned cabins, aft,
        With saloons 'n' smoke-rooms, aft—
There is sheets 'n' best of tucker for the first-salooners, aft.

Our beef is just like scrapin's from the inside of a hide,
And the spuds were pulled too early, for they're mostly green inside;
But from somewhere back amidships there's a smell o' cookin' waft,
An' I'd give my earthly prospects for a real good tuck-out aft—
      Ham an' eggs, 'n' coffee, aft,
        Say, cold fowl for luncheon, aft,
Juicy grills an' toast 'n' cutlets—Tucker a-lor-frongsy, aft.

They feed our women separate, an' they make a blessed fuss,
Just as if they couldn't trust 'em for to eat along with us!
Just because our hands are horny an' our hearts are rough with graft—
But the gentlemen and ladies always "dine" together aft—
      With their ferns an' mirrors, aft,
        With their flowers an' napkins, aft—
"I'll assist you to an orange"—"Kindly pass the sugar", aft.

We are shabby, rough, 'n' dirty, an' our feelin's out of tune,
An' it's hard on fellers for'ard that was used to go saloon;
There's a broken swell amongst us—he is barracked, he is chaffed,
An' I wish at times, poor devil, for his own sake he was aft;
      For they'd understand him, aft
        (He will miss the bath-rooms aft),
Spite of all there's no denying that there's finer feelin's aft.

Last night we watched the moonlight as it spread across the sea—
"It is hard to make a livin'," said the broken swell to me;
"There is ups and downs," I answered, an' a bitter laugh he laughed—

There were brighter days an' better when he always travelled aft—
        With his rug an' gladstone, aft,
        With his cap an' spyglass, aft—
A careless, rovin', gay young spark as always travelled aft.

There's a notice by the gangway, an' it seems to come amiss.
For it says that second-classers ain't allowed abaft o' this;
An' there ought to be a notice for the fellows from abaft—
But the smell an' dirt's a warnin' to the first-salooners, aft;
        With their tooth- and nail-brush, aft,
        With their cuffs an' collars, aft—
Their cigars an' books, an' papers, an' their cap-peaks for-'n'-aft.

I want to breathe the mornin' breeze that blows against the boat,
For there's a swellin' in my heart, a tightness in my throat.
We are for'ard when there's trouble! We are for'ard when there's
    graft!
But the men who never battle always seem to travel aft;
        With their dressin'-cases, aft,
        With their swell pyjamas, aft—
Yes! the idle and the careless, they have ease an' comfort aft.

I feel so low and wretched, as I mooch about the deck,
That I'm ripe for jumpin' over—an' I wish there was a wreck!
We are driven to New Zealand to be shot out over there,
Scarce a shillin' in our pockets, nor a decent rag to wear,
With the everlastin' worry lest we don't get into graft—
Oh, there's little left to land for if you cannot travel aft.
        No anxiety abaft,
        They have stuff to land with, aft—
There is little left to land for if you cannot travel aft.

But it's grand at sea this mornin', an' Creation almost speaks,
Sailin' past the Bay of Islands with its pinnacles an' peaks,
With the sunny haze all round us an' the white-caps on the blue,
An' the orphan rocks an' breakers—oh, it's glorious sailin' through!
To the south a distant steamer, to the west a coastin' craft,
An' we see the beauty for'ard—can they see it better aft?—
        Spite of op'ra glasses, aft;
        But, ah well, they're brothers aft—
Nature seems to draw us closer—bring us nearer for-'n'-aft.

What's the use of bein' bitter? What's the use of gettin' mad?
What's the use of bein' narrer just because yer luck is bad?
What's the blessed use of frettin' like a child that wants the moon?
There is broken hearts an' trouble in the gilded First Saloon!
We are used to bein' shabby—we have got no overdraft—
We can laugh at troubles for'ard that they couldn't laugh at aft!
    Spite o' pride an' tone abaft
    (Keepin' up appearance, aft),
There's anxiety an' worry in the breezy cabins aft.

But the curse of class distinctions from our shoulders shall be hurled,
An' the sense of Human Kinship revolutionize the world;
There'll be higher education for the toilin', starvin' clown,
An' the rich an' educated shall be educated down;
Then we all will meet amidships on this stout old earthly craft,
An' there won't be any friction 'twixt the classes for-'n'-aft.
    We'll be brothers, fore-'n'-aft!
    Yes, an' sisters, fore-'n'-aft!
When the people work together, and there ain't no fore-'n'-aft.

TO AN OLD MATE

Old Mate! In the gusty old weather,
When our hopes and our troubles were new,
In the years spent in wearing out leather,
I found you unselfish and true—
I have gathered these verses together
For the sake of our friendship and you.

You may think for awhile, and with reason,
Though still with a kindly regret,
That I've left it full late in the season
To prove I remember you yet;
But you'll never judge me by their treason
Who profit by friends—and forget.

I remember, Old Man, I remember—
The tracks that we followed are clear—
The jovial last nights of December,
The solemn first days of the year,
Long tramps through the clearings and timber,
Short partings on platform and pier.

I can still feel the spirit that bore us,
And often the old stars will shine—
I remember the last spree in chorus
For the sake of that other Lang Syne
When the tracks lay divided before us,
Your path through the future, and mine.

Through the frost-wind that cut like whip-lashes,
Through the ever-blind haze of the drought—
And in fancy at times by the flashes
Of light in the darkness of doubt—
I have followed the tent-poles and ashes
Of camps that we moved farther out.

You will find in these pages a trace of
That side of our past which was bright,
And recognize sometimes the face of
A friend who has dropped out of sight—
I send them along in the place of
The letters I promised to write.

SAYS YOU

When the heavy sand is yielding backward from your blistered feet,
And across the distant timber you can *see* the flowing heat;
When your head is hot and aching, and the shadeless plain is wide,
And it's fifteen miles to water in the scrub the other side—
Don't give up, don't be downhearted, to a man's strong heart be true!
Take the air in through your nostrils, set your lips and see it through—
For it can't go on for ever, and—"I'll have my day!" says you.

When you're camping in the mulga, and the rain is falling slow,
While you nurse your rheumatism 'neath a strip of calico,
Short of tucker or tobacco, short of sugar or of tea,
And the scrubs are dark and dismal, and the plains are like a sea;
Don't give up and be downhearted—to the soul of man be true!
Grin, if you've a mate to grin for! grin and joke, and don't look blue;
For it can't go on for ever, and "I'll rise again!" says you.

When you've tramped the Sydney pavements till you've counted
    all the flags,
And your flapping boot-soles trip you, and your clothes are mostly
    rags,
When you're called a city loafer, shunned, abused, moved on,
    despised—
Fifty hungry beggars after every job that's advertised—
Don't be beaten! Hold your head up! To your wretched self be true;
Set your pride to fight your hunger! Be a *man* in all you do!
For it can't go on for ever, and "I'll rise again!" says you.

When you're dossing out in winter, in the darkness and the rain,
Crouching, cramped and cold and hungry, 'neath a seat in The
    Domain,
And a cloaked policeman stirs you with that mighty foot of his—
"Phwat d'ye mane? Phwat's this? Who are ye? Come, move on—
    git out av this!"
Don't get mad; that's only foolish; there is nothing you can do,
Save to mark his beat and time him—find another hole or two;
But it can't go on for ever—"I'll have money yet!" says you.

· · · · ·

Don't you fret about the morrow, for sufficient to the day
Is the evil (rather more so). Put your trust in God and pray!
Study well the ant, thou sluggard. Blessed are he meek and low.
Ponder calmly on the lilies—how they idle, how they grow.
A man's a man! Obey your masters! Do not blame the proud and fat,
For the poor are always with them, and they cannot alter that.
Lay your treasure up in heaven—cling to life and see it through!
For it cannot last for ever—"I shall die some day," says you.

ANDY'S RETURN

With pannikins all rusty,
    And billy burnt and black,
And clothes all torn and dusty
    That scarcely hide his back;
With sun-cracked saddle-leather,
    And knotted green-hide rein,
His face burnt brown with weather,
    Our Andy's home again!

His unkempt hair is faded
  With sleeping in the wet,
He's looking old and jaded;
  But he is hearty yet.
With eyes sunk in their sockets—
  But merry as of yore;
With big cheques in his pockets,
  Our Andy's home once more!

Old Uncle's bright and cheerful;
  He wears a smiling face;
And Aunty's never tearful
  Now Andy's round the place.
Old Blucher barks for gladness;
  He broke his rusty chain,
And leapt in joyous madness
  When Andy came again.

With tales of flood and famine
  On distant northern tracks,
And shady yarns—"baal gammon!"
  Of dealings with the blacks,
From where the skies hang lazy
  On many a northern plain,
From regions dim and hazy
  Our Andy's home again!

His toil is nearly over;
  He'll soon enjoy his gains.
No more he'll be a drover,
  And cross the lonely plains.
Where sheoaks bend and quiver
  Far from the hot North-west,
At home by some cool river
  He means to build our nest.

SONG OF THE OLD BULLOCK-DRIVER

FAR back in the days when the blacks used to ramble
  In long single file 'neath the evergreen tree,
The wool-teams in season came down from Coonamble,
  And journeyed for weeks on their way to the sea.

'Twas then that our hearts and our sinews were stronger,
    For those were the days when tough bushmen were bred.
We journeyed on roads that were rougher and longer
    Than roads which the feet of our grandchildren tread.

We never were lonely, for, camping together,
    We yarned and we smoked the long evenings away,
And little I cared for the signs of the weather
    When snug in my hammock slung under the dray.
We rose with the dawn, were it ever so chilly,
    When yokes and tarpaulins were covered with frost,
And toasted the bacon and boiled the black billy—
    Then high on the camp-fire the branches we tossed.

On flats where the air was suggestive of possums,
    And homesteads and fences were hinting of change,
We saw the faint glimmer of apple-tree blossoms,
    And far in the distance the blue of the range;
Out there in the rain there was small use in flogging
    The poor tortured bullocks that tugged at the load,
When, down to the axles, the waggons were bogging
    And traffic was making a slough of the road.

Oh, hard on the beasts were those terrible pinches
    Where two teams of bullocks were yoked to a load,
And tugging and slipping, and moving by inches,
    Half-way to the summit they clung to the road.
And then, when the last of the pinches was bested,
    (You'll surely not say that a glass was a sin?)
The bullocks lay down 'neath the gum-trees and rested—
    The bullockies steered for the door of the inn.

Then slowly we crawled by the trees that kept tally
    Of miles that were passed on the long journey down.
We saw the wild beauty of Capertee Valley,
    As slowly we rounded the base of the Crown.
But, ah! the poor bullocks were cruelly goaded
    While climbing the hills from the flats and the vales;
'Twas here that the teams were so often unloaded
    That all knew the meaning of "counting your bales".

The best-paying load that I ever have carried
  Was one to the run where my sweetheart was nurse.
We courted awhile, and agreed to get married,
  And couple our futures for better or worse.
And when my old feet were too weary to drag on
  The miles of rough metal they met by the way,
My eldest grew up and I gave him the waggon—
  He's plodding along by the bullocks today.

I'M A REBEL TOO

The mighty King of Virland—
  Oh! he was angry then—
Who rode to crush rebellion
  With twenty thousand men.
His enemies he scattered
  And hanged on every side,
Because their creed was rapine,
  Their motive greed and pride.

They searched for Outlaw Eric,
  They hunted everywhere—
(Most honest of the rebels
  If aught was honest there).
King Hertzberg swore to hang him;
  But, when the day was done,
They had not caught the Outlaw,
  But found his little son.

He had not seen his father.
  Nor knew where he had gone;
And someone asked him thoughtless,
  Which side himself was on.
And straightaway he made answer,
  That child so brave and true,
"My father is a rebel,
  And I'm a rebel too."

King Hertzberg, he dismounted,
  And kindly bent his head:
"Now, why are you a rebel,
  My little man?" he said.

The boy nor paused nor faltered,
   But stood like Eric's son,
And answered Hertzberg simply—
   "Because my father's one."

King Hertzberg sank beside him
   And rested on one knee.
"I would my royal children
   As loyal were," said he.
"Go, seek and tell your father
   That he and his go free,
And if his wrongs be real
   Then let him come to me.

"And let him come with plain words,
   With plain words in the light,
And ride not with armed rebels
   And outlaws in the night.
And let him not mistrust me—
   To all that is untrue,
Wherever Wrong's the ruler,
   I am a rebel too."

SONG OF THE DARLING RIVER

THE skies are brass and the plains are bare,
Death and ruin are everywhere—
And all that is left of the last year's flood
Is a sickly stream on the grey-black mud;
The salt-springs bubble and quagmires quiver,
And—this is the Song of the Darling River:

"I rise in the drought from the Queensland rain,
I fill my branches again and again;
I drown dry gullies and lave bare hills,
I turn drought-ruts into rippling rills—
I form fair islands and glades all green
Till every bend is a sylvan scene.
I have watered the barren land ten leagues wide!
But in vain I have tried, ah! in vain I have tried
To show as a sign from the Great All-Giver,
His Word to a people: 'Oh, lock your river.'

"I want no blistering barge aground,
But racing steamers the seasons round;
I want fair homes on my lonely ways,
A people's love and a people's praise—
And rosy children to dive and swim—
And fair girls' feet in my rippling brim;
And cool, green forests, and gardens ever—"
So runs the Song of the Darling River.

The sky is brass, and the scrub-lands glare,
Death and ruin are everywhere;
Thrown high to bleach, or deep in the mud
The bones lie buried by last year's flood,
And the Demons dance from the Never Never
To laugh at the rise of the Darling River.

THE GOOD SAMARITAN

He comes from out the ages dim—
    The good Samaritan;
I somehow never pictured him
    A fat and jolly man.
But one who'd little joy to glean,
    And little coin to give—
A sad-faced man, and lank and lean,
    Who found it hard to live.

His eyes were haggard in the drought,
    His hair was iron-grey—
His dusty gown was patched, no doubt,
    Where we patch pants today.
His faded turban, too, was torn—
    But darned and folded neat,
And leagues of desert sand had worn
    The sandals on his feet.

He'd been a fool, perhaps, and would
    Have prospered had he tried,
But he was one who never could
    Pass by the other side.

An honest man whom men called soft,
    While laughing in their sleeves—
No doubt in business ways he oft
    Had fallen amongst thieves.

And, I suppose, by track and tent,
    And other ancient ways,
He drank, and fought, and loved, and went
    The pace in his young days.
And he had known the bitter year
    When love and friendship fail—
I wouldn't be surprised to hear
    That he had been in jail.

And if he was a married man,
    As many are that roam,
I guess the good Samaritan
    Was rather glum at home.
Howbeit—in a study brown—
    He had, for all we know,
His own thoughts as he journeyed down
    The road to Jericho.

(And so "by chance there came that way",
    It reads not like romance—
The truest friends on earth today,
    They mostly come by chance.)
He saw a stranger left by thieves
    Sore hurt and like to die—
He also saw (my heart believes)
    The others pass him by.

(Perhaps that good Samaritan
    Knew Levite well, and priest)
He lifted up the wounded man
    And sat him on his beast,
And took him on towards the inn—
    All Christlike, unawares—
Still pondering, perhaps, on sin
    And virtue—and his cares.

He bore him in and fixed him right
    (Helped by the local drunk),
And wined and oiled him well at night,
    And thought beside his bunk.

And on the morrow ere he went
    He left a quid and spoke
Unto the host in terms which meant
    "Look after that poor bloke".

He must have known them at the inn,
    They must have known him too—
Perhaps on that same track of sin
    He'd seen a sick mate through;
For "whatsoe'er thou spendest more"
    (The parable is plain)
"I will repay," he told the host,
    "When I return again."

It seems he was a good sort, too,
    The boss of that old pub—
(As even now there are a few
    At shanties in the scrub).
The good Samaritan jogged on
    Through Canaan's dust and heat,
And pondered on the good days gone
    Or ways to make ends meet.

(He was no Christian, understand,
    For Christ had not been born—
He journeyed later through the land
    To hold priests up to scorn;
To tell the world of "certain men"
    Like that Samaritan,
And preach the simple creed again—
    Man's duty, man to man!)

"Once on a time there lived a man"—
    But he has lived alway,
And that gaunt, good Samaritan
    Is with us here today;
He passed through the city streets
    Unnoticed and unknown,
He helps the sinner that he meets—
    His sorrows are his own.

He shares his tucker on the track
    When things are at their worst
(And often shouts in bars outback
    For souls that are athirst).

Today you see him staggering down
  The blazing watercourse,
And making for the distant town—
  A sick man on his horse.

He'll live while nations find their graves
  And mortals suffer pain—
Though colour rule, and whites be slaves
  And savages again.
And, after all is past and done,
  He'll rise up, the Last Man,
From tending to the last but one—
  The good Samaritan.

TO HANNAH

Spirit girl, to whom 'twas given
  To revisit scenes of pain,
From the hell I thought was heaven
  You have lifted me again;
Through the world that I inherit,
  Where I loved you ere you died,
I am walking with the spirit
  Of a dead girl by my side.

Through my old possessions only
  For a very little while;
And they say that I am lonely,
  And they pity—but I smile:
For the brighter side has won me
  By the calmness that it brings,
And the peace that is upon me
  Does not come of earthly things.

Spirit girl, the good is in me,
  But the flesh, we know, is weak,
And with no pure soul to win me
  I might miss the path I seek;
Lead me by the love you bore me
  When you trod the earth with me,
Till the light is clear before me
  And my spirit, too, is free.

SHEARERS

No church-bell rings them from the Track
  No pulpit lights their blindness—
'Tis hardship, drought, and homelessness
  That teach those Bushmen kindness:
The mateship born, in barren lands,
  Of toil and thirst and danger,
The camp-fare for the wanderer set,
  The first place to the stranger.

They do the best they can today—
  Take no thought of the morrow;
Their way is not the old-world way—
  They live to lend and borrow.
When shearing's done and cheques gone wrong,
  They call it "time to slither!"—
They saddle up and say "So-long!"
  And ride the Lord knows whither.

And though he may be brown or black,
  Or wrong man there, or right man,
The mate that's steadfast to his mates
  They call that man a "white man!"
They tramp in mateship side by side—
  The Protestant and Roman—
They call no biped lord or sir,
  And touch their hat to no man!

They carry in their swags, perhaps,
  A portrait and a letter—
And, maybe, deep down in their hearts,
  The hope of "something better".
Where lonely miles are long to ride,
  And long, hot days recurrent,
There's lots of time to think of men
  They might have been—but weren't.

They turn their faces to the west
  And leave the world behind them
(Their drought-dry graves are seldom set
  Where even mates can find them).

>They know too little of the world
>   To rise to wealth or greatness:
>But in these lines I gladly pay
>   My tribute to their straightness.

THE ARMY OF THE REAR

I listened through the music and the sounds of revelry,
And all the hollow noises of the year of Jubilee;
I heard behind the music and beyond the loyal cheer
The steady tramp of thousands who were marching in the rear.
>   Tramp! tramp! tramp!
>   They seemed to shake the air,
Those never-ceasing footsteps of the outcasts in the rear.

I hate the wrongs I read about, I hate the wrongs I see—
The tramping of that army sounds as music unto me!
A music that is terrible, that frights the anxious ear,
Is beaten from the weary feet slow-tramping in the rear.
>   Tramp! tramp! tramp!
>   In dogged, grim despair—
They have a goal, those footsteps of the Army of the Rear!

I looked upon the nobles, with their lineage so old,
I looked upon their mansions, on their acres and their gold,
I saw their women radiant in jewelled robes appear—
And then I joined the army of the outcasts in the rear.
>   Tramp! tramp! tramp!
>   We'll show what Want can dare,
My brothers and my sisters of the Army of the Rear!

I looked upon the mass of poor, in filthy alleys pent,
And on the rich men's Edens, that are built on grinding rent,
I looked o'er London's miles of slums—I saw the horrors here,
And swore to die a soldier of the Army of the Rear.
>   Tramp! tramp! tramp!
>   I've sworn to do and dare,
I've sworn to die a soldier of the Army of the Rear!

"They're brutes," so say the wealthy, "and by steel must be dismayed"—
Be there brutes among us, nobles, they are brutes that *ye* have made;

We want what God hath given us, we want our portion here.
And that is why we're marching—and we'll march beyond the rear!
    Tramp! tramp! tramp!
    Awake and have a care,
Ye proud and haughty spurners of the wretches in the rear.

We'll nurse our wrongs to strengthen us, our hate that it may grow,
For, outcast from society, Society's our foe.
Beware! who grind out human flesh, for human life is dear!
There's menace in the marching of the Army of the Rear.
    Tramp! tramp! tramp!
    There's danger in despair,
There's danger in the marching of the Army of the Rear!

The wealthy care not for our wants, nor for the pangs we feel;
Our hands have clutched in vain for bread, and now they clutch
 for steel!
Come, men of rags and hunger, come! There's work for heroes here!
There's room still in the vanguard of the Army of the Rear!
    Tramp! tramp! tramp!
    O men of want and care!
There's glory in the vanguard of the Army of the Rear!

NEW-CHUM JACKEROOS

He may not ride as you can ride,
 Or do what you can do;
But sometimes you'd seem small beside
 The new-chum jackeroo.

His share of work he never shirks,
 And through the blazing drought
He lives the old things down, and works
 His own salvation out.

When older, wiser chums despond,
 He battles brave of heart—
'Twas he who sailed of old beyond
 The margin of the chart.

He crossed wide deserts, hot and bare,
    From barren, hungry shores—
Grim wastes that you would scarcely dare
    With all your tanks and bores.

He fought a way through stubborn hills
    Towards the setting sun—
Our fathers all, and Burke and Wills,
    Were new chums, every one.

When England fought with all the world,
    In those brave days gone by,
And felt its strength against her hurled,
    They held her honour high.

By southern palm and northern pine,
    Where'er was life to lose,
They held their own—the thin red line
    Of new-chum jackeroos.

THE CAMBAROORA STAR

So you're writing for a paper? Well, it's nothing very new
To be writing yards of drivel for a tidy little screw;
You are young and educated, and a clever chap you are,
But you'll never run a paper like the Cambaroora *Star*.
Though in point of education I am nothing but a dunce,
I myself—you mayn't believe it—helped to run a paper once
With a chap on Cambaroora, by the name of Charlie Brown,
And I'll tell you all about it, if you'll take the story down.

On a golden day in summer, when the sunrays were aslant,
Brown arrived in Cambaroora with a little printing plant
And his worldly goods and chattels—rather damaged on the way—
And a weary-looking woman who was following the dray.
He had bought an empty humpy, and, instead of getting tight,
Why, the diggers heard him working like a lunatic all night:
And next day a sign of canvas, writ in characters of tar,
Claimed the humpy as the office of the Cambaroora *Star*.

Well, I cannot read, that's honest, but I had a digger friend
Who would read the paper to me from the title to the end;
The first number had a leader running thieves and spielers down,
With a slap against claim-jumping, and a poem made by Brown.
Once I showed it to a critic, and he said 'twas very fine,
Though he wasn't long in finding glaring faults in every line;
But the poem sang of Freedom—all the clever critic said
Couldn't stop that song from ringing, ringing, ringing in my head.

So I went where Brown was working in his little hut hard by:
"My old mate has been a-reading of your writings, Brown," said I—
"I have studied on your leader, I agree with what you say,
You have struck the bedrock certain, and there ain't no getaway;
Your new paper's just a thumper for a young and growing land,
And your principles is honest, Brown; I want to shake your hand,
And if there's any lumping in connection with the *Star*,
Well, I'll find the time to do it, and I'll help you—there you are!"

Brown was every inch a digger (bronzed and bearded, from the
 South),
But a kind of weakness hovered round the corners of his mouth
As he took the hand I gave him; and he gripped it like a vice,
While he tried his best to thank me, and he stuttered once or twice.
But there wasn't need for talking—we'd the same old loves and hates,
And we understood each other—Charlie Brown and I were mates.
So we worked a little paddock on a place they called the Bar,
And we sank a shaft together, and at night we worked the *Star*.

Charlie thought, and did his writing, when we left the claim at
 night,
And the missus set the "copy" near as quick as he could write.
Well, I didn't shirk my promise, and I helped the thing, I guess,
For I worked the heavy lever of the crazy printing-press;
Brown himself would do the feeding, and the missus used to "fly"—
She is flying with the angels, if there's justice up on high,
For she died on Cambaroora when the *Star* began to go,
And was buried as the diggers buried diggers long ago.

. . . . . .

Lord, that press! It was a jumper—we could seldom get it right,
And were lucky if we averaged a hundred in a night.
Then we'd sit, all three together, in the windy hut and fold,
And I helped the thing a little when I struck a patch of gold.

But we battled for the diggers as the papers seldom do,
Though at times, when diggers errored, then we touched the diggers too.
Yet the paper took the fancy of that roaring mining town,
And the diggers sent a nugget, with their sympathy to Brown.

Oft I sat and smoked beside him in the listening hours of night,
When the shadows from the corners seemed to gather round the light—
When his weary, aching fingers, closing stiffly round the pen,
Wrote defiant truth in language that could touch the hearts of men—
Wrote until his eyelids shuddered—wrote until the East was grey,
Wrote the stern and awful lessons that were taught him in his day;
And they knew that he was honest, and they read his smallest par,
For I think the diggers' Bible was the Cambaroora *Star*.

Diggers then had little mercy for the loafer and the scamp—
If there wasn't law and order, there was justice in the camp;
And the manly independence that is found where diggers are
Had a sentinel to guard it in the Cambaroora *Star*.
There was strife about the Chinkies who came down in days of old
Like a crowd of thieves and loafers when the diggers found the gold—
Like the sneaking fortune-hunters who are only found behind,
And who always shepherd diggers till they track them to the "find".

Charlie wrote a slinging leader, calling on his digger mates,
And he said: "We think that Asia is as bad as syndicates.
What's the good of holding meetings where you only talk and swear?
Get a move upon the Pig-tails when you've got an hour to spare."
It was nine o'clock next morning when the Chows began to swarm,
But they weren't so long in going, for the white men's blood was warm.
Then the diggers held a meeting, and they shouted: "Hip hoorar!
Give three ringing cheers, my hearties, for the Cambaroora *Star*."

But the Cambaroora petered, and the diggers' sun went down,
And another sort of people came and settled in the town;
Reefing matters were conducted by a syndicate or two,
And they changed the name to Queenville, for their blood was very blue.

Then they wanted Brown to help them put the feathers in their
    nests,
But his leaders went like thunder for their vested interests,
And he fought for right and justice, and he raved about the dawn
Of the reign of Man and Reason till his ads were all withdrawn.

He was offered shares for nothing in the richest of the mines,
Might have made a tidy fortune had he run on other lines;
They abused him for his leaders, and they parodied his rhymes,
And they told him that his paper was a mile behind the times.
"Let the times alone," said Charlie, "they're all right, you needn't
    fret;
For I started long before them, and they haven't caught me yet.
But," says he to me, "they're coming, and they're not so very far—
Though I left the times behind me, they are following the *Star*.

"Let them do their worst," said Charlie, "but I'll never drop the reins
While a single scrap of paper or an ounce of ink remains:
I've another truth to tell them, though they tread me in the dirt,
And I'll print another issue if I print it on my shirt."
So we fought the battle bravely, and we did our very best
Just to make the final issue quite as lively as the rest.
And the swells of Cambaroora talked of feathers and of tar
When they read that final issue of the Cambaroora *Star*.

Gold is stronger than the tongue is—gold is stronger than the pen:
They'd have squirmed in Cambaroora had I found a nugget then;
But in vain we scraped together every penny we could get,
For they fixed us with their boycott, and the plant was seized for
    debt.
'Twas the "General Store" that did it, and it sealed the paper's doom,
Though we gave it ads for nothing when the *Star* began to boom:
Just a paltry bill for tucker—and the crawling, sneaking clown
Sold the debt for twice its value to the men who hated Brown.

I was digging up the river, and I swam the flooded bend
With a little cash and comfort for my literary friend.
Brown was sitting sad and lonely with his head bowed in despair,
While a single tallow candle threw a flicker on his hair,
And the gusty wind that whistled through the crannies of the door
Stirred the scattered files of paper that were lying on the floor.
Charlie took my hand in silence—but at last he turned and said:
"Tom, old mate, we did our damnedest, but the brave old *Star* is
    dead."

.   .   .   .   .   .

Then he stood up on a sudden, with a face as pale as death,
And he gripped my hand a moment, while he seemed to fight for
> breath:
"Tom, old friend," he said, "I'm going, and I'm ready to—to start;
I have always known there's something—something crooked with
> my heart.
Tom, my first child died. I loved her even better than the pen,
Tom—and while the *Star* was dying, why, I felt as I did *then* . . . .
Listen! Like the distant thunder of the rollers on the bar—
Listen, Tom! I hear the—diggers—shouting: 'Bully of the *Star*!'"

THE WATER-LILY

A lonely young wife
In her dreaming discerns
A lily-decked pool
With a border of ferns,
And a beautiful child,
With butterfly wings,
Trips down to the edge of the water and sings:
"Come, mamma! come!
Quick! follow me!
Step out on the leaves of the water-lily!"

And the lonely young wife,
Her heart beating wild,
Cries, "Wait till I come,
Till I reach you, my child!"
But the beautiful child
With butterfly wings
Steps out on the leaves of the lily and sings:
"Come, mamma! come!
Quick! follow me!
And step on the leaves of the water-lily!"

And the wife in her dreaming
Steps out on the stream,
But the lily leaves sink
And she wakes from her dream
Ah, the waking is sad,
For the tears that it brings,

And she knows 'tis her dead baby's spirit that sings:
"Come, mamma! come!
Quick! follow me!
Step out on the leaves of the water-lily!"

TRACKS THAT LIE BY INDIA

Now this is not a dismal song, like some I've sung of late,
When I've been brooding all day long about my muddled fate;
For, though I've had a rocky time I'll never quite forget,
And though I never was so deep in trouble and in debt,
And though I never was so poor nor in a fix so tight—
The tracks that run by India are shining in my sight.

The roads that run by India, and all the ports of call—
I'm going back to London first to raise the wherewithal.
I'll call at Suez and Port Said as I am going past
(I was too worried to take notes when I was that way last),
At Naples and at Genoa, and, if I get the chance,
Who knows but I might run across the pleasant land of France.

The track that runs by India goes up the hot Red Sea—
The other side of Africa is far too dull for me.
(I fear that I have missed a chance I'll never get again
To see the land of chivalry and bide awhile in Spain.)
I'll graft a year in London, and if fortune smiles on me
I'll take the track to India by France and Italy.

'Tis sweet to court some foreign girl with eyes of lustrous glow,
Who does not know your language and whose language you don't know;
To loll on gently rolling decks beneath the softening skies,
While she sits knitting opposite, and courting with her eyes—
The glance that says far more than words, the old half-mystic smile—
The track that runs by India must wait for me awhile.

NEW LIFE, NEW LOVE

The cool breeze ripples the river below,
  And the fleecy clouds float high,
And I mark how the dark green gum-trees match
  The bright blue vault of the sky.
The rain has been, and the grass is green
  Where the slopes were bare and brown,
And I see the things that I used to see
  In the days ere my head went down.

I have found a light in my long dark night,
  Brighter than stars or moon;
I have lost the fear of the sunset drear,
  And the sadness of afternoon.
Here let us stand while I hold your hand,
  Where the light's on your golden head—
Oh! I feel the thrill that I used to feel
  In the days ere my heart was dead.

The storm's gone by, but my lips are dry
  And the old wrong rankles yet—
Sweetheart or wife, I must take new life
  From your red lips warm and wet!
So let it be, you may cling to me,
  There is nothing on earth to dread,
For I'll be the man that I used to be
  In the days ere my heart was dead!

MAY NIGHT ON THE MOUNTAINS

'Tis wonderful time when these hours begin,
  These long "small hours" of night,
When the grass is crisp, and the air is thin,
  And the stars come close and bright.
The moon hangs caught in a silvery veil
  From clouds of a steely grey,
And the hard, cold blue of the sky grows pale
  In the wonderful Milky Way.

There is something wrong with this star of ours,
    A mortal plank unsound,
That cannot be charged to the mighty powers
    Who guide the high stars round.
Though man is greater than bird or beast,
    Though wisdom is still his boast,
He surely resembles Nature least,
    And the things that vex her most.

Oh, say, some muse of a larger star,
    Some muse of the Universe,
If they who people those planets far
    Are better than we, or worse.
Are they exempted from deaths and births,
    And have they greater powers,
And higher heavens, and grander earths,
    And mightier Gods than ours?

Are our lies theirs? Is our truth their truth?
    Are they cursed for pleasure's sake?
Do they make their hells in their reckless youth
    Ere they know what hells they make?
And do they toil through each weary hour
    Till the tedious day is o'er.
For food that gives but the fleeting power
    To toil and strive for more?

THE CAPTAINS

The Captains sailed from Portugal, from England, France, and Spain;
Each sought to win his country's ease, her glory and her gain;
The Captains sailed to Southern Seas, and sailed the Spanish Main;
And some sailed out beyond the world, and some sailed home again.

And when a storm was on the coast, and spray leapt o'er the quays,
Then little Joan or Dorothy, or Inez or Louise,
Would kneel her down on such a night beside her mother's knees,
And fold her little hands and pray for those beyond the seas.

Now some will pray at Christ His feet, and some at Mary's shrine;
And some to heathen goddesses, as I have prayed to mine;
To Mecca or to Bethlehem, to Fire, or Joss, or Sol,
And some will pray to sticks or stones—and one to her rag doll.

But we are stubborn men and vain, and though we rise or fall,
Our children's prayers and women's prayers, God knows we need
    them all!
And no one fights the bitter gale, or strives in combat grim,
But somewhere in the world a child is praying hard for him.

The Captains sailed to India, to China and Japan,
Received the Strangers' Welcome, met the Friendliness of Man;
The Captains sailed to southern seas, and wondrous sights they
    saw—
The Rights of Man in savage lands, and law without a law.

They found fresh worlds for crowded folk from cities old and worn,
They found the new great, empty lands where Nations might be
    born;
They found new foods, they found new wealth, and newer ways
    to live,
Where sons might grow in strength and health, with all that
    God would give.

They tracked their ways through unknown seas where Danger
    still remains,
And sailed back poor and broken men—and some sailed back in
    chains.
But, bound or free, or ill or well, where'er their sails were furled,
They brought to weary, worn-out lands glad tidings from the World.

A VOICE FROM THE CITY

On western plain and eastern hill,
    Where once my fancy ranged,
The station hands are riding still
    And they are little changed.
But I have lost in London gloom
    The glory of the day—
The old, sweet scent of wattle-bloom
    Is faint and far away.

I warp my life on pavement stones
    That drag me ever down,
A paltry slave to little things,
    By custom chained to town.
I've lost the strength to strike alone,
    The heart to do and dare—
When swag and will were still my own
    I'd tramp to God-knows-where.

I mind the time when I was shy
    To meet the brown Bush girls—
I've lunched with lords since then, and I
    Have been at home with earls:
I learned to smile and learned to bow
    And lie to ladies gay—
But to a gaunt Bushwoman now
    What should I have to say?

And if I sought her home out west
    From scenes of show and sham,
The hard bare place would grimly test
    The poor weak thing I am.
I could not meet her hopeless eyes
    That look one through and through,
The haggard woman, hardship-wise,
    Who once thought I was true.

But nought on earth can last for aye,
    And, wild with care and pain,
Some day by chance I'll break away
    And seek the Bush again.
And find awhile from bitter years
    The rest the Bush can bring,
And hear, perhaps, with truer ears,
    The songs it has to sing.

CAMERON'S HEART

The diggings were just in their glory when Alister Cameron came,
With recommendations, he told me, from friends and a parson
    "at hame";

He read me his recommendations—he called them a part of his
    plant—
The first one was signed by the parson, another by Cameron's aunt.
The meenister called him "ungodly"—"a stray frae the fauld o' the
    Lord,"
And his aunt set him down as a spendthrift, "a rebel at hame and
    abroad".

He got drunk now and then and he gambled (such heroes are often
    the same);
That's all they could say in connection with Alister Cameron's name.
He was straight, and he stuck to his country and spoke with respect
    of his kirk;
He did his full share of the cooking, and more than his share
    of the work.
And many a poor devil knew, when his strength and his money
    were spent,
He'd be sure of a shakedown, and tucker—and a lecture in
    Cameron's tent.

He shunned all the girls near the diggings; they said he was
    proof to the dart—
That nothing but whisky and gaming had ever a place in his
    heart;
He carried a packet about him, well hid; but I saw it at last,
And—well, 'tis a very old story—the story of Cameron's past:
A ring and a sprig of white heather, a letter or two and a curl,
A bit of a worn chain of silver, and the portrait of Cameron's girl.

    .   .   .   .   .

It chanced in the first of the Sixties that Ally and I and McKean
Were sinking a shaft on Mundoorin, near Fosberry's puddle-machine.
The bucket we used was a big one, and rather a weight when
    'twas full,
Though Alister wound it up easy, for he had the strength of a bull.
He'd hinted at heart-disease often; but, setting his fancy apart,
I always believed there was nothing the matter with Cameron's heart.

One day I was working below—I was filling the bucket with clay,
When Alister cried, "Pack it on, mon! we ought to reach bottom
    today."
He wound, and the bucket rose steady and swift to the surface
    until

It reached the first log on the top, when it suddenly stopped, and hung still,
I knew what was up in a moment when Cameron shouted to me:
"Climb up for your life by the footholes. *I'll stick tae th' haun'le—or dee!*"

The strength of despair was upon me; I started, and scarcely drew breath,
But climbed to the top for dear life in the fear of a terrible death.
And there, with his waist on the handle, I saw the dead form of my mate,
And over the shaft hung the bucket, suspended by Cameron's weight.
He'd thought of my danger, not his, when he felt in his bosom the smart,
And stuck to the handle in spite of the Finger of Death on his heart.

GENOA

A long farewell to Genoa,
  That rises to the skies
Where the barren coast of Italy
  Like our own coastline lies.
A sad farewell to Genoa—
  And long my heart shall grieve—
The only city in the world
  That I was loth to leave.

No sign of rush or stress is there,
  No war of greed they wage.
The deep cool streets of Genoa
  Are rock-like in their age.
No garish signs of commerce there
  Against the sky are flung;
The rag that drapes a balcony
  An artist's hands have hung.

I've said farewell to tinted days
  And glorious starry nights,
I've said farewell to Naples
  With her long straight lines of lights;

Yet it is not for Naples that I grieve,
But for Genoa that I grieve,
The only city in the world
That I was loth to leave.

EUREKA

(A Fragment.)

Roll up, Eureka's heroes, on that Grand Old Rush afar,
For Lalor's gone to join you in the big camp where you are;
Roll up and give him welcome such as only diggers can,
For well he battled for the rights of miner and of Man.
In that bright, golden country that lies beyond our sight,
The record of his honest life shall be his Miner's Right;
But many a bearded mouth shall twitch, and many a tear be shed,
And many a grey old digger sigh to hear that Lalor's dead.
Yet wipe your eyes, old fossickers, o'er worked-out fields that roam,
You need not weep at parting from a digger going home.

. . . .

Now from the strange wild seasons past, the days of golden strife,
Now from the Roaring Fifties comes a scene from Lalor's life:
All gleaming white amid the shafts o'er gully, hill, and flat
Again I see the tents that form the camp at Ballarat.
I hear the shovels and the picks, and all the air is rife
With the rattle of the cradles and the sounds of digger-life;
The clatter of the windlass-boles, as spinning round they go,
And then the signal to his mate, the digger's cry, "Below!"
From many a busy pointing-forge the sound of labour swells,
The tinkling at the anvils is as clear as silver bells.
I hear the broken English from the mouth of many a one
From every state and nation that is known beneath the sun;
The homely tongue of Scotland and the brogue of Ireland blend
With the dialects of England, right from Berwick to Land's End;
And to the busy concourse here the States have sent a part,
The land of gulches that has been immortalized by Harte;
The land where long from mining-camps the blue smoke upward curled;
The land that gave the "Partner" true and "Mliss" unto the world;
The men from all the nations in the New World and the Old,
All side by side, like brethren here, are delving after gold.

But suddenly the warning cries are heard on every side
As, closing in around the field, a ring of troopers ride.
Unlicensed diggers are the game—their class and want are sins,
And so, with all its shameful scenes, the digger-hunt begins.
The men are seized who are too poor the heavy tax to pay,
Chained man to man as convicts were, and dragged in gangs away.
Though in the eye of many a man the menace scarce was hid,
The diggers' blood was slow to boil, but scalded when it did.

. . . . . .

But now another match is lit that soon must fire the charge,
A digger murdered in the camp; his murderer at large!
"Roll up! Roll up!" the poignant cry awakes the evening air,
And angry faces surge like waves around the speakers there.
"What are our sins that we should be an outlawed class?" they say,
"Shall we stand by while mates are seized and dragged like lags away?
Shall insult be on insult heaped? Shall we let these things go?"
And with a roar of voices comes the diggers' answer—"No!"
The day has vanished from the scene, but not the air of night
Can cool the blood that, ebbing back, leaves brows in anger white.
Lo, from the roof of Bentley's inn the flames are leaping high;
They write "Revenge!" in letters red across the smoke-dimmed sky.
"To arms! To arms!" the cry is out; "To arms and play your part;
For every pike upon a pole will find a tyrant's heart!"
Now Lalor comes to take the lead, the spirit does not lag,
And down the rough, wild diggers kneel beneath the Diggers' Flag;
Then, rising to their feet, they swear, while rugged hearts beat high,
To stand beside their leader and to conquer or to die!
Around Eureka's stockade now the shades of night close fast,
Three hundred sleep beside their arms, and thirty sleep their last.

. . . . . .

About the streets of Melbourne town the sound of bells is borne
That call the citizens to prayer that fateful Sabbath morn;
But there, upon Eureka's hill, a hundred miles away,
The diggers' forms lie white and still above the blood-stained clay.
The bells that toll the diggers' death might also ring a knell
For those few gallant soldiers, dead, who did their duty well.
The sight of murdered heroes is to hero-hearts a goad,
A thousand men are up in arms upon the Creswick road,
And wildest rumours in the air are flying up and down,
'Tis said the men of Ballarat will march on Melbourne town.

But not in vain those diggers died. Their comrades may rejoice,
For o'er the voice of tyranny is heard the people's voice;
It says: "Reform your rotten law, the diggers' wrongs make right,
Or else with them, our brothers now, we'll gather to the fight."

.   .   .   .

'Twas of such stuff the men were made who saw our nation born,
And such as Lalor were the men who led the vanguard on;
And like such men may we be found, with leaders such as they,
In the roll-up of Australians on our darkest, grandest day!

KNOCKING AROUND

Weary old wife, with the bucket and cow,
"How's your son Jack? and where is he now?"
Haggard old eyes that turn to the west—
"Boys will be boys, and he's gone with the rest!"
Grief without tears and grief without sound;
"Somewhere up-country he's knocking around."
    Knocking around with a vagabond crew,
    Does for himself what a mother would do;
    Maybe in trouble and maybe hard-up,
    Maybe in want of a bite or a sup;
    Dead of the fever, or lost in the drought,
    Lonely old mother! he's knocking about.

Wiry old man at the tail of the plough,
"Heard of Jack lately? and where is he now?"
Pauses a moment his forehead to wipe,
Drops the rope reins while he feels for his pipe,
Scratches his grey head in sorrow or doubt:
"Somewhere or other he's knocking about."
    Knocking about on the runs of the West,
    Holding his own with the worst and the best,
    Breaking in horses and risking his neck,
    Droving or shearing and making a cheque;
    Straight as a sapling—six-foot, and sound,
    Jack is all right when he's knocking around.

THE BUSH FIRE

On the runs to the west of the Dingo Scrub there was drought, and ruin, and death,
And the sandstorm came from the dread north-east with the blast of a furnace-breath;
Till at last one day, at the fierce sunrise, a boundary-rider woke,
And saw in the place of the distant haze a curtain of light-blue smoke.

There is saddling-up by the cocky's hut, and out in the station yard,
And away to the north, north-east, north-west, the bushmen are riding hard.
The pickets are out, and many a scout, and many a mulga wire,
While Bill and Jim, their faces grim, are riding to meet the fire.

It roars for days in the trackless scrub, and across, where the ground seems clear,
With a crackle and rush, like the hissing of snakes, the fire draws near and near;
Till at last, exhausted by sleeplessness, and the terrible toil and heat,
The squatter is crying, "My God! the wool!" and the farmer, "My God! the wheat!"

But there comes a drunkard (who reels as he rides) with news from the roadside pub:—
"Pat Murphy—the cocky—cut off by the fire!—way back in the Dingo Scrub!
Let the wheat and the woolshed go to ——" Well, they do as each great heart bids;
They are riding a race for the Dingo Scrub—for Pat and his wife and kids.

And who are leading the race with Death? An ill-matched three, you'll allow;
Flash Jim, the Breaker, and Boozing Bill (who is riding steadily now),
And Constable Dunn, of the Mounted Police, on the grey between the two
(He wants Flash Jim, but that job can wait till they get the Murphys through).

As they strike the track through the blazing scrub, the trooper is heard to shout:
"We'll take them on to the Two-mile Tank, if we cannot bring them out!"
A half-mile more, and the rest rein back, retreating, half-choked, half-blind;
And the three are gone from the sight of men, and the bush fire roars behind.

The Bushmen wiped the smoke-made tears, and like Bushmen laughed and swore
"Poor Bill will be wanting his drink tonight as never he did before."
"And Dunn was the best in the whole damned force!" says a client of Dunn's, with pride;
"I reckon he'll serve his summons on Jim—when they get to the other side."

.   .   .   .   .

It is daylight again, and the fire is past, and the black scrub silent and grim
Except for the blaze in an old dead tree, or the crash of a falling limb;
And the Bushmen are riding across the waste, with hearts and with eyes that fill,
To look at the bodies of Constable Dunn, Flash Jim, and Boozing Bill.

They are found in the mud of the Two-mile Tank, where a fiend might scarce survive,
But the Bushmen gather from words they hear that the bodies are much alive.
There is Swearing Pat, with his grey beard singed, and language of lurid hue,
And his tough old wife, and his half-baked kids, and the three who dragged them through.

Old Pat is deploring his burnt-out home, and his wife the climate warm;
And Jim the loss of his favourite horse and Dunn of his uniform;
And Boozing Bill, with a raging thirst, is cursing the Dingo Scrub,
But all he'll ask is the loan of a flask and a lift to the nearest pub.

.   .   .   .   .

Flash Jim the Breaker is lying low—blue-paper is after Jim,
But Dunn, the trooper, is riding his rounds with a blind eye out
    for him;
And Boozing Bill is fighting D.Ts. in the township of Sudden Jerk—
When they're wanted again in the Dingo Scrub, they'll be there
    to do the work.

THE DRUNKARD'S VISION

A PUBLIC parlour in the slums,
    The haunt of vice and villainy,
Where things are said that none should hear,
    And things are done unfit to see;
'Mid ribald jest and reckless song
    That mock at all that's pure and right,
The drunkard drinks the whole day long,
    And raves through half the dreadful night.

There in the morning hours he sits
    With staring eyes and trembling limb;
The harbour in the sunlight laughs,
    But morning is as night to him
While, staring blankly at the wall,
    He sees the tragedy complete—
He sees the man he used to be
    Go striding proudly up the street,

And turn the corner with a swing,
    Where at the vine-framed cottage gate,
With outstretched arms and laughing eyes,
    His little son and daughter wait:
They race to meet him as he comes—
    And—oh! this memory is worst—
Her dimpled arms go round his neck,
    She pants, "I dot my daddy first!"

He sees his bright-eyed, smiling wife,
    The little cottage, neat and clean—
He sees the shipwreck of his life . . . .
    And all the joys that might have been!

Then, sunk in tearless, black despair
    That drink shall ne'er have power to drown,
Upon the beer-stained table there
    The hopeless drunkard's head goes down.

    .   .   .   .   .   .

But even I, in dread of wreck,
    Have drifted long before the storm:
I know, when all seems lost on earth,
    How hard it can be to reform.
I, too, have sinned, and we have both
    Drunk to the dregs the bitter cup—
Give me your hand, O brother mine,
    And even I might help you up.

DONS OF SPAIN

The Eagle screams at the beck of Trade; so Spain, as the world goes round,
Must wrest the right to live or die from the sons of the land she found;
For, as in the days when the buccaneer was abroad on the Spanish Main,
The national honour's the thing most dear to the heart of the Dons of Spain.

She had slaughtered thousands with fire and sword, as the Christian world doth know;
We murder millions—but, thank the Lord! we only starve 'em slow.
The times have changed since the days of old, but the same old rules obtain;
We fight for Freedom, and God, and Gold, and the Spaniards fight for Spain.

We fought with the strength of moral right, but they, as their ships went down,
Fought on because they were fighting-men—and their armour helped them drown.
It mattered little what chance or hope, for ever the path was plain;
The Church was the Church, and the Pope the Pope—but the Spaniards fought for Spain.

Their Yankee foes* may be kin to us (we are English, heart and soul),
And proud of their national righteousness, and proud of the lands they stole;
But we yet might pause while those brave men die, and the death-pledge drink again—
For the sake of the past, if you're doomed, say I, may your end be a grand one, Spain!

Then here's to the bravest of Freedom's foes that ever with death have stood,
To the men with the courage to die on steel as their fathers died on wood;
And here's a cheer for the flag unfurled in a hopeless cause again,
For the sake of the days when the Christian world was saved by the Dons of Spain.

* Written during the Spanish-American War of 1898.

THE CATTLE-DOG'S DEATH

The plains lay bare on the homeward route,
And the march was heavy on man and brute;
For the Spirit of Drouth was on all the land,
And the white heat danced on the glowing sand.

The best of our cattle-dogs lagged at last;
His strength gave out ere the plains were passed;
And our hearts were sad as he crept and laid
His languid limbs in the nearest shade.

He saved our lives in the years gone by,
When no one dreamed of the danger nigh,
And treacherous blacks in the darkness crept
On the silent camp where the white men slept.

"Rover is dying," a stockman said,
As he knelt and lifted the shaggy head;
"'Tis a long day's march ere the run be near,
And he's going fast; shall we leave him here?"

But the super cried, "There's an answer there!"
As he raised a tuft of the dog's grey hair;
And, strangely vivid, each man descried
The old spear-mark on the shaggy hide.

We laid a bluey and coat across
A camp-pack strapped on the lightest horse,
Then raised the dog to his deathbed high,
And brought him far 'neath the burning sky.

At the kindly touch of the stockmen rude
His eyes grew human with gratitude;
And though we were parched, when his eyes grew dim
The last of our water was given to him.

The super's daughter we knew would chide
If we left the dog in the desert wide;
So we carried him home o'er the burning sand
For a parting stroke from her small white hand.

But long ere the station was seen ahead,
His pain was o'er, for Rover was dead;
And the folks all knew by our looks of gloom
'Twas a comrade's corpse that we carried home.

SECOND CLASS WAIT HERE

At suburban railway stations—you may see them as you pass—
There are signboards on the platforms saying "Wait here second class";
And to me the whirr and thunder and the cluck of running gear
Seem to be for ever saying, saying "Second class wait here—
        Wait here second class,
        Second class wait here."
Seem to be forever saying, saying "Second class wait here".

Yes, the second class were waiting in the days of serf and prince,
And the second class are waiting—they've been waiting ever since.
There are gardens in the background, and the line is bare and drear,
Yet they wait beneath a signboard, sneering "Second class wait here".

I have waited oft in winter, in the mornings dark and damp,
When the asphalt platform glistened underneath the lonely lamp,
Glistened on the brick-faced cutting "Sellum's Soap" and "Blower's Beer",
Glistened on enamelled signboards with their "Second class wait here".

And the others seemed like burglars, slouched and muffled to the throats,
Standing round apart and silent in their shoddy overcoats;
And the wind among the poplars, and the wires that thread the air,
Seemed to be for ever snarling, snarling "Second class wait here".

Out beyond a further suburb, 'neath a chimney-stack alone
Lay the works of Grinder brothers, with a platform of their own;
And I waited there and suffered, waited there for many a day,
Slaved beneath a phantom signboard, telling all my hopes to stay.

Ah! a man must feel revengeful for a boyhood such as mine.
God! I hate the very houses near the workshop by the line;
And the smell of railway stations, and the roar of running gear,
And the scornful-seeming signboards, saying "Second class wait here".

There's a train, with Death for driver, that is ever going past;
There will be no class compartments when it's "all aboard" at last
For the long white jasper platform with an Eden in the rear;
And there won't be any signboards, saying "Second class wait here".

THE OUTSIDE TRACK

There were ten of us there on the moonlit quay,
    And one on the for'ard hatch;
No straighter mate to his mates than he
    Had ever said: "Len's a match!"
" 'Twill be long, old man, ere our glasses clink,
    'Twill be long ere we grip your hand"—
So we dragged him ashore for a final drink
    And the whole wide world seemed grand.

For they marry and go as the world rolls back,
    They marry and vanish and die;
But their spirit shall live on the Outside Track
    As long as the years go by.

The port-lights glowed in the morning mist
    That rolled from the waters green;
And over the railing we grasped his fist
    As the dark tide came between.
We cheered the captain and cheered the crew,
    And our mate, times out of mind;
We cheered the land he was going to
    And the land he had left behind.

We roared "Lang Sync" as a last farewell,
    But my heart seemed out of joint;
I well remember the hush that fell
    When the steamer had passed the point.
We drifted home through the public bars,
    We were ten times less by one
Who sailed out under the morning stars,
    And under the rising sun.

And one by one, and two by two,
    They have sailed from the wharf since then;
I have said good-bye to the last I knew,
    The last of the careless men.
And I can't but think that the times we had
    Were the best times after all,
As I turn aside with a lonely glass
    And drink to the bar-room wall.

But I'll try my luck for a cheque Out Back,
    Then a last good-bye to the bush;
For my heart's away on the Outside Track,
    On the track of the steerage push.

THE STORM THAT IS TO COME

By our place in the midst of the farthest seas we are fated to stand alone—
When the nations fly at each other's throats let Australia look to her own;

Let her spend her gold on the barren West for the land and its
    manhood's sake;
For the South must look to herself for strength in the storm that
    is yet to break.

Now who shall gallop from cape to cape, and who shall defend
    our shores—
The crowd that stands on the kerb agape and glares at the cricket
    scores?
And who will hold the invader back when the shells tear up
    the ground—
The weeds that yelp by the cycling track while a nigger scorches
    round?

There may be many to man the forts in the big towns by the sea—
But the East will call to the West for scouts in the storm that is
    to be:
The West cries out to the East in drought, but the coastal towns
    are dumb;
And the East must look to the West for food in the war that is
    to come.

The rain comes down on the Western land and the rivers run
    to waste,
While the townsfolk rush for the special tram in their childish,
    senseless haste,
And never a pile of a lock we drive—but a few mean tanks we
    scratch—
For the fate of a nation is nought compared with the turn of
    a cricket match!

There's a gutter of mud where there spread a flood from the
    land-long western creeks,
There is dust and drought on the plains far out where the water
    lay for weeks,
There's a pitiful dam where a dyke should stretch and a tank
    where a lake should be,
And the rain goes down through the silt and sand and the floods
    waste into the sea.

I saw a vision in days gone by, and would dream that dream
    again,
Of the days when the Darling shall not back her billabongs up
    in vain.

There were reservoirs and grand canals where the sad, dry lands had been,
And a glorious network of aqueducts mid fields that were always green.

I have pictured long in the land I love what the land I love might be,
Where the Darling rises from Queensland rains and the floods rush out to the sea.
And is it our fate to wake too late to the truth that we have been blind,
With a foreign foe at our harbour-gate and a blazing drought behind?

MEN WE MIGHT HAVE BEEN

When God's wrath-cloud is o'er me,
  Affrighting heart and mind;
When days seem dark before me,
  And days seem black behind;
Those friends who think they know me—
  Who deem their insight keen—
They ne'er forget to show me
  The man I might have been.

He's rich and independent,
  Or rising fast to fame;
His bright star is ascendant,
  The country knows his name;
His houses and his gardens
  Are splendid to be seen;
His fault the wise world pardons—
  The man I might have been.

His fame and fortune haunt me;
  His virtues wave me back;
His name and honours daunt me
  When I would take the track;
But you, my friend true-hearted—
  God keep our friendship green!—
You know how I was parted
  From all I might have been.

But what avails the ache of
    Remorse or weak regret?
We'll battle for the sake of
    The men we might be yet!
We'll strive to keep in sight of
    The brave, the true, and clean,
And triumph yet in spite of
    The men we might have been.

BOOTH'S DRUM

They were ratty—they were hooted by the meanest and the least,
When they woke the Drum of Glory long ago in London East.
They were often mobbed by hoodlums; they were few, but unafraid;
And their Lassies were insulted, but they banged the drum, and
    prayed—
Prayed in public for the sinners, prayed in private for release,
Till they saved some brawny lumpers; *then* they banged the drum
    in peace.

Oh, they drummed it ever onward, with old Blood-and-Fire unfurled,
Ever onward, ever outward to the corners of the world,
Till they banged it up in Greenland, and they banged in Ispahan,
And they banged it round to India and China and Japan;
Then they took it through the Islands, where each seasoned Son
    of Rum
Thought he'd got new-fangled jim-jams when he heard the Army
    Drum.
And they banged it in the desert, and they banged it in the snow—
They'd have banged it up in Mecca with the shadow of a "show"
(But Mohammed cut their heads off, so they had to let him go).

Somewhere in the early eighties they had banged the drum to
    Bourke—
But the job of fighting Satan there was hot and dusty work.
There the local Lass was withered in the heat that bakes and glares,
And we sent her food and firewood, but we heeded not her prayers.
We were blasphemous and beery, we had neither Creed nor Care—
Till they sent their prettiest Lassies—and that broke our centre
    there.
Often, moderately sober, we would stand to hear them sing,
And we'd chaff their Testifiers, but throw quids into the ring.
(Never less than bobs or dollars—sometimes quids—into the ring.)

They have stormed our sinful cities—banged for all that they were worth
From Port Darwin to Port Melbourne, and from Sydney round to Perth.
We'd no use for them in good times; if there came a rotten spell,
They would take us out of prison, they would keep us out of Hell.
And they saved our fallen sisters, who'd gone down for such as we,
And our widows and our orphans in distress and poverty,
And they made us fit for Glory (or another Glorious Spree).

But, our blindness to the Future! We had never reckoned much
That they'd beat the quids we gave them into bayonets and such,
That our coin would be devoted, when the world was looking blue,
To make German children orphans, and their mothers widows, too.
But the times have changed most sudden, and the past is very dim;
They have found a real Devil, and they're going after him.
(With the Bible *and* a Rifle they are going after him.)

For the Old Salvation Army, and their Country, and their King,
They are marching to the trenches, shouting, "Comrades! Let us Sing!"
They'll find foreign "Army" soldiers here and there and everywhere
Who will speak their tongue, and help them. They will surely breathe a prayer
For the spy, before they shoot him, and another when he's still;
And they're going to "fire" their "volleys" at the host of Kaiser Bill.

They are "Ensigns", "Captains", "Colonels", but oh say what it shall be
If a few come back the real thing, if but one comes back V.C.!
They will bang the drum at Crow's Nest, they will bang it on "The Shore",
They will bang the drum in Kent-street as they never banged before.
Then, at last, they'll frighten Satan from the mansion and the slum—
He'll have never, *never* suffered such a Banging of the Drum.
    Booth was hook-nosed, he was scrawny,
    He was nothing of a Don,
    And his business ways seemed Yiddish,
    And his speeches "kid", or kiddish;
    And we doubted his "convictions"—
    But his drum is thudding on.

MOUNT BUKAROO

Only one old post is standing—
   Solid yet, but only one—
Where the milking, and the branding,
   And the slaughtering were done.
Later years have brought dejection,
   Care, and sorrow; but we knew
Happy days on that selection
   Underneath old Bukaroo.

Then the light of day commencing,
   Found us at the gully's head,
Splitting timber for the fencing,
   Stripping bark to roof the shed.
Hands and heart with labour strengthened,
   Weariness we never knew,
Even when the shadows lengthened
   Round the base of Bukaroo.

There for days below the paddock
   How the wilderness would yield
To the spade, and pick, and mattock,
   While we toiled to win the field.
Hard brown hands are hard to sully,
   Ours to deepest blackness grew
"Burning off" down in the gully
   At the back of Bukaroo.

When we came the baby brother
   Left in haste his broken toys,
Shouted to the busy mother:
   "Here is dadda and the boys!"
Strange one woman's arms were able
   All those rough bush tasks to do—
How she'd bustle round the table
   In the hut 'neath Bukaroo!

When the cows were safely yarded,
   And the calves were in the pen,
All the cares of day discarded,
   Round the fire we clustered then.

Rang the roof with boyish laughter
  While the flames o'er-topped the flue—
Happy nights remembered after
  Far away from Bukaroo.

But the years are full of changes,
  And a sorrow found us there;
For our home amid the ranges
  Was not safe from searching Care.
On he came, a silent creeper;
  And another mountain threw
O'er our lives a shadow deeper
  Than the shade of Bukaroo.

BOURKE

I've followed all my tracks and ways, from old bark school to Leicester Square;
I've been right back to boyhood's days, and found no light or pleasure there.
But every dream and every track—and there were many that I knew—
They all lead on, or they lead back, to Bourke in Ninety-one and two.

No sign that green grass ever grew in scrubs that blazed beneath the sun;
The plains were dust in Ninety-two, and hard as bricks in Ninety-one.
On glaring iron-roofs of Bourke the scorching, blinding sandstorms blew,
No hint of beauty lingered there in Ninety-one and Ninety-two.

Save grit and pulse of generous hearts—great hearts that broke and healed again—
The hottest drought that ever blazed could never parch the souls of men;
And they were men in spite of all, and they were straight, and they were true;
The hat went round at trouble's call in Ninety-one and Ninety-two.

They drank—when all is said and done—they gambled, and their
    speech was rough;
You'd only need to say of one "He was my mate!" That was enough.
But hint a bushman was not white, nor to his Union straight and
    true—
'Twould mean a long and bloody fight in Ninety-one and Ninety-
    two.

The yard behind the Shearers' Arms was reckoned best of battle-
    grounds,
And there in peace and quietness they fought their ten or fifteen
    rounds;
And then they wiped the blood away, and then shook hands—
    as strong men do—
And washed away the bitterness, in Ninety-one and Ninety-two.

The "Army" on the grand old creek was mighty in those days
    gone by,
For they had sisters who could shriek, and brothers who could
    testify;
And by the muddy waterholes they tackled sin till all was blue—
They took our bobs and damned our souls in Ninety-one and
    Ninety-two.

By shanty-bar and shearing-shed they took their toll and did their
    work;
But now and then they lost their heads, and raved of hotter hells
    than Bourke:
The only message from the dead that ever came distinctly through
Was "Send my overcoat to hell"; it came to Bourke in Ninety-two.

They're scattered wide and scattered far—by fan-like tracks, north,
    east, and west—
The cruel New Australia star drew off the bravest and the best.
The Cape and Klondyke claim their bones, the streets of London
    damned a few,
And jingo-cursed Australia mourns for Ninety-one and Ninety-two.

They say the world has changed out there, and western towns
    have altered quite:
They don't know how to drink and swear—they've half forgotten
    how to fight;

They've almost lost the strength to trust, they leave their mate to
    battle through—
Their hearts beat true in drought and dust in Ninety-one and
    Ninety-two.

And could I roll the summers back, or bring the dead time here
    again,
Or from the grave or world-wide track recall to Bourke the vanished
    men,
With mind content I'd go to sleep, and leave those mates to judge
    me true,
And leave my name to Bourke to keep—the Bourke of Ninety-one
    and two.

STICKING TO BILL

There's a thing that sends a lump to my throat,
    And cuts my heart like a knife:
'Tis the woman who waits at the prison gate,
    When the woman is not his wife.
You may preach and pray till the dawn of day,
    Denounce or damn as you will,
But the soul of that woman will cleave for aye
    To the sin-stained soul of Bill.

She has no use for our sympathy
    And her face is hard as a stone—
A rag of a woman, at war with the world
    And fiercely fighting alone.
At the kindly touch of the janitor's hand
    The eyes of a wife would fill,
But Sal replies with a "Blast yer eyes!"—
    She is only stickin' to Bill.

In spite of herself there is help that comes—
    And it comes from a source well hid—
To buy the tucker and pay the rent
    Of a roost for herself and kid.
For the "talent" has sent round its thievish hat
    By one with a fist and a will,
For a quid or two just to see Sal through—
    For Sal is stickin' to Bill.

A furtive figure from Nowhere comes
    To Red Rock Lane by night,
And it softly raps at a dingy door
    While it scowls to left and right:
It jerks its arm in a half salute,
    By habit—against its will;
'Tis a fellow felon of Bill's, discharged,
    And it brings her a message from Bill.

    . . . .

There's a woman who comes to the gate alone
    (Bill's Gaol Delivery's near),
With a face a little less like a stone
    And a sign of a savage tear;
With a suit of clobber done up and darned—
    For William is leaving "The Hill",
And the tear is the first she ever has shed
    Since she's been stickin' to Bill.

There's tucker at home, and a job to come
    And no one to wish him ill,
There's a bottle of beer, and a minded kid
    In a brand-new suit of drill.
There's an old-time mate who will steer him straight,
    And the sticks of furniture still—
He can take a spell for a month if he likes,
    And—she's done her best for Bill.

DRUMS OF BATTERSEA

THEY can't hear in West o' London, where the worst dine with
    the best—
Deaf to all save empty laughter, they can't hear in London West—
Tailored brutes and splendid harlots, and the parasites that be—
They can't hear the warning thunder of the Drums of Battersea.
                More drums! War drums!
                Drums of misery—
Beating from the hearts of men—the Drums of Battersea.

Where the hearses hurry ever, and where man lives like a beast,
They can feel the war-drums beating—men of Hell! and London
    East.

And the far-off foreign farmers, fighting fiercely to be free,
Found new courage in the echo of the Drums of Battersea.
          More drums! War drums!
          Beating for the free—
Beating on the hearts of men—the Drums of Battersea.

And the drummers! Ah! the drummers!—stern and haggard men are those
Standing grimly at their meeting; and their washed and mended clothes
Speak of worn-out wives behind them and of grinding poverty—
But the English of the English beat the Drums of Battersea!
          More drums! War drums!
          Drums of agony—
The big bruised heart of England's in the Drums of Battersea.

In the fields are slaving women—oh! the sound of drums is there:
I have heard it in the laughter of the night of Leicester Square—
Sailing southward with the summer, London but a dream to me,
Still I feel the distant thunder of the Drums of Battersea!
          More drums! War drums!
          Drums of liberty—
Rolling round the English world—the Drums of Battersea.

Oh! I heard them in the Queen's Hall—ay! and London heard that night—
As we formed up round the leaders while they struck one blow for right!
And the ancient fire and courage that I thought were dead in me,
Blazed up fiercely at the beating of the Drums of Battersea!
          More drums! War drums!
          They beat for victory—
When above the roar of Jingoes rolled the Drums of Battersea.

And where'er my feet may wander, and howe'er I lay my head,
I shall hear them while I'm dreaming—I shall hear them when I'm dead!
For they beat for men and women, beat for Christ and you and me;
There is hope and there is terror in the Drums of Battersea!
          More drums! War drums!
          Drums of destiny—
There's hope!—there's hope for England in the Drums of Battersea.

THE WRECK OF THE *DERRY CASTLE*

Day of ending for beginnings!
Ocean hath another innings,
  Ocean hath another score;
And the surges sing his winnings,
And the surges shout his winnings,
And the surges shriek his winnings,
  All along the sullen shore.

Sing another dirge in wailing,
For another vessel sailing
  With the shadow-ships at sea;
Shadow-ships for ever sinking—
Shadow-ships whose pumps are clinking,
And whose thirsty holds are drinking
  Pledges to Eternity.

Pray for souls of ghastly, sodden
Corpses, floating round untrodden
  Cliffs, where nought but sea-drift strays:
Souls of dead men, in whose faces
Of humanity no trace is—
Not a mark to show their races—
  Floating round for days and days.

. . . .

Ocean's salty tongues are licking
  Round the faces of the drowned,
And a cruel blade seems sticking
  Through my heart, and turning round.
Heaven! shall *his* ghastly, sodden
  Corpse float round for days and days?
Shall it dash 'neath cliffs untrodden,
  Rocks where nought but sea-drift strays?

God in heaven! hide the floating,
  Falling, rising, face from me;
God in heaven; stay the gloating,
  Mocking singing of the sea!

RUTH

All is well—in a prison—tonight, and the warders are crying "All's Well!"
I must speak, for the sake of my heart—if it's but to the walls of my cell.
For what does it matter to me if tomorrow I go where I will?
I am free, as I never was free—there is nought in my life to fulfil.

Are the fields of my fancy less fair through a window that's narrow and barred?
Are the morning stars dimmed by the glare of the gas-light that flares in the yard?
I am free! I am haunted no more by the question that tortured my brain:
Was I sane, of a people gone mad—or mad, in a world that is sane?

I've had time to recover, and pray—and my reason no longer is vext
By the spirit that hangs you one day, and would hail you as martyr the next;
Yet I found in my raving a balm—in the worst that had come to the worst;
Let me think of it all. I grow calm; let me think it all out from the first.

. . . . . .

Beyond the horizon of Self the bare walls of my prison retreat,
And I stand in a gap of the hills with the scene of my life at my feet;
The range to the west, and the Peak, and the marsh where the dark ridges end,
And the spurs running down to the Creek, and the sheoaks that sigh in the bend;

A glimpse of the river below; and, away in the azure and green,
The old goldfield of Specimen Flat, and the township—a blotch on the scene;
The store, the hotels, and the bank—and the gaol; and the people who come
With a weatherboard box and a tank—the Australian idea of a home:

The scribe, spirit-broken; the "wreck", in his might-have-been glory
—or shame;
The townsman "respected" or "worthy"; the wor'nan respectful
and tame;
The clever young churchman, despised by the swaggering, popular
man;
The doctor with hands clasped behind, his head bowed as if under
a ban;

The boss of the pub with his fine sense of honour, grown moral
and stout
Like the spielers who came with the "line", on the "hauls" that
were made farther out;
The old local liar whose story was ancient when Egypt was young,
And the gossip who hangs on the fence, and poisons God's world
with her tongue.

And a lad with a cloud on his heart, who was lost in a world
vague and dim—
No one dreamt, as he drifted apart, it was genius that mattered
with him—
Who was doomed in that ignorant hole to its spiritless level to sink,
Till the iron had entered his soul, and his brain found a refuge
in drink.

. . . . . .

There was no one to understand me. I was lonely and shy as a lad;
I lived in a world of my own; so, of course, people said "He is mad".
Perhaps I was bitter because of the tongues of dispraise in the town,
Of a boy-nature misunderstood, and its nobler ambitions sneered
down.

And I was ambitious. Perhaps as a boy I could see things too plain;
How I wished I could write of the truths, of the visions, that
haunted my brain!
Of the bush-buried toiler denied e'en the last loving comforts of all;
Of my father, who slaved till he died in the scrub by his wedges
and maul.

Twenty years, and from daylight till dark—twenty years it was split,
fence, and grub;
The reward was a tumble-down hut, and a bare, dusty patch in
the scrub.

'Twas the first time he'd rested, they said; but the knit in his forehead was deep,
And to me the scarred hands of the dead seemed to *work* as I'd seen them in sleep.

And the mother who toiled by his side through hardship and trouble and drought,
And who fought for the home when he died till her heart—not her spirit—wore out:
I am shamed for Australia, and haunted by the face of the haggard bush wife
Who fights her grim battle undaunted, because she knows nothing of life.

By the barren track travelled by few men—poor victims of commerce, unknown—
E'en the troubles that woman tells woman she suffers, unpitied, alone,
Heart-numbed, and mind-dulled, and benighted—Eve's beauty in girlhood destroyed!
Till the wrongs (never felt) shall be righted, and the peace (never missed) be enjoyed.

There was Doctor Lebinski, my friend, and the friend, too, of all who were down;
Clever, gloomy, and generous drunkard, the pride—and disgrace—of the town;
He had learnt all the glory and shame of a wild life by city and sea,
And his tales of the land whence he came had a strong fascination for me.

And often in fancy or yarn, when the sheoaks grew misty and dim,
From the forest and straight for the camp of the Cossack I've ridden with him:
Ridden out in the dusk with a score, ridden back at the dawning with ten—
Have struck at three kingdoms, and Fate, for the fair land of Poland again!

He'd sorrow that drink couldn't drown, that his great heart was powerless to fight;
And I gathered the threads 'twixt the long, pregnant puffs of his last pipe at night;

For he'd say to me, sadly: "Jack Drew"—then he'd pause, as to
    watch the smoke curl—
"If a good girl should love you, be true, though you die for it—
    true to the girl!

"A man may be false to his people, a man may be false to his
    friend,
May be vagabond, drunkard, or spieler—yet his soul may come
    right in the end;
But no prayer, no atonement, no drink can banish the terrible shade
From your side, if you pause but to think, of a dead girl you loved
    and betrayed."

   .   .   .   .   .   .

'Twas Ruth, the bank-manager's niece, made the wretched old
    goldfield seem fair,
For she came like an angel of peace in an hour of revengeful despair.
A girl as God made her, and wise in a faith that was never
    estranged—
From childhood neglected and wronged, she had grown with her
    nature unchanged.

She was brave, and she never complained; for the hardships of
    youth, that had driven
My soul to the brink of perdition, but strengthened the girl's faith
    in Heaven.
In the home that her relatives gave she was tortured each hour
    of her life
By her cruel dependence—the slave of her aunt, the bank-manager's
    wife.

Does the world know how easy to lead and how hard to be driven
    are men?
She was leading me back, with her love, to the faith of my
    childhood again!
Ideals neglected or lost—high hopes that were strangled at birth—
She led me to goodness and truth—all the good that was left
    on the earth.

The sigh of the oaks seemed a hymn, and the waters were music
    for me
As I sat on the grass at her feet, and rested my head on her knee;
And we lived in a dreamland apart from the world's discontent
    and despair,
For the cynic went out of my heart at the touch of her hand on
    my hair.

She would talk like a matron at times, she would prattle at times
  like a child:
"I will trust you; I know you are good—you have only been
  careless and wild;
You are clever, you'll rise in the world; you must think of your
  future and me—
You will give up the drink for my sake, and you don't know
  how happy we'll be!

"I can work, I will help you," she said, and she'd plan out our
  future and home,
Yet it found no response in my heart, but revived the old craving
  to roam.
Could I follow the paths of the dead? I was young. Could my heart
  settle down
To the life that our parents had led by the dull, paltry-spirited town?

Could I sacrifice all for a wife, who was free now to put on my hat
And to go far away from the life—what they called "life" in
  Specimen Flat?
Could I live as our fathers had lived? And what, in the end,
  was it worth?
A woman's reproach at the last—of all things most unjust upon
  earth.

The old rebel stirred in my blood, and whispered, "What matter?"
  "Why not?"
Ruth trembled and paled, for the kiss that I gave her was reckless
  and hot.
And the angel that watched o'er her slept, and the oaks sighed
  aloud in the creek
As we sat in a shadow that crept from a storm-cloud high up on
  the Peak.

There's a voice warns the purest and best of her danger in love
  or in strife,
But that voice is a knell to her peace if she loves with the love
  of her life!
And "Ruth—Ruth!" I whispered at last in a voice that was not
  like my own;
She trembled, and clung to me fast with a sigh that was almost
  a moan.

While you listen and doubt, and incline to the devil that plucks
    at your sleeve—
When the whispers of angels have failed—then Heaven may speak
    once, I believe.
The lightning leapt out, in a flash only seen by those ridges and
    creeks,
And the darkness shut down with a crash that I thought would
    have riven the peaks.

By the path through the saplings we ran, as the great drops came
    pattering down,
To the first of the low-lying hills that lay between us and the
    town;
There she suddenly drew me aside with her beautiful instinct of love
As the clatter of hoofs reached our ears, and a horseman loomed
    darkly above.

'Twas the Doctor; he reined up, and sat for the first moment
    pallid and mute;
Then lifted his hand to his hat with his old-fashioned martial salute,
And said with a glance at the ridge, looming black with its pine
    tops awhirl,
"Take my coat, you are caught in the storm!" and he whispered,
    "Be true to the girl!"

I wrapped the coat round her with care; I held her; I felt her
    heart thump
When the lightning leapt out, as we crouched in the lee of a
    fire-hollowed stump;
There seemed a strange fear in her eyes, and the colour had gone
    from her cheek;
She scarcely had uttered a word since the hot brutal kiss by the
    creek.

The storm rushed away to the west, to the ridges drought-stricken
    and dry;
To the eastward loomed far-away peaks 'neath the still, starry arch
    of the sky;
By the light of the full moon that swung from a curtain of cloud
    like a lamp
We saw that my tent had gone down in the storm, as we passed
    by the camp.

'Tis a small thing, a chance such as this, that decides between hero and cur
In one's heart. I was wet to the skin, and my comfort was precious to her.
Her aunt was away in the town—the dining-room fire was alight,
And the uncle was absent—he dined with some friends at the Royal that night.

He came late, and passed on to his room without glancing at her or at me—
Too straight and precise, be it said, for a man who was sober to be.
Then the drop of one boot on the floor (there was no wife to witness his guilt),
And a moment thereafter a snore that proclaimed him asleep on the quilt.

Was it vanity, love, or revolt? Was it joy that came into my life
As I sat there with her in my arms, and caressed her and called her "My wife!"
Ah, the coward! My heart shall still bleed, though I live on for fifty long years,
For she could not cry out, only plead with eyes that were brimming with tears.

Not the passion alone brings remorse, but the thought of the treacherous part
I had played—with my future planned out and already endorsed by my heart!
When a good woman falls for the sake of a love that has blinded her eyes,
There is pardon, perhaps, for the lust; but what heaven could pardon the lies?

And "What does it matter?" I said. "You are mine, I am yours—and for life.
He is drunk and asleep—he won't hear, and tomorrow you shall be my wife!"
There's an hour in the memory of most that we hate ever after and loathe. . . .
'Twas the daylight which came like a ghost to her window that startled us both.

'Twixt the door of her room and the door of the office I stood
  for a space,
When a treacherous board in the floor sent a crack like a shot
  through the place!
Then the creak of a step, and the click of a lock in the manager's
  room—
I grew cold to the stomach and sick, as I trembled and shrank
  in the gloom.

He faced me, revolver in hand—"Now I know you, you damnable
  whelp!
Stand still, where you are, or I'll fire!" and he suddenly shouted
  for help.
"Help! Burglary!" Yell after yell—such a voice would have wakened
  the tomb;
And I heard her scream once; then she fell like a log on the
  floor of her room.

I bethought myself then, in a flash, of the foul fiend of gossip
  that drags
A soul to perdition—I thought of the murderous tongues of the
  hags;
She would sacrifice all for my sake—she would tell the whole
  township the truth.
I'd escape, send the Doctor a word, then die—ere they took me—
  for Ruth!

Then I rushed him—a struggle—a flash—I was down with a shot
  in my arm—
Up again, and a desperate fight—hurried footsteps and cries of
  alarm—
Mad struggles, a blow on the head—and the gossips will fill in
  the blank
Where the tale of the capture of Drew on the night he broke into
  the bank.

In the cell at the lock-up all day and all night, without pause,
  through my brain
Whirled the scenes of my life to the last one; and over and
  over again
I paced the small cell, till exhaustion brought sleep; and I woke
  to the past
A man changed in heart and clear-headed—a man strong in purpose
  at last.

She would sacrifice all for my sake—she would tell the whole township the truth—
In the mood I was in I'd have given my life for a moment with Ruth;
Just then, as I thought, from without came the voice of the constable's wife:
"They say it's brain fever, poor girl, and the doctor despairs of her life.

"He has frightened the poor girl to death—such a pity—so fair and so young,"
And the voice of her gossip chimed in: "Ah, the wretch! he deserves to be hung.
They were always a bad lot, the Drews, and I knowed *he* was more rogue than crank—
He only pretended to court her to find his way into the bank!"

Came the doctor, his voice hard and cold, and his face as if sculptured in stone,
Hands behind—but it mattered not then—'twas a fight I must fight out alone:
"You have cause to be thankful," he said, as though speaking a line from the past—
"She was conscious an hour; she is dead, and she called for you, Drew, till the last!"

. . . . . .

The curious crowd in the court seemed to me but as ghosts from the past,
And the words of the charge were read out, like a hymn from the first to the last;
"I am guilty," I said, when they asked; and again, "I have nothing to say."
Every eye, as I looked 'round the court, was turned in aversion away,

Save the doctor's; it seemed to me then that Lebinski and I stood alone;
For a moment he looked in my eyes with a wonderful smile in his own,
Slowly lifted his hand in salute, turned and walked from the courtroom, and then
From the rear of the crowd came the whisper: "The Doctor's been boozing again!"

Next, the Judge spoke in harshness; I stood with my fluttering
    senses awhirl.
"Your crime," he said sternly, "has cost the young life of an innocent
    girl;
You brought sorrow and death to a home; you are worse than
    a murderer now."
And the sentence he passed on me then was the longest the law
    would allow.

.   .   .   .

Let me rest—I grow weary and faint. Let me breathe—but what
    value has breath?
Ah! the pain in my heart, as of old! and I know what it is—it
    is Death.
It is death—it is rest—it is sleep. 'Tis the world and I drifting
    apart.
I have been through a sorrow too deep to have passed without
    breaking my heart.

There's a breeze! And a light without bars! Let me drink the
    free air till I drown.
'Tis the sheoaks—the Peak—and the stars. Lo, a dead angel's spirit
    floats down!
This will pass—ay, and all things will pass. Oh, my Love, have
    you come back to me?
I am tired—let me lie on the grass at your feet, with my head on
    your knee.

TO MY CULTURED CRITICS

Fight through ignorance, want, and care—
    Through the griefs that crush the spirit;
Push your way to a fortune fair,
    And the smiles of the world you'll merit.
Long, as a boy, for the chance to learn—
    For the chance that Fate denies you;
Win degrees where the Life-lights burn,
    And scores will teach and advise you.

My cultured friends! you have come too late
    With your bypath nicely graded;
I've fought thus far on my track of Fate,
    And I'll follow the rest unaided.

Must I be stopped by a college gate
  On the track of Life encroaching?
Be dumb to Love, and be dumb to Hate,
  For the lack of a pedant's coaching?

You grope for Truth in a language dead—
  In the dust 'neath tower and steeple!
What do you know of the tracks we tread,
  And what of the living people?
I *"must* read this, and that, and the rest",
  And write as the cult expects me?—
I'll read the book that may please me best,
  And write as my heart directs me!

You were quick to pick on a faulty line
  That I strove to put my soul in:
Your eyes were keen for a dash of mine
  In the place of a semi-colon—
And blind to the rest. And is it for such
  As you I must brook restriction?
"I was taught too little?" I learnt too much
  To care for a scholar's diction!

Must I turn aside from my destined way
  For a task your Joss would find me?
I come with strength of the living day,
  And with half the world behind me;
I leave you alone in your cultured halls
  To drivel and croak and cavil:
Till your voices goes farther than college walls,
  Keep out of the tracks we travel!

PIGEON TOES

A DUSTY clearing in the scrubs
  Of barren, western lands—
Where, out of sight or sign of hope,
  The wretched school-house stands;
A roof that glares at glaring days,
  A bare, unshaded wall,
A fence that guards no blade of green—
  A dust-storm over all.

The books and slates are packed away,
    The maps are rolled and tied,
And for an hour I breathe, and lay
    My ghastly mask aside;
I linger here to save my head
    From voices shrill and thin,
That rasp for ever in the shed—
    The "home" I'm boarding in.

I had ideals when I came here—
    A purpose made me glad;
But all that they can understand
    Is "axe to grind" or "mad".
The children call me "Pigeon Toes",
    "Green Eyes" and "Carrot Head"—
They do not think the Teacher knows
    What cruel things are said.

There is a thought that haunts my dreams,
    And gathers strength each day:
Shall I as narrow-minded grow
    And mean of soul as they?
I brood at times till comes a fear
    That sets my brain awhirl—
I fight a strong man's battle here,
    And I am but a girl.

On phantom seas my dreams, adrift,
    Too near to madness roam;
The only thing that keeps me here
    Is thought of those at home—
The hearts that love and cling to me,
    That I love best on earth,
My mother, left in poverty,
    A brother, blind from birth.

On burning West Australian fields
    In that great, dreadful land
Where all day long the heat-waves flow
    O'er seas of glowing sand,
My elder brother toils and breaks
    That great true heart of his
To rescue us from poverty—
    To rescue me from this.

And one is with him where he goes,
  My brother's mate and mine;
He never called me Pigeon Toes—
  He said my eyes were "fine";
His face comes up before me now,
  And hope and courage rise—
The lines of life, the troubled brow,
  Firm mouth and kind grey eyes.

I preach content and gentleness,
  And meek example give;
They little think the Teacher hates
  And loathes the life they live.
I told the infants fairy tales
  But half an hour since—
They little dream that Pigeon Toes
  Prays for her fairy Prince.

I have one prayer (and God forgive
  A selfish prayer and wild)—
I kneel down by the infants' stool
  (For I am but a child),
And pray, as I've prayed times untold,
  That Heaven will set a sign
To guide my brother to the gold,
  For mother's sake and mine.

A dust-cloud swirls above the road
  And I am here alone—
I lock the door till it be past,
  So nervous have I grown.
No. Leave it open. Come what may,
  I'll not give in, or hide;
No bushman hurts a girl, I know—
  I'll watch them as they ride.

. . . . .

A voice, a form I seem to know
  That stops beside the gate—
God spare me disappointment's blow!
  My brother? or his mate?
His eyes! *His* proud, triumphant smile!
  His voice, so sweet to hear:
"Come! Jack and I have made our pile,
  I'm here to fetch you, Dear!"

THE BATTLING DAYS

So, sit you down in a straight-backed chair, with your pipe and your wife content,
And cross your knees with your wisest air, and preach of the "days misspent";
Grown fat and moral apace, old man! you prate of the change "since then"—
In spite of it all, I'd as lief be back in those hard old days again.

We travel first, or we sail saloon—on the planned-out trips we go
With those who are neither rich nor poor, and we find that the life is slow;
It's "A pleasant trip!" where they cried "So long". There was fun in the steerage then—
In spite of it all, I would fain be back in those vagabond days again.

On Saturday night we've a pound to spare—a pound for a trip down town—
We got more joy in those hard old days from a hardly spared half-crown;
We took more pride in the pants we patched than the suits we have had since then—
In spite of it all, I would rather be back in those hard-up times again.

'Twas We and the World—and the rest go hang—when the Outside Tracks we trod;
Each thought of himself as a man and mate, and not as a martyred god;
The world goes wrong when your heart is strong and this is the way with men—
The world goes right when your liver is white, and you preach of the change "since then".

They were hard old days; they were battling days; they were cruel times—but then,
In spite of it all, we shall live tonight in those hard old days again.

THE FIRE AT ROSS'S FARM

The squatter saw his pastures wide
  Decrease, as one by one
The farmers moving to the west
  Selected on his run;
Selectors took the water up
  And all the black-soil round;
The best grass-land the squatter had
  Was spoilt by Ross's ground.

Now many schemes to shift old Ross
  Had racked the squatter's brains,
But Sandy had the stubborn blood
  Of Scotland in his veins;
He held the land and fenced it in,
  He cleared and ploughed the soil,
And year by year a richer crop
  Repaid him for his toil.

Between the homes for many years
  The devil left his tracks:
The squatter 'pounded Ross's stock,
  And Sandy 'pounded Black's.
A well upon the lower run
  Was filled with earth and logs,
And Black laid baits about the farm
  To poison Ross's dogs.

It was, indeed, a deadly feud
  Of class and creed and race,
So Fate supplied a Romeo
  And a Juliet in the case;
And more than once across the flats,
  Beneath the Southern Cross,
Young Robert Black was seen to ride
  With pretty Jenny Ross.

One Christmas time, when months of drought
  Had parched the western creeks,
The bush-fires started in the north
  And travelled south for weeks.

At night along the river-side
  The scene was grand and strange—
The hill-fires looked like lighted streets
  Of cities in the range.

The cattle-tracks between the trees
  Were like long dusky aisles,
And on a sudden breeze the fire
  Would sweep along for miles;
Like sounds of distant musketry
  It crackled through the brakes,
And o'er the flat of silver grass
  It hissed like angry snakes.

It leapt across the flowing streams
  And raced the pastures through;
It climbed the trees, and lit the boughs,
  And fierce and fiercer grew.
The bees fell stifled in the smoke
  Or perished in their hives,
And with the stock the kangaroos
  Went flying for their lives.

The sun had set on Christmas Eve,
  When through the scrub-lands wide
Young Robert Black came riding home
  As only natives ride.
He galloped to the homestead door
  And gave the first alarm:
"The fire is past the granite spur,
  And close to Ross's farm.

"Now, father, send the men at once,
  They won't be wanted here;
Poor Ross's wheat is all he has
  To pull him through the year."
"Then let it burn," the squatter said;
  "I'd like to see it done—
I'd bless the fire if it would clear
  Selectors from the run.

"Go if you will," the squatter said,
  "You shall not take the men—
Go out and join your precious friends,
  But don't come here again."

"I won't come back," young Robert cried,
  And, reckless in his ire,
He sharply turned his horse's head
  And galloped towards the fire.

And there for three long weary hours,
  Half-blind with smoke and heat,
Old Ross and Robert fought the flames
  That neared the ripened wheat.
The farmer's hand was nerved by fear
  Of danger and of loss;
And Robert fought the stubborn foe
  For love of Jenny Ross.

But serpent-like the curves and lines
  Slipped past them, and between
Until they reached the boundary where
  The old coach-road had been.
"The track is now our only hope,
  There we must stand," cried Ross,
"For nought on earth can stop the fire
  If once it gets across."

Then came a cruel gust of wind,
  And, with a fiendish rush,
The flames leapt o'er the narrow path
  And lit the fence of brush.
"The crop must burn!" the farmer cried,
  "We cannot save it now,"
And down upon the blackened ground
  He dashed his ragged bough.

But wildly, in a rush of hope,
  His heart began to beat,
For o'er the crackling fire he heard
  The sound of horses' feet.
"Here's help at last," young Robert cried,
  And even as he spoke
The squatter with a dozen men
  Came racing through the smoke.

Down on the ground the stockmen jumped
  And bared each brawny arm;
They tore green branches from the trees
  And fought for Ross's farm:

And when before the gallant band
　　The beaten flames gave way,
Two grimy hands in friendship joined—
　　And it was Christmas Day.

THE SHAME OF GOING BACK

When you've come to make a fortune, and you haven't made your salt,
And the reason of your failure isn't anybody's fault—
When you haven't got a billet, and the times are very slack,
There is nothing that can spur you like the shame of going back;
　　　　Crawling home with empty pockets,
　　　　Going back hard-up;
Oh! it's then you learn the meaning of "humiliation's cup".

When the place and you are strangers and you struggle all alone,
And you have a mighty longing for the town where you are known;
When your clothes are very shabby, and the future's very black,
There is nothing that can hurt you like the shame of going back.

When we've fought the battle bravely and are beaten to the wall,
'Tis the sneer of man, not conscience, that makes cowards of us all;
And the while you are returning, oh! your brain is on the rack,
And your heart is in the shadow of the shame of going back.

When a beaten man's discovered with a bullet in his brain,
They post-mortem him, and try him, and they say he was insane;
But it very often happens that he'd lately got the sack,
And his onward move was owing to the shame of going back.

Ah! my friend, you call it nonsense, and your upper lip is curled—
You have had no real trouble in your passage through the world;
But when fortune rounds upon you and the rain is on the track,
You will learn the bitter meaning of the shame of going back;
　　　　Going home with empty pockets,
　　　　Going home hard-up;
Oh, it's then you'll taste the poison in humiliation's cup.

FAREWELL TO THE BUSHMEN

Some carry their swags in the Great North-west,
  Where the bravest battle and die,
And a few have gone to their last long rest,
  And a few have said "Good-bye!"
The coast grows dim, and it may be long
  Ere the Gums again I see;
So I put my soul in a farewell song
  To the chaps who barracked for me.

Their days are hard at the best of times,
  And their dreams are dreams of care—
God bless them all for their big soft hearts,
  And the brave, brave grins they wear!
God keep me straight as a man can go,
  And true as a man may be,
For the sake of the hearts that were always so,
  Of the men who had faith in me!

And a ship-side word I would say, you chaps
  Of the blood of the Don't-give-in!
The world will call it a boast, perhaps—
  But I'll win, if a man can win!
And not for gold or the world's applause—
  Though ways to an end they be—
I'll win, if a man might win, because
  Of the men who believe in me.

BREAK O' DAY

You love me, you say, and I think you do,
  But I know so many who don't,
And how can I say I'll be true to you
  When I know very well that I won't?
I have journeyed long and my goal is far
  I love, but I cannot bide,
For as sure as rises the morning star,
  With the break of day I'll ride.
    I was doomed to ruin or doomed to mar
      The home wherever I stay,
    But I'll think of you as the Morning Star
    And they call me Break o' Day.

They well might have named me the Fall o' Night,
    For drear is the track I mark,
But I love fair girls and I love the light,
    For I and my tribe were dark.
You may love me, dear, for a day and a night,
    You may cast your life aside;
But as sure as the morning star shines bright
    With the break of day I'll ride.

There was never a lover so proud and kind,
    There was never a friend so true;
But the song of my life I have left behind
    In the heart of a girl like you.
There was never so deep or cruel a wrong
    In the land that is far away,
There was never so bitter a broken heart
    That rode at the break of day.

God bless you, dear, with your red-gold hair
    And your pitying eyes of grey—
Oh! my heart forbids that a star so fair
    Should be marred by the Break o' Day.
Live on, my girl, as the girl you are,
    Be a good and a true man's bride,
For as sure as the set of the evening star
    With the fall o' night I'll ride.
    I was born to ruin or born to mar
        The home wherever I light.
    Oh, I wish that you were the Evening Star
        And that I were the Fall o' Night.

CROSS-ROADS

Once more I write a line to you,
    While darker shadows fall;
Dear friends of mine who have been true,
    And steadfast through it all.
If I have written bitter rhymes,
    With many lines that halt,
And if I have been false at times,
    It was not all my fault.

To Heaven's decree I would not bow,
    And I sank very low—
The bitter things are printed now,
    And we must let them go.
But I feel softened as I write;
    The better spirit springs,
And I am very sad tonight
    Because of many things:—

The friendships that I have abused,
    The trust I dared betray,
The talents that I have misused,
    The gifts I threw away.
But I have done with barren strife
    And dark imaginings,
And in my future work and life
    Will seek the better things.

MEN WHO COME BEHIND

There's a class of men (and women) who are always on their guard—
Cunning, treacherous, suspicious—feeling softly, grasping hard—
Brainy, yet without the courage to forsake the beaten track—
Warily they feel their way behind a bolder spirit's back.

If you save a bit of money, and you start a little store—
Say an oyster-shop, for instance, where there wasn't one before—
When the shop begins to pay you, and the rent is off your mind,
You will see another opened by a chap who comes behind.

So it is, my friend, and might be with the likes of me and you,
When a friend of both, and neither, interferes between the two;
We might fight like fiends, forgetting in our passion mad and blind
That the row is mostly started by the folks who come behind.

They will stick to you as sin does, while your money comes and goes,
But they'll leave you when you haven't got a shilling in your clothes.
You may get some help from others, but you'll nearly always find
That you cannot get assistance from the men who come behind.

There are many, far too many, in the world of prose and rhyme,
Always looking for another's "footprints on the sands of time".
Journalistic imitators are the meanest of mankind;
And the grandest themes are hackneyed by the pens that come
    behind.

If you strike a novel subject, write it up, and do not fail,
They will rhyme and prose about it till your very own is stale,
As they raved about the bushland that the wattle-boughs perfume
Till the reader cursed that region and the stink of wattle-bloom.

They will follow in your footsteps while you're groping for the light;
But they'll run to get before you when they see you're going right;
And they'll trip you up and balk you in their blind and greedy heat,
Like a stupid pup that hasn't learned to trail behind your feet.

Take your load of sin and sorrow on an energetic back!
Go and strike across the country, where there isn't any track!
And—we fancy that the subject could be further treated here,
But we'll leave it to be hackneyed by the fellows in the rear.

RIDING ROUND THE LINES

Dust and smoke against the sunrise out where grim disaster lurks,
And a broken skyline looming like unfinished railway works,
And a trot, trot, trot and canter down inside the belt of mines:
It is General Greybeard Shrapnel who is riding round his lines.

All the scarecrows from the trenches, haggard eyes and hollow
    cheeks,
Uniforms war-stained and ragged, that have not been off for weeks;
They salute him and they cheer him and they watch his face for
    signs;
Ah! they try to read old Greybeard while he's riding round the lines.

There's a crack, crack, crack and rattle; there's a thud and there's a
    crash;
In a battery over yonder there is something gone to smash,
Then a hush and sudden movement, and its meaning he divines,
And he patches up a blunder while he's riding round his lines.

There are fifty thousand rifles and a hundred batteries
Making fitful battle-music, with his fingers on the keys,
And if for an hour, exhausted, on his camp-bed he reclines,
In his mind he still is riding—riding round his tattered lines.

He's the brain of fifty thousand. blundering at their country's call;
He's the one hope of his nation, and the loneliest man of all;
But for all that can be gathered from his eyes of steely blue
He might be a great contractor who has some big job to do.

There's the son who died in action—it may be a week ago;
There's the wife and other troubles that most men have got to
    know—
(And we'll say the grey-haired mother underneath the porch of
    vines):
Does he ever think of these things while he's riding round his lines?

He is bossed by brainless placemen who can never understand;
He is hampered by the profiteers who rob their native land,
And I feel inclined to wonder what his own opinions are
Of the Government, the country, of the war and of the Czar.

He's the same when he's advancing, he's the same in grim retreat;
For he wears one mask in triumph and the same mask in defeat;
Of the brave he is the bravest, he is strongest of the strong:
Not from General Greybeard Shrapnel will you know when things
    go wrong.

THE CHRIST OF THE NEVER

With eyes that are narrowed to pierce
  To the awful horizons of land,
Through the haze of hot days, and the fierce
  White heat-waves that flow on the sand;
Through the Never Land westward and nor'ward,
  Bronzed, bearded, and gaunt on the track,
Low-voiced and hard-knuckled, rides forward
  The Christ of the Outer Out-back.

For the cause that will ne'er be relinquished
  Despite all the cynics on earth—
In the ranks of the bush undistinguished
  By manner or dress—if by birth;

God's preacher, of Churches unheeded—
    God's vineyard, though barren the sod—
Plain spokesman where spokesman is needed,
    Rough link 'twixt the bushman and God.

He works where the hearts of a nation
    Are withered in flame from the sky,
Where the sinners work out their salvation
    In a hell-upon-earth ere they die.
In the camp or the lonely hut lying
    In a waste that seems out of God's sight,
He's the doctor—the mate of the dying
    Through the smothering heat of the night.

By his work in the hells of the shearers,
    Where the drinking is ghastly and grim,
Where the roughest and worst of his hearers
    Have listened bareheaded to him;
By his paths through the parched desolation,
    Hot rides, and long, terrible tramps;
By the hunger, the thirst, the privation
    Of his work in the farthermost camps;

By his worth in the light that shall search men
    And prove—ay! and justify—each,
I place him in front of all churchmen
    Who feel not, who *know* not—but preach!

A PROUDER MAN THAN YOU

IF you fancy that your people came of better stock than mine,
If you hint at higher breeding by a word or by a sign,
If you're proud because of fortune, or the clever things you do—
Then I'll play no second fiddle: I'm a prouder man than you!

If you think that your profession has the more gentility,
And that you are condescending to be seen along with me;
If you notice that I'm shabby, while your clothes are spruce and new—
You have only got to hint it: I'm a prouder man than you!

If you have a swell companion when you see me on the street,
And you think that I'm too common for your toney friend to meet,
So that I, though passing closely, fail to come within your view—
Then be blind to me for ever; I'm a prouder man than you!

If your character be blameless, if your outward past be clean,
While 'tis known my antecedents are not what they should have been,
Do not risk contamination; save your name whate'er you do—
Birds o' feather fly together: I'm a prouder bird than you!

Keep your patronage for others! Gold and station cannot hide
Friendship that can laugh at fortune, friendship that can conquer pride!
Offer this as to an equal—let me see that you are true,
And my wall of pride is shattered: I am not so proud as you!

FROM THE BUSH

The Channel fog has lifted—
  And see where we have come!
Round all the world we've drifted,
  A hundred years from "home".
The fields our parents longed for—
  Ah! we shall ne'er know how—
The wealth that they were wronged for
  We'll see as strangers now!

The Dover cliffs have passed on
  In morning light aglow,
That our fathers looked their last on
  A weary time ago.
Now grin, and grin your bravest!
  We need be strong to fight;
For you go home to picture
  And I go home to write.

Hold up your head in England,
  Tread firm the London streets;
We come from where the strong heart
  Of all Australia beats!

Hold up your head in England,
   However poor you roam,
For no man is your better
   Who's never sailed from home!

From a hundred years of hardship—
   'Tis ours to tell the cost—
From a thousand miles of silence
   Where London would be lost;
From where the glorious sunset
   On sweeps of mulga glows—
Ah! we know more than England,
   And more than Europe knows!

THE SEPARATION

We knew too little of the world,
   And you and I were good—
But paltry bickerings wrecked our lives
   As well I knew they would.
The people said our love was dead,
   But how were they to know?
Ah! had we loved each other less
   We'd not have quarrelled so.

We knew too little of the world,
   And you and I were kind,
We listened to what others said
   And both of us were blind.
The people said 'twas selfishness,
   But how were they to know?
Ah! had we both been selfish then
   We'd not have parted so.

But still, when all seems lost on earth
   Then heaven sets a sign—
Kneel down beside your lonely bed,
   And I will kneel by mine,
And let us pray for happy days—
   Like those of long ago.
Ah! had we knelt together once
   We'd not have parted so.

CHERRY-TREE INN

The rafters are open to sun, moon, and star,
The thistles and nettles grow high in the bar;
The chimneys are crumbling, the log fires are dead,
And green mosses spring from the hearthstone instead.
The voices are silent, the bustle and din,
For the railroad has ruined the Cherry-tree Inn.

Save the glimmer of stars, or the moon's pallid streams,
And the sounds of the possums that camp on the beams,
The bar-room is dark and the stable is still,
For the coach comes no more over Cherry-tree Hill.
No riders push on through the darkness to win
The rest and the comfort of Cherry-tree Inn.

I drift from my theme, for my memory strays
To the carrying, digging, and bushranging days—
Far back to the years that I still love the best,
When a stream of wild diggers rushed into the west;
But the rushes grew feeble, and sluggish, and thin,
Till scarcely a swagman passed Cherry-tree Inn.

Do you think, my old mate (if it's thinking you be),
Of the times when you tramped to the goldfields with me?
Do you think of the day of our thirty-mile tramp,
When never a fire could we light on the camp,
And, weary and footsore and drenched to the skin,
We tramped o'er the ranges from Cherry-tree Inn.

Then I had a sweetheart and you had a wife,
And Johnny was more to his mother than life;
But we solemnly swore, ere that evening was done,
That we'd never return till our fortunes were won . . .
Next morning to harvests of folly and sin
We tramped o'er the ranges from Cherry-tree Inn.

FOREIGN LANDS

You may roam the wide seas over, follow, meet, and cross the sun,
Sail as far as ships can sail, and travel far as trains can run;
You may ride and tramp wherever range or plain or sea expands,
But the crowd has been before you, and you'll not find "Foreign Lands";

    For the Early Days are over,
     And no more the white-winged rover
Sinks the gale-worn coast of England bound for bays in Foreign Lands.

Foreign lands are in the distance dim and dream-like, faint and far,
Long ago, and over yonder, where our boyhood fancies are;
All the earth is yoked with railways, fettered in their iron bands;
Oceans, spanned by steam and cables, lead no more to Foreign Lands.
    Ah! the days of blue and gold!
     When all news was six months old—
But the news was worth the telling in the days of Foreign Lands.

When the gipsies stole the children still, in village tale and song,
And the world was wide to travel, and the roving spirit strong;
When they dreamed of South Sea Islands, summer seas and coral strands—
Then the bravest hearts of England sailed away to Foreign Lands,
    "Fitting foreign"—flood and field—
     Half the world and orders sealed—
And the first and best of Europe went to fight in Foreign Lands.

Canvas towers along the ocean—homeward bound and outward bound—
Glint of topsails over islands—splash of anchors in the sound;
Then they landed in the forests, took their strong lives in their hands,
And they fought and toiled and conquered, making homes in Foreign Lands,
    Through the cold and through the drought—
     Farther on and farther out—
Winning half the world for England in the wilds of Foreign Lands.

Love and pride of life inspired them when the simple village hearts
Followed Master Will and Harry, gone abroad to "furrin parts".
By our townships and our cities, and across the desert sands
Are the graves of those who battled—died for us in Foreign Lands—
    Gave their young lives for our sake
     (Was it all a grand mistake?)
Sons of Master Will and Harry born abroad in Foreign Lands!

*Here we slave the dull years hopeless for the sake of Wool and
    Wheat—*
Hive in homes of ugly Commerce—niggard farm and haggard street;
But with all the world before us, God above us—hearts and hands—
I can sail the seas in fancy far away to Foreign Lands.

PASSING OF SCOTTY

We throw ourselves down on the dusty plain
    When the gold has gone from the west,
But we rise and tramp on the track again,
    For we're tired—too tired to rest.
Darker and denser the shadows fall,
    Yet ease not the aching brow—
Scotty the Wrinkler!* you've solved it all,
    Give us a wrinkle now.

But no one lieth so still in death
    As the rover who never could rest;
He is free of thought as he's free of breath,
    And his hands are crossed on his breast.
You have earned your rest, you brave old tramp,
    As I hope in the end we will.
Ah me! 'tis a long, long way to camp
    Since the days when we called you "Phil".

What have they done with your quaint old soul
    Now they have passed you through?
We can't but think, as our swags we roll,
    That it's right, old man, with you;
You learned some truth in the storm and strife
    Of the outcast battler's ways;
And you left some light in the vagabond's life
    Ere you vanished beyond the haze.

One by one in the far ahead,
    In the smothering haze of drought—
Where hearts are loyal and hopes are dead—
    The forms of our mates fade out.
'Tis a distant goal, and a weary load,
    But we follow the Wrinkler home,
As, staggering into the short, straight road,
    From the blind branch-tracks we come.

* *Nom de plume* of the late Phil Moubray.

THE THREE KINGS*

The East is dead and the West is done, and again our course lies thus:—
South-east by Fate and the Rising Sun where the Three Kings wait for us.
While our hearts are young, and the world is wide, and the heights seem made to climb,
We are off and away to the Sydney-side—but the Three Kings bide their time.

"I've been to the West," the digger said: he was bearded, bronzed and old:
Ah, the smothering curse of the East is wool, and the curse of the West is gold.
I went to the West in the golden boom, with Hope and a life-long mate;
"They sleep in the sand by the Boulder Soak, and long may the Three Kings wait."

"I've had my fling on the Sydney-side," said a black-sheep to the sea,
"Let the young forlorn learn what he can't be taught: I've learnt what's good for me."
And he gazed ahead on the sea-line dim—grown dim to his softened eyes—
With a pain in his heart that was good for him, as he saw the Three Kings rise.

A pale girl sits on the fo'c'sle-head—she is back, Three Kings! so soon;
But it seems to her that a lifetime's dead since she fled with a man "saloon".
There's a refuge still in the old folks' arms for the child that has loved too well;
They will hide her shame on the Southern farm—and the Three Kings will not tell.

Our hearts are young, and the old hearts old, and life on the farms is slow,
And away in the world there is fame and gold—and the Three Kings watch us go.

* Three sea-girt pinnacles off North Cape, New Zealand.

*Our heads seem wise, and the world seems wide, and its heights
  are ours to climb,
So it's off and away in our youthful pride—but the Three Kings
  bide their time.*

ROVERS

Some born of homely parents,
    For ages settled down—
For steady generations
    Of village, farm, and town;
And some of dusky fathers
    Who've wandered since the Flood—
The fairest skin or darkest
    May hold the roving blood.

Some born of brutish peasants,
    And some of stately peers,
In poverty or plenty
    They pass their early years
But, born in pride of purple,
    Or straw and squalid sin,
In all the far world-corners
    The wanderers are kin.

A rover or a rebel,
    Conceived and born to roam,
As babies they will toddle
    With faces turned from home;
They've fought beyond the vanguard
    Wherever storm has raged,
And home is but a prison
    They pace like lions caged.

They smile, and are not happy;
    They sing, and are not gay;
They weary, yet they wander;
    They love, and cannot stay;
They marry, yet are single
    Who watch the roving star;
The closer home-ties bind them,
    The lonelier they are.

They die of peace and quiet,
　The deadly ease of life;
They die of home and comfort;
　They *live* in storm and strife;
No poverty can tie them,
　Nor wealth nor place restrain—
Girl, wife, or child may draw them.
　But they'll be gone again!

Across the glowing desert,
　Through naked trees and snow,
Across the rolling prairies
　The skies have seen them go;
They fought to where the ocean
　Receives the setting sun;—
What room for these bold rovers
　When all the lands are won?

They starve on Greenland snowfields,
　On Never-Never sands;
Where there's no man to conquer
　They conquer barren lands;
They feel that most are cowards,
　That all depends on "nerve",
They lead, who cannot follow,
　They rule, who cannot serve.

Across the plains and ranges,
　Away across the seas,
On blue and green horizons
　They camp by twos and threes;
Upholding in the turmoil
　Of States that trouble earth
The honour of the country
　That only gave them birth.

Unlisted, uncommissioned,
　Untaught of any school,
In far-away world-corners
　Unconquered tribes they rule;
Sure hand on the revolver—
　Sad eyes that never quail—
Firm hands that grip the rifle
　And win where armies fail.

Theirs, while they slumber soundly,
    And treachery is bare,
The bull-dog's self-reliance,
    The daring of despair;
Thin brown men in pyjamas—
    The thin brown wiry men!—
The helmet and revolver
    That lie beside the pen.

Through drought and desolation
    They won the way Out Back;
The commonplace and selfish
    Have followed in their track;
They conquer lands for others,
    For others find the gold—
What room, what room for rovers
    When all the lands are old?

THE BUSH GIRL

So you rode from the range where your brothers "select",
    Through the ghostly grey bush in the dawn—
You rode slowly at first, lest her heart should suspect
    That you were so glad to be gone;
You had scarcely the courage to glance back at her
    By the homestead receding from view,
And you breathed with relief as you rounded the spur,
    For the world was a wide world to you.

Grey eyes that grow sadder than sunset or rain,
    Fond heart that is ever more true,
Firm faith that grows firmer for watching in vain—
    She'll wait by the sliprails for you.

Ah! the world is a new and a wide one to you,
    But the world to your sweetheart is shut,
For a change never comes to the lonely Bush girl
    From the stockyard, the bush, and the hut;

And the only relief from its dullness she feels
    Is when ridges grow softened and dim,
And away in the dusk to the sliprails she steals
    To dream of past meetings "with him".

Do you think, where, in place of bare fences, dry creeks,
    Clear streams and green hedges are seen—
Where the girls have the lily and rose in their cheeks,
    And the grass in midsummer is green—
Do you think now and then, now or then, in the whirl
    Of the city, while London is new,
Of the hut in the Bush, and the freckled-faced girl
    Who is eating her heart out for you?

Grey eyes that are sadder than sunset or rain,
    Bruised heart that is ever more true,
Fond faith that is firmer for trusting in vain—
    She waits by the sliprails for you.

MARSHALL'S MATE

You almost heard the surface bake, and saw the gum-leaves turn—
You could have watched the grass scorch brown had there been
    grass to burn.
In such a drought the strongest heart might well grow faint and
    weak—
'Twould frighten Satan to his home—not far from Dingo Creek.

The tanks went dry on Ninety Mile, as tanks go dry Out Back.
The Half-Way Spring had failed at last when Marshall missed
    the track;
Beneath a dead tree on the plain we saw a pack-horse reel—
Too blind to see there was no shade, and too done-up to feel.
And charcoaled on the canvas bag ('twas written pretty clear)
We read the message Marshall wrote. It said: "I'm taken queer—
I'm somewhere off of Deadman's Track, half-blind and nearly dead;
Find Crowbar, get him sobered up, and follow back," it said.

"Let Mitchell go to Bandicoot. You'll find him there," said Mack.
"I'll start the chaps from Starving Steers, and take the dry-holes
    back."
We tramped till dark, and tried to track the pack-horse on the sands,
And just at daylight Crowbar came with Milroy's station-hands.
His cheeks were drawn, his face was white, but he was sober then—
In time of trouble, fire, and flood, 'twas Crowbar led the men.
"Spread out as widely as you can each side the track," said he;
"The first to find him make a smoke that all the rest can see."

We took the track and followed back where Crowbar challenged fate,
We found a dead man in the scrub—but 'twas not Crowbar's mate.
The station-hands from Starving Steers were searching all the week—
But never news of Marshall's end came back to Dingo Creek.
And no one, save the spirit of the sand-waste, fierce and lone,
Knew where Jack Marshall crawled to die—but Crowbar might have known.

He'd scarcely closed his quiet eyes or drawn a sleeping breath—
They say that Crowbar slept no more until he slept in death.
And, when we spelled at night, he'd lie with eyes still open wide,
And watched the stars as if they'd point the place where Marshall died.

The search was made as searches are (and often made in vain),
And on the seventh day we saw a smoke across the plain.
We left the track and followed back; 'twas Crowbar still that led,
And when his horse gave out at last he walked—or ran—ahead.
We reached the place and turned again—dragged back, and no man spoke—
It was a bush-fire in the scrub that made the cursed smoke.
And when we gave it best at last, he said, *"I'll see it through"*,
Although we knew we'd done as much as mortal men could do.

"I'll not—I won't give up!" he said, his hand pressed to his brow;
"My God! the cursed flies and ants, they might be at him now.
I'll see it so in twenty years, 'twill haunt me all my life—
I could not face his sister so—I could not face his wife.
It's no use talking to me now—I'm going back," he said,
"I'm going back to find him, and I will—alive or dead!"

. . . . . .

He got his horse and loaded up with tucker for a week,
And then, at sunset, crossed the plain, away from Dingo Creek.
We watched him tramp beside the horse till we, as it grew late,
Scarce knew which shade was Bonypart and which was Marshall's mate.
The dam went dry at Dingo Creek, and we were driven back,
And none dared face the Ninety Mile when Crowbar took the track.

They saw him at Dead Camel and along the Dry Hole Creeks—
There came a time when none had heard of Marshall's mate for
    weeks;
They'd seen him at No Sunday, he had called at Starving Steers—
There came a time when none had heard of Marshall's mate for
    years.
They found old Bonypart at last, picked clean by hungry crows,
But no one knew how Crowbar died—the soul of Marshall knows!

And now, way out on Dingo Creek, when winter days are late,
The bushmen talk of Crowbar's ghost "what's looking for his mate";
For—let the fool indulge his mirth, and let the wise man doubt—
The soul of Crowbar and his mate have travelled farther out.
Beyond the farthest two-rail fence, Colanne and Nevertire—
Beyond the farthest rabbit-proof, barbed wire and common wire—
Beyond the farthest Gov'ment tank, and past the farthest bore—
The Never-Never, No Man's Land, No More, and Nevermore—
Beyond the Land o' Break-o'-Day, and Sunset and the Dawn,
The soul of Marshall and the soul of Marshall's mate have gone
Unto that Loving, Laughing Land where life is fresh and clean—
Where rivers flow the summer long, and grass is always green.

THE OLD JIMMY WOODSER

THE old Jimmy Woodser comes into the bar
    Unwelcomed, unnoticed, unknown,
Too old and too odd to be drunk with, by far;
So he glides to the end where the lunch-baskets are
    And they say that he tipples alone.

His frockcoat is green and the nap is no more,
    And his hat is not quite at its best;
He wears the peaked collar our grandfathers wore,
The black-ribbon tie that was legal of yore,
    And the coat buttoned over his breast.

When first he came in, for a moment I thought
    That my vision or wits were astray;
For a picture and page out of Dickens he brought—
'Twas an old file dropped in from the Chancery Court
    To the wine-vault just over the way.

But I dreamed, as he tasted his "bitter" tonight
    And the lights in the bar-room grew dim,
That the shades of the friends of that other day's light,
And of girls that were bright in our grandfathers' sight.
    Lifted shadowy glasses to him.

Then I opened the door, and the old man passed out,
    With his short, shuffling step and bowed head;
And I sighed; for I felt, as I turned me about,
An odd sense of respect—born of whisky no doubt—
    For the life that was fifty years dead.

And I thought—there are times when our memory trends
    Through the future, as 'twere, on its own—
That I, out-of-date ere my pilgrimage ends,
In a new-fashioned bar to dead loves and dead friends
    Might drink, like the old man, alone.

WARATAH AND WATTLE

Though poor and in trouble I wander alone,
    With a rebel cockade in my hat;
Though friends may desert me, and kindred disown,
    My country will never do that!
You may sing of the Shamrock, the Thistle, the Rose,
    Or the three in a bunch, if you will;
But I know of a country that gathered all those,
And I love the great land where the Waratah grows,
    And the Wattle-bough blooms on the hill.

Australia! Australia! so fair to behold—
    While the blue sky is arching above;
The stranger should never have need to be told,
That the Wattle-bloom means that her heart is of gold,
    And the Waratah's red with her love.

Australia! Australia! most beautiful name,
    Most kindly and bountiful land;
I would die every death that might save her from shame,
    If a black cloud should rise on the strand;

But whatever the quarrel, whoever her foes,
   Let them come! Let them come when they will!
Though the struggle be grim, 'tis Australia that knows
That her children shall fight while the Waratah grows,
   And the Wattle blooms out on the hill.

AUSTRALIAN ENGINEERS

Ah, well! but the case seems hopeless, and the pen might write in vain;
The people gabble of old things over and over again.
For the sake of the sleek importer we slave with the pick and the shears,
While hundreds of boys in Australia long to be engineers.

A new generation has risen under Australian skies,
Boys with the light of genius deep in their dreamy eyes—
Not as of artists or poets with their vain imaginings,
But born to be thinkers and doers, and makers of wonderful things.

Born to be builders of vessels in the Harbours of Waste and Loss,
That shall carry our goods to the nations, flying the Southern Cross;
And fleets that shall guard our seaboard—while the East is backed by the Jews—
Under Australian captains, and manned by Australian crews.

Boys who are slight and quiet, but boys who are strong and true
Dreaming of great inventions—always of something new;
With brains untrammelled by training, but quick where reason directs—
Boys with imagination and keen, strong intellects.

They long for the crank and the belting, the gear and the whirring wheel,
The stamp of the giant hammer, the glint of the polished steel,
For the mould, and the vice, and the turning-lathe—they are boys who long for the keys
To the doors of the world's mechanics and science's mysteries.

They would be makers of fabrics, of cloth for the continents—
Makers of mighty engines and delicate instruments,
It is they who would set fair cities on the western plains far out.
They who would garden the deserts—it is they who would conquer the drought!

They see the dykes to the skyline, where a dust-waste blazes today,
And they hear the lap of the waters on the miles of sand and clay;
They see the rainfall increasing, and the bountiful sweeps of grass,
And all the year on the rivers long strings of their barges pass.

But still are the steamers loading with our timber and wool and gold,
To return with costly shoddy stacked high in the foreign hold,
With cardboard boots for our leather, and Brummagem goods and slops
For thin, white-faced Australians to sell in our sordid shops.

EURUNDEREE

There are scenes in the distance where beauty is not,
On the desolate flats where gaunt apple-trees rot.
Where the brooding old ridge rises up to the breeze
From his dark lonely gullies of stringy-bark trees,
There are voice-haunted gaps, ever sullen and strange;
But Eurunderee lies like a gem in the range.

Still I see in my fancy the dark-green and blue
Of the box-covered hills where the five-corners grew;
And the rugged old sheoaks that sighed in the bend
O'er the lily-decked pools where the dark ridges end,
And the scrub-covered spurs running down from the Peak
To the deep grassy banks of Eurunderee Creek.

On the knolls where the vineyards and fruit-gardens are
There's a beauty that even the drought cannot mar:
For it came to me oft, in the days that are lost,
As I strolled on the sidling where lingered the frost,
And, the shadows of night from the gullies withdrawn,
The hills in the background were flushed by the dawn.

I was there in late years, but there's many a change
Where the Cudgegong River flows down through the range;
For the curse of the town with the railroad has come,
And the goldfields are dead. And the girl, and the chum,
And the old home were gone; yet the oaks seemed to speak
Of the hazy old days on Eurunderee Creek.

And I stood by that creek, ere the sunset grew cold,
When the leaves of the sheoaks were traced on the gold,
And I thought of old days, and I thought of old folks,
Till I sighed in my heart to the sigh of the oaks;
For the years waste away like the waters that leak
Through the pebbles and sand of Eurunderee Creek.

DO YOU THINK THAT I DO NOT KNOW?

They say that I never have written of love,
  As a writer of songs should do;
They say that I never could touch the strings
  With a touch that is firm and true;
They say I know nothing of women and men
  In the fields where Love's roses grow,
I must write, they say, with a halting pen—
  Do you think that I do not know?

My love-burst came, like an English Spring,
  In the days when our hair was brown,
And the hem of her skirt was a sacred thing,
  And her hair was an angel's crown.
The shock when another man touched her arm,
  Where the dancers sat in a row,
The hope, the despair, and the false alarm—
  Do you think that I do not know?

By the arbour lights on the western farms,
  You remember the question put,
While you held her warm in your quivering arms
  And you trembled from head to foot.
The electric shock from her finger-tips,
  And the murmuring answer low,
The soft, shy yielding of warm red lips—
  Do you think that I do not know?

She was buried at Brighton, where Gordon sleeps,
  When I was a world away;
And the sad old garden its secret keeps,
  For nobody knows today.

179

She left a message for me to read,
    Where the wild, wide oceans flow;
Do you know how the heart of a man can bleed?—
    Do you think that I do not know?

I stood by the grave where the dead girl lies,
    When the sunlit scene was fair,
'Neath white clouds high in the autumn skies
    I answered the message there.
But the haunting words of the dead to me
    Shall go wherever I go.
She lives in the Marriage that Might Have Been—
    Do you think that I do not know?

THE GHOST

Down the street as I was drifting with the city's human tide,
Came a ghost, and for a moment walked in silence by my side.
Now my heart was hard and bitter, and a bitter spirit he,
So I felt no great aversion to his ghostly company.
Said the shade: "At finer feelings let your lip in scorn be curled,
'Self and Pelf', my friend, has ever been the motto for the world."

And he said: "If you'd be happy, you must clip your fancy's wings,
Stretch your conscience at the edges to the size of earthly things;
Never fight another's battle, for a friend can never know
When he'll gladly fly for succour to the bosom of the foe.
At the power of truth and friendship let your lip in scorn be
    curled—
'Self and Pelf', my friend, remember, is the motto of the world.

"Where Society is mighty, always truckle to her rule;
Never send an 'i' undotted to the teacher of a school;
Only fight a wrong or falsehood when the crowd is at your back,
And, till Charity can pay you, shut the purse, and let her pack;
At the fools who will not truckle let your lip in scorn be curled,
'Self and Pelf', my friend, remember, that's the motto of the world.

"Ne'er assail the shaky ladders Fame has from her niches hung,
Lest unfriendly heels above you grind your fingers from the rung;
Or the fools who idle under, envious of your fair renown,
Heedless of the pain you suffer, do their best to shake you down.

At the praise of men, or censure, let your lip in scorn be curled,
'Self and Pelf', my friend, remember, is the motto of the world.

"Flowing founts of inspiration leave their sources parched and dry,
Scalding tears of indignation sear the hearts that beat too high;
Chilly waters thrown upon it drown the fire that's in the bard;
And the banter of the critic hurts his heart till it grows hard.
At the fame your muse may offer let your lip in scorn be curled,
'Self and Pelf', my friend, remember, that's the motto of the world.

"Shun the fields of love, where lightly to a low and mocking tune
Strong and useful lives are ruined, and the broken hearts are strewn.
Not a farthing is the value of the honest love you hold;
Call it lust, and make it serve you! Set your heart on nought but
    gold.
At the bliss of purer passions let your lip in scorn be curled—
'Self and Pelf', my friend, shall ever be the motto of the world."

Here he ceased, and looked intently in my face, and nearer drew;
But a sudden deep repugnance to his presence thrilled me through.
Then I saw his face was cruel, by the look that o'er it stole,
Then I felt his breath was poison, by the shuddering of my soul,
Then I guessed his purpose evil, by his lip in sneering curled,
And I knew mankind he slandered, by my knowledge of the world.

But he vanished as a purer, brighter presence gained my side—
"Heed him not! there's truth and friendship in this wondrous world,"
    she cried,
"And of those who cleave to virtue in their climbing for renown
Only they who faint, or falter, from the heights are shaken down.
At a cynic's baneful teaching let your lip in scorn be curled!
'Brotherhood, and Love, and Honour!' is the motto for the world."

THE LAST REVIEW

Turn the light down, nurse, and leave me, while I hold my
    last review,
For the Bush is slipping from me, and the town is going too.
Draw the blinds. The streets are lighted, and I hear the tramp
    of feet—
And I'm weary, very weary, of the Faces in the Street.

In the dens of Grind and Heartbreak, in the streets of Never-Rest,
I have lost the scent and colour and the music of the West:
I would fain recall old faces with the memories they bring—
Where are Bill and Jim and Mary and the Songs They Used
    to Sing?

They are coming! They are coming! they are passing through the
    room
With the smell of gum-leaves burning, and the scent of wattle-bloom!
And behind them in the timber, after dust and heat and toil,
Others sit beside the camp-fire, yarning While the Billies Boil.

In the Gap above the ridges there's a flash and there's a glow—
Swiftly down the scrub-clad sidling come the Lights of Cobb
    and Co.,
Red face from the box-seat beaming—oh, how plain those faces grow!
From his Golden Hole 'tis Peter—Peter McIntosh, I know.

Dusty patch in desolation, bare slab walls and earthen floor,
And a blinding drought that blazes from horizon to the door:
Milkless tea and ration sugar, damper, junk, and pumpkin mash—
And a Day on our Selection passes by me in a flash.

Rush of big, wild-eyed, store bullocks while the sheep crawl
    hopelessly,
And the loaded wool-teams rolling, lurching on like ships at sea—
With his whip across his shoulder (and the wind just now abeam)
There goes Jimmy Nowlett, ploughing through the dust beside
    his team!

Sunrise on the olden diggings! (Oh, what life and hopes are here.)
From a hundred pointing-forges comes a tinkle, tinkle, clear—
Strings of drays with wash to puddle, clack of countless windlass-
    boles,
Here and there the red flag flying, flying over golden holes.

Picturesque, unspoiled, romantic, chivalrous, and brave and free
Clean in living, true in mateship—reckless generosity—
Mates are buried here as comrades who on fields of battle fall;
And the dreams—the aching, hoping lover-hearts beneath it all!

Rough-built theatres and stages where the world's best actors trod;
Singers bringing reckless rovers nearer boyhood, home, and God;
Paid in laughter, tears, and nuggets in the drama fortune plays—
'Tis the palmy days of Gulgong—Gulgong in the Roaring Days.

Pass the same old scenes before me—and again my heart will ache—
There the Drover's Wife sits watching (not as Eve did) for a snake.
And I see the drear deserted goldfields when the night is late,
And the stony face of Mason, watching by his Father's Mate.

And I see my Haggard Women plainly as they were in life;
'Tis the form of Mrs Spicer and her friend, Joe Wilson's wife,
Sitting hand in hand, Past Carin'—not a sigh and not a moan—
Staring steadily before them, while the slow tears trickle down.

It was No Place for a Woman where the women worked like men;
From the Bush and Jones's Alley come their haunting forms again.
Let this also be recorded when I've answered to the roll,
That I pitied haggard women—wrote for them with all my soul.

Narrow bedroom in the city in the hard days that are dead,
An alarm clock on the table, and a pale boy on the bed:
Arvie Aspinall's Alarm Clock with its harsh and startling call
Never more shall break his slumbers—*I* was Arvie Aspinall.

Maoriland and cynic Steelman, stiff-lipped spieler, battle-through
(Kept a wife and child in comfort, but of course they never knew—
Thought he was an honest bagman). Well, old man, you needn't hug—
Sentimental? you of all men!—Steelman, oh! I *was* a mug!

Ghostly lines of scrub at daybreak—dusty daybreak in the drought—
See a lonely swagman tramping on the track to Further Out:
Like a shade the form of Mitchell, nose-bag full and bluey up,
And between the swag and shoulders lolls his foolish cattle-pup.

Kindly cynic, sad comedian! Mitchell, when you've left the Track,
And have shed your load of sorrow as we slipped our swags Out Back,
We shall have a yarn together in the land of Rest Awhile—
And across his ragged shoulder Mitchell smiles his quiet smile.

Shearing-sheds, and tracks, and shanties—girls that wait at homestead gates—
Camps and stern-eyed Union leaders, and Joe Wilson and his Mates,
True and straight; and to my fancy, each one as he passes through
Deftly down upon the table slips a dusty "note" or two.

. . . . . .

So at last the end has found me (end of all the human push),
And again in silence round me come my Children of the Bush!
Listen, who are young, and let them—if in late and bitter days
Reckless lines I wrote—forget them; there is little there to praise.

I was human, very human; and if in the days misspent
I have injured man or woman, it was done without intent.
If at times I blundered blindly—bitter heart and aching brow—
If I wrote a line unkindly—I am sorry for it now.

Days in London like a nightmare—dreams of foreign lands and sea—
Dreams—for far Australia only is a real land to me.
Tell the Bushmen to Australia and each other to be true—
Tell the boys to stick together! I have held my Last Review.

THE OLD BARK SCHOOL

It was built of bark and poles, and the roof was full of holes
    And each leak in rainy weather made a pool;
And the walls were mostly cracks lined with calico and sacks—
    There was little need for windows in the school.

Then we rode to school and back by the rugged gully-track,
    On the old grey horse that carried three or four;
And he looked so very wise that he lit the Master's eyes
    Every time he put his head in at the door.

(He had run with Cobb and Co.—"That grey leader, let him go!"
    There were men "as knowed the brand upon his hide",
Some "as knowed him on the course"—Funeral service: "Good old horse!"
    When we burnt him in the gully where he died.)

Kevin was the master's name, 'twas from Ireland that he came,
    Where the tanks are always full, and feed is grand;
And the joker then in vogue said his lessons wid a brogue—
    'Twas unconscious imitation, understand.

And we learnt the world in scraps from some ancient dingy maps
    Long discarded by the public-schools in town;
And as nearly every book dated back to Captain Cook
    Our geography was somewhat upside-down.

It was "in the book" and so—well, at that we'd let it go,
   For we never would believe that print could lie;
And we all learnt pretty soon that when school came out at noon
   "The sun is in the south part of the sky".

And Ireland!—*that* was known from the coast-line to Athlone,
   But little of the land that gave us birth;
Save that Captain Cook was killed (and was very likely grilled)
   And "our blacks are just the lowest race on earth".

And a woodcut, in its place, of the same degraded race,
   More like camels than the blackmen that we knew;
Jimmy Bullock, with the rest, scratched his head and gave it best;
   But he couldn't stick a bobtailed kangaroo!

Now the old bark school is gone, and the spot it stood upon
   Is a cattle-camp where curlews' cries are heard;
There's a brick school on the flat—an old school-mate teaches that—
   It was built when Mr Kevin was "transferred".

But the old school comes again with exchanges 'cross the plain—
   With the *Out-Back Press* my fancy roams at large
When I read of passing stock, of a western mob or flock,
   With James Bullock, Grey, or Henry Dale in charge.

When I think how Jimmy went from the old bark school content,
   "Eddicated", with his packhorse after him,
Well . . . perhaps, if I were back, I would follow in his track,
   And let Kevin "finish" me as he did Jim.

PAROO RIVER

It was a week from Christmas-time,
   As near as I remember,
And half a year since, in the rear,
   We'd left the Darling Timber.
The track was hot and more than drear;
   The day dragged out for ever;
But now we knew that we were near
   Our Camp—the Paroo River.

With blighted eyes and blistered feet,
   With stomachs out of order,
Half-mad with flies and dust and heat
   We'd crossed the Queensland Border.
I longed to hear a stream go by
   And see the circles quiver;
I longed to lay me down and die
   That night on Paroo River.

The "nose-bags" heavy on each chest
   (God bless one kindly squatter!),
With grateful weight our hearts they pressed—
   We only wanted water.
The sun was setting in a spray
   Of colour like a liver—
We'd fondly hoped to camp and stay
   That night by Paroo River.

A cloud was on my mate's broad brow,
   And once I heard him mutter:
"What price the good old Darling, now?—
   God bless that grand old gutter!"
And then he stopped and slowly said
   In tones that made me shiver:
"It cannot well be on ahead—
   I think we've crossed the river."

But soon we saw a strip of ground
   Beside the track we followed,
No damper than the surface round,
   But just a little hollowed.
His brow assumed a thoughtful frown—
   This speech he did deliver:
"I wonder if we'd best go down
   Or up the blessed river?"

"But where," said I, " 's the blooming stream?"
   And he replied, "We're at it!"
I stood awhile, as in a dream,
   "Great Scott!" I cried, "is *that* it?
Why, that is some old bridle-track!"
   He chuckled, "Well, I never!
It's plain you've never been Out Back—
   This *is* the Paroo River!"

BILLY'S SQUARE AFFAIR

Long Bill, the captain of the push, was tired of his estate,
And wished to change his life and win the love of something "straight";
Twas rumoured that the Gory B.'s had heard Long Bill declare
That he would turn respectable and wed a "square affair".

He craved the kiss of innocence; his spirit longed to rise;
The Crimson Streak, his faithful piece, grew hateful in his eyes;
(And though, in her entirety, the Crimson Streak "was there",
I grieve to state the Crimson Streak was not a square affair.)

He wanted clothes, a masher suit, he wanted boots and hat;
His girl had earned a quid or two—he couldn't part with that;
And so he went to Brickfield Hill, and from a draper there
He shook the proper kind of togs to fetch a square affair.

Long Bill went to the barber's shop and had a shave and singe,
And down his narrow forehead combed his darling Mabel fringe;
Long Bill put on a "square cut", and he brushed his boots with care,
And roved about the Gardens till he mashed a square affair.

She was a toney servant-girl from somewhere on "The Shore";
She dressed in style that suited Bill—he could not wish for more.
While in her guileless presence he had ceased to chew or swear—
He knew the sort of guyver that will fetch a square affair.

He took her to the stalls; 'twas dear, but Billy said "Wot odds?
You couldn't take a square affair amongst the crimson gods!"
They wandered in the park at night, and hugged each other there—
But, ah! the Crimson Streak got wind of Billy's square affair!

"The blank and space and stars!" she yelled; "the nameless crimson dash!
I'll smash the blanky smooger and his square affair, I'll smash"—
In short, she drank and raved and shrieked and tore her crimson hair,
And swore to murder Billy and to pound his square affair.

And so one summer evening, as the day was growing dim,
She watched her bloke go out and foxed his square affair and him.
That night the park was startled by the shrieks that rent the air—
The Streak had gone for Billy and for Billy's square affair.

The "Gory" push had foxed the Streak; they'd foxed her to the park,
And so, of course, were close at hand to see the bleedin' lark;
A cop arrived in time to hear a Gory B. declare
"Good Lord, here's Billy's Crimson Streak foul of his square affair".

Now Billy scowls about The Rocks, his manly beauty marred,
The Crimson Streak, upon her head, is doing six months' hard;
Bill's swivel eye is in a sling, his heart is in despair,
And in the Sydney Hospital lies Billy's square affair.

THE BOSS-OVER-THE-BOARD

When in charge of a rough and unpopular shed,
With the sins of the bank and the men on his head,
And he mustn't look black or indulge in a grin,
For thirty or forty men hate him like sin—
One is moved to admit—when the total is scored—
That it's just a bit off for the Boss-of-the-board.
  I have battled a lot,
   But in dreams never soared
To the lonely position of Boss-of-the-board.

'Twas a blacklisted shed down the Darling: the Boss
Was a small man to see—though a big man to cross.
We had nought to complain of—except what we thought,
And the Boss didn't boss any more than he ought;
But the Union was booming, and Brotherhood soared,
So we hated like poison the Boss-of-the-board.
  We could tolerate "hands",
   We respected the cook;
But the name of a Boss was a blot in our book.

He'd a row with Big Duggan—a rough sort was Jim—
Or, rather, Jim Duggan was "laying" for him!
Jim's hate of injustice and greed was so deep
That his shearing grew rough, and he ill-used the sheep.
But I fancied that Duggan his manliness lowered
When he took off his shirt to the Boss-of-the-board.
  For the Boss was ten stone,
   And the shearer full-grown,
And he might have, we said, let the crawler alone.

Though some of us there wished the fight to the strong.
Yet we knew in our hearts that the shearer was wrong,
And the crawler was plucky, it can't be denied,
For he had to fight Freedom and Justice beside;
But he came up so gamely, as often as floored,
That a blackleg stood up for the Boss-of-the-board!
      Oh, the fight was a sight,
          And we pondered that night
How surprisingly some of those blacklegs can fight!

Next day at the office, when sadly the wreck
Of Jim Duggan came up like a lamb for his cheque,
Said the Boss, "Don't be childish! It's all past and gone;
I'm short of good shearers. You'd *better* stay on."
And we fancied Jim Duggan *our* dignity lowered
When he stopped to oblige a damned Boss-of-the-board.
      We said nothing to Jim—
          Such a joke might be grim
For the subject, we saw, was distasteful to him.

The Boss just went on as he'd done from the first,
And he favoured Big Duggan no more than the worst;
And when we'd cut out and the steamer came down—
With the hawkers and spielers—to take us to town,
And we'd all got aboard, 'twas Jim Duggan, good Lord!
Who yelled for three cheers for the Boss-of-the-board.
      'Twas a bit off, no doubt—
          And with Freedom about—
But a lot is forgot when a shed is cut out!

ROBBIE'S STATUE

Grown tired of mourning for my sins—
    And brooding over merits—
The other night with puckered brow
    I went amongst the spirits;
And I met one that I knew well:
    "Oh, Scotty's Ghost, is that you?
And did you see the fearsome crowd
    At Robbie Burns's statue?

"They hurried up in hansom cabs,
   Tall-hatted and frock-coated;
They trained it in from all the towns,
   The weird and hairy-throated;
They spoke in some outlandish tongue,
   They cut some comic capers,
And ilka man was wild to get
   His name intil the papers.

"They showed no gleam of intellect,
   Those frauds who rushed before us;
They knew one verse of *Auld Lang Syne*—
   The first one—and the chorus:
They clacked and clashed o' Scotlan's Bard
   They glibly talked of "Rabbie";
But what if he had come to them
   Without a groat, and shabby?

"They sighed and wept for Robbie's sake,
   They stood and brayed like asses
(The living bard's a drunken rake,
   The dead one loved the lasses);
If Robbie Burns were here, they'd sit
   As still as any mouse is;
If Robbie Burns should come their way,
   They'd chase him from their houses.

"Oh, weep for Bonnie Scotland's bard!
   And praise the Scottish nation,
Who made him spy, and let him die
   Heart-broken in privation:
Exciseman, so that he might yet
   Survive their winters' rigours—
Just as in southern lands they set
   The rhymer counting figures.

"We need some lines of stinging fun
   To wake the States and light 'em;
I wish a man like Robert Burns
   Were here today to write 'em!
But still the mockery shall survive
   Till Day o' Judgment crashes—
The men we scorn when we're alive
   With praise insult our ashes."

> But Scotty's Ghost said: "Never mind
> The fleas that you inherit;
> The living bard can flick them off—
> They cannot hurt his spirit.
> The crawlers round the bardie's name
> Shall crawl through all the ages;
> His work's the living thing, and they
> Are fly-dirt on the pages."

TAMBAROORA JIM

He never drew a sword to fight a dozen foes alone,
Nor gave a life to save a life no better than his own.
He lived because he had been born—the hero of my song—
And fought the battle with his fist whene'er he fought a wrong.
Yet there are many men who would do anything for him—
A simple chap as went by name of Tambaroora Jim.

He used to keep a shanty in the Come-and-find-it Scrub,
And there were few but knew the name of Tambaroora's pub.
He wasn't great at lambing-down (which many landlords are),
And never was a man less fit to stand behind a bar;
Off-hand, as most bush natives are, and freckled, tall, and slim,
A careless native of the land was Tambaroora Jim.

When people said that loafers took the profit from his pub,
He'd ask them how they thought a chap could do without his grub;
He'd say, "I've gone for days myself without a bite or sup—
Oh! I've been through the mill and know the meaning of 'hard-up'."
He might have made his fortune, but he wasn't in the swim—
No bushman e'er had softer heart than Tambaroora Jim.

One dismal day I tramped across the Come-and-find-it Flats,
With Ballarat Adolphus and a mate of Ballarat's;
'Twas nearly dark, and raining fast, and all our things were damp;
We'd no tobacco, and our legs were aching with the cramp;
We couldn't raise a cent, and so our lamp of hope was dim;
'Twas thus we struck the shanty kept by Tambaroora Jim.

We dropped our swags beneath a tree, and squatted in despair,
But Jim came out to watch the rain, and saw us sitting there;

He came and muttered, "I suppose you haven't half-a-crown,
But come and get some tucker, and a drink to wash it down."
We hitched our blueys up again, and went along with him,
And then we learned why bushmen swore by Tambaroora Jim.

We sat beside his kitchen fire and nursed our aching knees,
And blessed him when we heard the rain go wooshing through the
    trees.
He made us stay, although he knew we couldn't raise a bob,
And tuckered us until we made some money on a job.
Ah, many a time since then we've filled our glasses to the brim,
And drunk in various pubs the health of Tambaroora Jim.

A man need never want a meal while Jim had "junk" to carve,
For Tambaroora always said a fellow mustn't starve.
And this went on until they put a bailiff in his pub
For helping chaps who couldn't raise the money for their grub.
At last, one rainy evening, as the distant range grew dim,
He humped his bluey from the Flats, did Tambaroora Jim.

I miss the fun in Jim's old bar—the laughter and the noise,
The jolly hours I used to spend on pay-nights with the boys.
But that's all past, and vain regrets are useless, I'll allow;
They say the Come-and-find-it Flats are all deserted now.
Poor Tambaroora's dead, perhaps—but that's all right for him,
Saint Peter cottons on to chaps like Tambaroora Jim.

REJECTED

She says she's "very sorry", as she sees you to the gate;
    You calmly say "Good-bye" to her while standing off a yard,
Then you lift your hat and leave her, walking mighty stiff and
    straight—
    But you're hit, old man—hit hard.

In your brain the words are burning of the answer that she gave,
    As you turn the nearest corner and you stagger just a bit;
But you pull yourself together, for a man's strong heart is brave
    When it's hit, old man—hard hit.

You may try to drown the sorrow, but the drink has no effect;
   You cannot stand the barmaid with her coarse and vulgar wit:
And so you seek the street again, and start for home direct,
   When you're hit, old man—hard hit.

You see the face of her you lost, the pity in her smile—
   Ah! she is to the barmaid much as snow to chimney grit;
You're a better man and nobler, in your sorrow, for a while,
   When you're hit, old man—hard hit.

And arriving at your lodgings, with a face of deepest gloom,
   You shun the other boarders and your manly brow you knit;
You take a light and go upstairs directly to your room—
   For you're hit, old man—hard hit.

You clutch your scarf and collar, and you tear them from your throat,
   You rip your waistcoat open like a fellow in a fit;
And you fling them in a corner with the made-to-order coat,
   When you're hit, old man—hard hit.

You throw yourself, despairing, on your hateful single bed—
   In the future not a twinkle, in your black sky not a split—
And then lie blindly staring at the plaster overhead—
   You are hit, old man—hard hit.

You think, and think, and think, till you go mad almost;
   The spectres of the bygone years across your vision flit;
The very girl herself seems dead, and comes back as a ghost,
   When you're hit, like this—hard hit.

You long and hope for nothing save the rest that sleep can bring,
   But you find that in the morning things have brightened up a bit;
Still, you're dull for many evenings, with a cracked heart in a sling,
   When you're hit, old man—hard hit.

O'HARA, J.P.

JAMES Patrick O'Hara, the Justice of Peace,
Bossed the local P.M. as he bossed the police;
A parent, a landlord, a sportsman was he—
A townsman of weight was O'Hara. J.P.

He gave out the prizes, foundation-stones laid,
He shone when the Governor's visit was paid;
And twice re-elected as Mayor was he—
The flies couldn't roost on O'Hara, J.P.

Now Sandy Macleod of the Axe-and-the-Saw,
Was charged with a breach of the Licensing Law—
He sold after hours whilst talking too free
On matters concerning O'Hara, J.P.

Each witness the next contradicted so flat,
Concerning back-parlours, side-doors, and all that;
'Twas very conflicting as all must agree—
"Ye'd betther take care!" said O'Hara, J.P.

When "Baby", the barmaid, her evidence gave—
A poor, timid darling who tried to be brave—
"Now, *don't* be afraid—if it's frightened ye be—
Speak out, my good girl," said O'Hara, J.P.

Her hair was so golden, her eyes were so blue,
Her face was so fair, and her words seemed so true—
So green in the ways of sweet woman was he
That she jolted the heart of O'Hara, J.P.

He turned to the other grave Justice of Peace,
And whispered, "You can't always trust the police;
I'll visit the premises during the day
And see for myself," said O'Hara, Jay Pay.

                                                     (*Case postponed*)

.   .   .   .   .

'Twas early next morning, or late the same night—
"'Twas early next morning" I think would be right—
That sounds which betokened a breach of the law
Escaped through the cracks of the Axe-and-the-Saw.

And Constable Dogherty, out in the street,
Met Constable Clancy a bit off his beat;
He took him with finger and thumb by the ear,
And led him around to a lane in the rear.

On a blind, where he pointed, strange shadows were seen,
And pantomime hinting of revels within;
"We'll drop on Macleod, if ye'll listen to me,
And prove we are right to O'Hara, J.P."

But Clancy was up to the lay of the land;
He cautiously shaded his mouth with his hand—
"Wisht, man! Howld yer whisht! or it's ruined we'll be,
It's the Justice himself—it's O'Hara, J.P."

They hished and they whishted, and turned themselves round,
And got themselves off like two cats on wet ground;
Agreeing to be, on their honour as men,
A deaf-dumb-and-blind institution just then.

Inside on a sofa, two barmaids between
(Plus one on his knee), was a gentleman seen;
And any chance eye at the keyhole could see
In less than a wink 'twas O'Hara, J.P.

The first in the chorus of songs that were sung,
The loudest who laughed at the jokes that were sprung,
The guest of the evening, the soul of the spree,
The daddy of all was O'Hara, J.P.

And hard-cases chuckled, and hard-cases said
That Baby and Alice conveyed him to bed;
In subsequent storms it was joyful to see
Those hard-cases side with the sinful J.P.

Next day in the court, when the case came in sight,
O'Hara declared he was satisfied, quite;
The case was dismissed—it was destined to be
The final ukase of O'Hara, J.P.

The law and religion came down on him first—
The Christians were hard, but his wife was the worst!
Half ruined and half driven crazy was he—
It made an old man of O'Hara, J.P.

Now, young men who come from the bush, do you hear?
You who know not the power of barmaids and beer—
Don't see for yourself! from temptation steer free,
Remember the fall of O'Hara, J.P.

BILL AND JIM FALL OUT

Bill and Jim are mates no longer—they would scorn the name of mate—
Those two bushmen hate each other with a soul-consuming hate;
They were once as brothers should be, though henceforth they never will:
Ne'er were mates to one another half so true as Jim and Bill.

Bill was one of those who have to argue all the day, or die—
Though, of course, he swore, 'twas Jim who always itched to argufy.
They'd discuss most abstract subjects, contradict each other flat
And at times in lurid language—but were mates in spite of that.

Bill believed the Bible story *re* the origin of him—
He was sober, he was steady, he was orthodox; while Jim,
Who, we grieve to state, was always getting into drunken scrapes,
Held that man degenerated from degenerated apes.

Bill was British to the backbone, he was loyal through and through;
Jim declared that Blucher's Prussians won the fight at Waterloo,
And he hoped the coloured races would in time wipe out the white—
'Twas a strain upon their mateship, but it didn't burst it quite.

Round in Maoriland they battled—there they saw it through and through—
Once they argued on the rata, what it was and how it grew;
Bill believed the vine grew downward, Jim declared that it grew up—
Yet they always shared their fortunes to the final bite and sup.

Night by night they used to argue how the kangaroo was born;
Each believed the other's theory stupid, only fit for scorn;
Bill said that it was "born inside", Jim declared it was born out—
Each about his own opinion never had the slightest doubt.

Then they left the earth to argue and they went among the stars;
Re conditions atmospheric, Bill believed "the hair of Mars
Was too thin for human beins to exist in mortal states".
Jim declared it thick as treacle—yet they lived and worked as mates.

Bill for Free Trade—Jim, Protection—argued as to which was best
For the welfare of the workers—and their mateship stood the test!
Then they argued over meanings that they didn't mean at all,
As to what they said and didn't—and were mates in spite of all.

Till one night the pair, *together*, tried to light a fire in camp,
When they had a leaky billy, and the wood was scarce and damp.
And.... No matter: let the moral be distinctly understood:
One alone should tend the fire, while the other brings the wood.

BALLAD OF MABEL CLARE

YE children of the Land of Gold,
   I sing this song to you,
And if the jokes are somewhat old
   The central facts are new.
So be it sung, by hut and tent,
   Where tall the native grows;
And understand, the song is meant
   For singing through the nose.

There dwelt a hard old cockatoo
   On western hills far out,
Where everything is green and blue
   (Except, of course, in drought);
A crimson Anarchist was he—
   Held other men in scorn—
Yet preached that every man is free,
   And also "ekal born".

He lived in his ancestral hut—
   His missus wasn't there—
There was none other with him but
   His daughter, Mabel Clare.
Her eyes and hair were like the sun;
   Her foot was like a mat;
Her cheeks a trifle overdone;
   She was a democrat.

A manly independence, born
   Among the hills, she had;
She treated womankind with scorn,
   And often cursed her dad.

She hated swells and shining lights,
  For she had seen a few,
And she believed in Women's Rights
  (She mostly got 'em, too).

A stranger on the neighbouring run
  Sojourned, the squatter's guest;
He was unknown to anyone,
  But exquisitely dress'd;
He wore the latest toggery,
  The loudest thing in ties—
'Twas generally reckoned he
  Was something in disguise.

Once strolling in the noontide heat
  Beneath the blinding glare,
This noble stranger chanced to meet
  The radiant Mabel Clare.
She saw at once he was a swell—
  According to her lights—
But, ah! 'tis very sad to tell,
  She met him oft of nights.

And, rambling through the moonlit gorge,
  She chatted all the while
Of Ingersoll, and Henry George,
  And Bradlaugh and Carlyle:
In short, he learned to love the girl,
  And things went on like this,
Until he said he was an Earl,
  And asked her to be his.

"Oh, say no more, Lord Kawlinee,
  Oh, say no more!" she said;
"Oh, say no more, Lord Kawlinee,
  I wish that I was dead:
My head is in an awful whirl,
  The truth I dare not tell—
I am a democratic girl,
  And cannot wed a swell!"

"O Love!" he cried, "but you forget
  That you are most unjust;
'Twas not my fault that I was set
  Within the upper crust.

Heed not the yarns the poets tell—
  O Darling, do not doubt
A simple lord can love as well
  As any rouseabout!

"For you I'll give my fortune up—
  I'd go to work for you!
I'll put the money in the cup
  And drop the title, too.
Oh, fly with me! Oh, fly with me
  Across the mountains blue!
Hoh, fly with me! *Hoh, fly with me!*"
  That very night she flew.

They took the train and journeyed down,
  Across the range they sped
Until they came to Sydney town,
  Where shortly they were wed.
(And still upon the western wild
  Admiring teamsters tell
How Mabel's father cursed his child
  For clearing with a swell.)

"What ails my bird this bridal night?"
  Exclaimed Lord Kawlinee;
"What ails my bird this bridal night?"
  O Love, confide in me!"
"Oh now," she said, "that I am yaws
  You'll let me weep—I must—
For I've betrayed the people's caws
  And joined the upper crust."

Oh, proudly smiled his lordship then—
  His chimney-pot he floor'd;
"Look up, my love, and smile again,
  For I am not a lord!"
His eye-glass from his eye he tore,
  The dickey from his breast,
And turned and stood his bride before—
  A rouseabout, confess'd!

"Unknown I've loved you long," he said,
  "And I have loved you true—
A-shearing in a neighbour's shed
  I learned to worship you.

I do not care for place or pelf,
   For now, my love, I'm sure
That you will love me for myself
   And not because I'm poor.

"To prove your love I spent my cheque
   To buy this swell rig-out;
So fling your arms about my neck
   For I'm a rouseabout!"
At first she gave a startled cry,
   Then, safe from Care's alarms,
She sighed a soul-subduing sigh
   And sank into his arms.

He pawned the togs, and home he took
   His bride in all her charms;
The proud old cockatoo received
   The pair with open arms.
And long they lived, the faithful bride,
   The lowly rouseabout—
And if she wasn't satisfied
   She never let it out.

THE STRANGERS' FRIEND

I MET him in Bourke in the Union days—with which we have nought to do
(Their creed was narrow, their methods crude, but they stuck to the Cause like glue).
He came into town from the Lost Soul Run for his grim half-yearly "bend".
And because of a curious hobby he had, he was known as "The Strangers' Friend".

In the joyful mood, in the joyless mood—in his cynical stages too—
In the maudlin stage, in the fighting stage, in the stage when all was blue—
From the joyful hour when his spree commenced, right through to the awful end,
He never lost grip of the "fixed idee" that he was the Strangers' Friend.

"The feller as knows, *he* can battle around for his bloomin' self,"
 he'd say—
"I don't give a curse for the blanks I know—send the hard-up bloke
 this way;
Send the stranger round, and I'll see him through," and, e'en as
 the bushman spoke,
The chaps and fellers would tip the wink to a casual hard-up bloke.

And it wasn't only a bushman's bluff to the fame of the Friend
 they scored,
For he'd shout the stranger a suit of clothes, and he'd pay for
 the stranger's board;
But the worst of it was that he'd skite all night on the edge of
 the stranger's bunk,
And never get helplessly tight himself till he'd got the stranger
 drunk.

And the chaps and the fellers would speculate—by way of a
 ghastly joke—
As to who'd be caught by the jim-jams first—the Friend or the
 hard-up bloke?
And the Joker would say that there wasn't a doubt as to who'd
 be damned in the end,
When the Devil got hold of a hard-up bloke in the shape of the
 Strangers' Friend.

It was nothing at all to the Strangers' Friend what the rest might
 say or think;
He always held that the hard-up state was due to the curse of drink,
To the evils of cards, and of company: "But a young cove's built
 that way,
And I was that sort of a fool meself when I started out," he'd say.

At the end of the spree, in fresh white moles, clean-shaven, and
 cool as ice,
He'd give the stranger a bob or two, and some straight out-back
 advice;
Then he'd tramp away for the Lost Soul Run, where the hot dust
 rose like smoke,
Having done his duty to all mankind, for he'd stuck to a hard-up
 bloke.

THE CAPTAIN OF THE PUSH

As the night was falling slowly down on city, town, and bush,
From a slum in Jones's Alley sloped the Captain of the Push;
And he scowled towards the North, and he scowled towards the South,
As he hooked his little fingers in the corners of his mouth.
Then his whistle, loud and piercing, woke the echoes of "The Rocks",
And a dozen ghouls came sloping round the corners of the blocks.

There was nought to rouse their anger; yet the oath that each one swore
Seemed less fit for publication than the one that went before.
For they spoke the gutter language with the easy flow that comes
Only to the men whose childhood knew the gutters and the slums.
Then they spat in turn, and halted; and the one that came behind,
Spitting fiercely at the pavement, called on Heaven to strike him blind.

Let me first describe the captain, bottle-shouldered, pale and thin:
He was just the beau-ideal of a Sydney larrikin.
E'en his hat was most suggestive of the place where Pushes live,
With a gallows-tilt that no one, save a larrikin, can give;
And the coat, a little shorter than the fashion might require,
Showed a (more or less uncertain) lower part of his attire.

That which tailors know as "trousers"—known to him as "blooming bags"—
Hanging loosely from his person, swept, with tattered ends, the flags;
And he had a pointed sternpost to the boots that peeped below
(Which he laced up from the centre of the nail of his great toe),
And he wore his shirt uncollared, and the tie correctly wrong;
But I think his vest was shorter than should be on one so long.

Then the captain crooked his finger at a stranger on the kerb,
Whom he qualified politely with an adjective and verb,
And he begged the Gory Bleeders that they wouldn't interrupt
Till he gave an introduction—it was painfully abrupt—
"Here's the bleedin' push, my covey—here's a (something) from the bush!
Strike me dead, he wants to join us!" said the captain of the push.

Said the stranger: "I am nothing but a bushy and a dunce;
But I read about the Bleeders in the *Weekly Gasbag* once:
Sitting lonely in the humpy when the wind began to woosh,
How I longed to share the dangers and the pleasures of the push!
Gosh! I hate the swells and good uns—I could burn 'em in their beds;
I am with you, if you'll have me, and I'll break their blazing heads."

"Now, look here," exclaimed the captain to the stranger from the bush,
"Now, look here—suppose a feller was to split upon the push,
Would you lay for him and down him, even if the traps were round?
Would you lay him out and kick him to a jelly on the ground?
Would you jump upon the nameless—kill, or cripple him, or both?
Speak? or else I'll—SPEAK!" The stranger answered, "My kerlonial oath!"

"Now, look here," exclaimed the captain to the stranger from the bush,
"Now, look here—suppose the Bleeders let you come and join the push,
Would you smash a bleedin' bobby if you got the blank alone?
Would you stoush a swell or Chinkie—split his garret with a stone?
Would you have a 'moll' to keep you—like to swear off work for good?"
"Yes, my oath!" replied the stranger. "My kerlonial oath! I would!"

"Now, look here," exclaimed the captain to that stranger from the bush,
"Now, look here—before the Bleeders let you come and join the push.
You must prove that you're a blazer—you must prove that you have grit
Worthy of a Gory Bleeder—you must show your form a bit—
Take a rock and smash that winder!" and the stranger, nothing loth,
Took the rock and—smash! The Bleeders muttered "My kerlonial oath!"

So they swore him in, and found him sure of aim and light of heel,
And his only fault, if any, lay in his excessive zeal.
He was good at throwing metal, but I chronicle with pain
That he jumped upon a victim, damaging the watch and chain
Ere the Bleeders had secured them; yet the captain of the push
Swore a dozen oaths in favour of the stranger from the bush.

Late next morn the captain, rising, hoarse and thirsty, from his lair,
Called the newly-feathered Bleeder; but the stranger wasn't there!
Quickly going through the pockets of his bloomin' bags, he learned
That the stranger had been through him for the stuff his moll had
    earned;
And the language that he uttered I should scarcely like to tell
(Stars! and notes of exclamation!! blank and dash will do as well).

That same night the captain's signal woke the echoes of The Rocks,
Brought the Gory Bleeders sloping through the shadows of the
    blocks;
And they swore the stranger's action was a blood-escaping shame,
While they waited for the nameless—but the nameless never came.
And the Bleeders soon forgot him; but the captain of the push
Still is laying round, in ballast, for the stranger "from the bush".

CORNY BILL

His old clay pipe stuck in his mouth,
    His hat pushed from his brow,
His dress best fitted for the South—
    I think I see him now;
And when the streets are very still,
    And sleep upon me comes,
I often dream that me an' Bill
    Are humpin' of our drums.

I mind the time when first I came
    A stranger to the land;
And I was stumped, an' sick, an' lame
    When Bill took me in hand.
And when we'd journeyed damp an' far,
    An' clouds were in the skies,
We'd camp in some old shanty bar,
    And sit a-tellin' lies.

Though time had writ upon his brow
    And rubbed away his curls,
He always was—an' may be now—
    A favourite with the girls;

I've heard bush-wimmin scream an' squall—
   I've see'd 'em laugh until
They could not do their work at all,
    Because of Corny Bill.

He was the jolliest old pup
   As ever you did see,
And often at some bush kick-up
   They'd make old Bill M.C.
He'd make them dance and sing all night,
   He'd make the music hum,
But he'd be gone at mornin' light
   A-humpin' of his drum.

Though joys of which the poet rhymes
   Was not for Bill an' me,
I think we had some good old times
   Out on the wallaby.
I took a wife and left off rum,
   An' camped beneath a roof;
But Bill preferred to hump his drum
   A-paddin' of the hoof.

The lazy, idle loafers wot
   In toney houses camp
Would call old Bill a drunken sot,
   A loafer, or a tramp;
But if the dead get up again—
   As preachers say they will—
I'd take my chance of judgment then
   Along of Corny Bill.

His long life's day is nearly o'er,
   Its shades begin to fall;
He soon must sling his bluey for
   The last long tramp of all;
I trust that when, in bush an' town,
   He's lived and laughed his fill,
They'll let the golden sliprails down
   For poor old Corny Bill.

MARY CALLED HIM MISTER

They'd parted just a year ago—she thought he'd ne'er come back;
She stammered, blushed, held out her hand, and called him "Mister Mack".
How could he know that all the while she longed to murmur "John"?—
He called her "Miss le Brook", and asked "How she was getting on".

They'd parted but a year before; they'd loved each other well,
But he'd been down to Sydney since, and come back *such* a swell.
They longed to meet in fond embrace, they hungered for a kiss—
But Mary called him *Mister*, and the idiot called her *Miss*.

He paused, and leaned against the door—a stupid chap was he—
And, when she asked if he'd come in and have a cup of tea,
He looked to left, he looked to right, and then he glanced behind . . . .
And slowly doffed his cabbage-tree . . . and said he "didn't mind".

She made a shy apology because the meat was tough,
Then asked if he was quite, quite sure the tea was sweet enough;
He stirred his tea, and sipped it twice, and answered "plenty, quite".
And cut himself a slice of beef, and said that it was "right".

She glanced at him, at times, and coughed an awkward little cough;
He stared at anything but her and said, "I must be off".
That evening he went riding north—a sad and lonely ride—
She locked herself inside her room, and sat her down and cried.

They'd parted but a year before, they loved each other well—
But she was *such* a country girl and he'd grown such a swell;
They longed to meet in fond embrace, they hungered for a kiss—
But Mary called him *Mister*, and the idiot called her *Miss*.

UP THE COUNTRY*

I am back from up the country—very sorry that I went
Seeking out the Southern poets' land whereon to pitch my tent;
I have lost a lot of idols, which were broken on the track,
Burnt a lot of fancy verses, and I'm glad that I am back.

Farther out may be the pleasant scenes of which our poets boast,
But I think the country's rather more inviting round the coast.
Anyway, I'll stay at present at a boarding-house in town.
Drinking beer and lemon-squashes, taking baths and cooling down.

"Sunny plains!" Great Scott!—those burning wastes of barren soil
    and sand
With their everlasting fences stretching out across the land!
Desolation where the crow is! Desert where the eagle flies,
Paddocks where the luny bullock starts and stares with reddened
    eyes;
Where, in clouds of dust enveloped, roasted bullock-drivers creep
Slowly past the sun-dried shepherd dragged behind his crawling
    sheep.
Stunted peak of granite gleaming, glaring like a molten mass
Poured from some infernal furnace on a plain devoid of grass.

Miles and miles of thirsty gutters—strings of muddy waterholes
In the place of "shining rivers"—"walled by cliffs and forest boles".
Barren ridges, gullies, ridges! where the everlasting flies—
Fiercer than the plagues of Egypt—swarm about your blighted eyes!
Bush! where there is no horizon! where the buried bushman sees
Nothing—Nothing! but the sameness of the ragged, stunted trees!
Lonely hut mid drought eternal, suffocating atmosphere
Where the God-forgotten hatter dreams of city life and beer.
Treacherous tracks that trap the stranger, endless roads that gleam
    and glare,
Dark and evil-looking gullies, hiding secrets here and there!
Dull, dumb flats and stony rises, where the toiling bullocks bake,
And the sinister goanna joins the lizard and the snake!
Land of day and night—no morning freshness, and no afternoon,
When the great white sun in rising brings the summer heat in June.

*A retort to Paterson's "A Voice from the Town". "Banjo" replied with "In Defence of the Bush".

Dismal country for the exile! Shades of sudden night that fall
From the sad heart-breaking sunset hurt the new chum worst of all.

Dreary land in sodden weather, where the endless cloud-banks drift
O'er the bushmen like a blanket that the Lord will never lift—
Dismal land when it is raining—growl of floods, and, oh! the woosh
Of the rain and wind together on the dark bed of the bush—
Ghastly fires in lonely humpies, where the granite rocks are piled
In the rain-swept wildernesses that are wildest of the wild.
Land where gaunt and haggard women live alone and work like
    men
Till their husbands, gone a-droving, will return to them again;
Homes of men; if home had ever such a God-forgotten place,
Where the wild selector's children fly before a stranger's face.
Home of tragedy applauded by the dingoes' dismal yell,
Heaven of the shanty-keeper—fitting fiend for such a hell—
Full of wallaroos and wombats, and, of course, the "curlew's call"—
And the lone sundowner tramping ever onward through it all!

I am back from up the country, up the country where I went
Seeking for the Southern poets' land whereon to pitch my tent;
I have shattered many idols out along the dusty track,
Burnt a lot of fancy verses—and I'm glad that I am back.
I believe the Southern poets' dream will not be realized
Till the plains are irrigated and the land is humanized.
I intend to stay at present, as I said before, in town,
Drinking beer and lemon-squashes, taking baths and cooling down.

DAYS WHEN WE WENT SWIMMING

    The breezes waved the silver grass
        Waist-high along the siding,
    And to the creek we ne'er could pass,
        Three boys, on bare back riding;
    Beneath the sheoaks in the bend
        The waterhole was brimming—
    Do you remember yet, old friend,
        The times we went in swimming?

    The days we played the wag from school—
        Joys shared—but paid for singly—
    The air was hot, the water cool—
        And naked boys are kingly!

With mud for soap, the sun to dry—
    A well-planned lie to stay us,
And dust well rubbed on neck and face
    Lest cleanliness betray us.

And you'll remember farmer Kutz—
    Though scarcely for his bounty—
He'd leased a forty-acre block,
    And thought he owned the county;
A farmer of the old-world school,
    That men grew hard and grim in,
He drew his water from the pool
    That we preferred to swim in.

And do you mind when down the creek
    His angry way he wended,
A green-hide cartwhip in his hand
    For our young backs intended?
Three naked boys upon the sand—
    Half-buried and half-sunning—
Three startled boys without their clothes
    Across the paddocks running.

We'd had some scares, but we looked blank
    When, resting there and chumming,
We glanced by chance along the bank
    And saw the farmer coming!
Some home impressions linger yet
    Of cups of sorrow brimming;
I hardly think that we'll forget
    The last day we went swimming.

RIPPERTY! KYE! AHOO!

THERE was a young woman, as I've heard tell
        (Ripperty! Kye! Ahoo!),
Lived near the sea in a nice little hell
That she made for herself and her husband as well;
But that's how a good many married folk dwell—
        Ripperty! Kye! A-hoo!

She kept a big mongrel that murdered his fowls
        (Ripperty! Kye! Ahoo!)
She also had cats that assisted with yowls;
She gave him old dishcloths and nightgowns for tow'ls,
And called in the neighbours to witness his growls—
        Ripperty! Kye! A-hoo!

You'd think 'twas the limit, but *she* didn't—quite
        (Ripperty! Kye! Ahoo!);
He had to sleep out in the fowlhouse at night
And make his own breakfast before it was light;
Then go to his work and keep out of sight—
        Ripperty! Kye! A-hoo!

She'd find him and chase him with pot-stick and fist
        (Ripperty! Kye! Ahoo!)
Why *didn't* he give her a jolt or a twist?
Then, because she so crowed for the hiding she missed,
She'd shriek: "You great coward! why don't you enlist?"
        Ripperty! Kye! A-hoo!

She'd invite all her relatives down for the day
        (Ripperty! Kye! A-hoo!),
And also invite *his* relations to stay.
He found his own worst, as is often the way;
His red beard went white, and his brown hair went grey.
        (*Sadly*): Rip-per-ty! Kye! A-hoo!

Her parents were German, as he was aware.
        (Ripperty! Kye! Ahoo!),
He said to himself: "I had better be there!"
He went to the Depot and made himself bare,
Was straightway accepted, and passed then and there—
        Ripperty! Kye! A-hoo!

He came home for "final" and filled up with rum.
        (Ripperty! Kye! A-hic-hoo!)
She said, when she saw him: "I thought you would come!
Just fix the allowance, and don't look so glum!"
He did as she told him, and went away, dumb—
        Ripperty! Kye! A-hoo!

He went to the Front, and he fought for the French.
>   (Ripperty! Kye! Ahoo!)
He went for the Germans and cleared out a trench;
He finished them off with a jab and a wrench,
And loudly he yelled, in the mix-up and stench.
>   "Ripperty! Kye! A-hoo!"

He came back at last with ideas that were new.
>   (Ripperty! Kye! A-hoo!)
He went for the mongrel, and ran him right through;
North, southward and eastward the relatives flew;
Then he said: "Now, old woman, I'm coming for you!
>   RIPPERTY! KYE! A-HOO!"

Three times round the house and the fowlyard she fled
>   (Ripperty! Kye! A-hoo!)
Three inches in front of his bayonet red;
He yelled, and she shrieked fit to shriek off her head,
Till she fell on the wood-heap quite three-quarters dead.
>   Ripperty! Kye! A-hoo!

.   .   .   .   .   .

Now, there's a young woman, as I've heard tell
>   (*Sing softly*) Ripperty! Kye! A-hoo!
Resides in a nice little home at Rozelle:
She's fond of her husband, and he's doing well—
And that's how a good many married folk dwell.
>   (*Sing Exultantly*) Ripperty! Kye! A-hoo!

RISE YE! RISE YE!

RISE ye! rise ye! noble toilers! claim your rights with fire and steel!
Rise ye! for the cursed tyrants crush ye with the hiron 'eel!
They would treat ye worse than sl-a-a-ves! they would treat ye worse
>   than brutes!
Rise and crush the selfish tyrants! ker-r-rush them with your hob-
>   nailed boots!
>   Rise ye! rise ye! glorious toilers!
>   Rise ye! rise ye! noble toilers!
>   Erwake! er-rise!

Rise ye! rise ye! noble toilers! tyrants come across the waves!
Will ye yield the Rights of Labour? will ye? *will* ye still be sl-a-a-ves?
Rise ye! rise ye! mighty toilers and revoke the rotten laws!
Lo, your wives go out a-washing while ye battle for the caws!
    Rise ye! rise ye! glorious toilers!
    Rise ye! rise ye! noble toilers!
    Erwake! er-rise!

Our gerlorious dawn is breaking! Lo, the tyrant trembles now!
He shall star-r-rve us here no longer! toilers will not bend or bow!
Rise ye! rise ye! noble toilers! Rise! behold, revenge is near;
See the Leaders of the People! Come an' 'ave a pint o' beer!
    Rise ye! rise ye! noble toilers!
    Rise ye! rise ye! glorious toilers!
    Erwake! er-rise!

Lo, the poor are starved, my brothers Lo, our wives and children weep!
Lo, our women toil to keep us while the toilers are asleep!
Rise ye! rise ye! noble toilers! rise and break the tyrants' chain!
March ye! march ye! mighty toilers! even to the battle-plain
    Rise ye! rise ye! noble toilers!
    Rise ye! rise ye! noble toilers!
    Erwake! er-r-rise!

SONG OF OLD JOE SWALLOW

When I was up the country in the rough and early days,
I used to work along of Jimmy Nowlett's bullick-drays;
Then the reelroad wasn't heered on, an' the bush was wild an' strange,
An' we useter draw the timber from the saw-pits in the range—
Load provisions for the stations, an' we'd travel far and slow
Through the plains an' 'cross the ranges in the days of long ago.

> *Then it's yoke up the bullicks and tramp beside*
> *'em slow,*
> *An' saddle up yer horses an' a-ridin' we well go,*
> *To the bullick-drivin', cattle-drovin'*
> *Nigger, digger, roarin', rovin'*
> *Days o' long ago.*

Once me and Jimmy Nowlett loaded timber for the town,
But we hadn't gone a dozen mile before the rain come down,
An' me an' Jimmy Nowlett an' the bullicks an' the dray
Was cut off on some risin' ground while floods around us lay;
An' we soon run short of tucker an' terbaccer, which was bad,
An' pertaters dipped in honey was the only tuck we had.

Then half our bullicks perished, when a drought was on the land,
In the burnin' heat that dazzles as it dances on the sand;
But in spite of barren ridges, an' in spite of mud, an' heat,
An' the dust that browned the bushes when it rose from bullicks' feet,
An' in spite of modern progress, and in spite of all their blow,
'Twas a better land to live in, in the days o' long ago.

When the frosty moon was shinin' o'er the ranges like a lamp,
An' a lot of bullick-drivers was a-campin' on the camp,
When the fire was blazin' cheery an' the pipes was drawin' well,
Then our songs we useter chorus an' our yarns we useter tell;
An' we'd talk of lands we come from, and of chaps we useter know,
For there always was behind us other days o' long ago.

Ah, them early days was ended when the reelroad crossed the plain,
But in dreams I often tramp beside the bullick-team again:
Still we pauses at the shanty just to have a drop o' cheer,
Still I feels a kind of pleasure when the campin'-ground is near;
Still I smells the old tarpaulin me an Jimmy useter throw
'Cross the timber-track for shelter in the days of long ago.

I have been a-drifting back'ards with the changes of the land,
An' if I spoke to bullicks now they wouldn't understand;
But when Mary wakes me sudden in the night I'll often say:
"Come here, Spot, an' stan' up, Bally, blank an' blank an' come-eer-way."
An' she says that, when I'm sleepin', oft my elerquince 'ill flow
In the bullick-drivin' language of the days o' long ago.

Well, the pub will soon be closin', so I'll give the thing a rest;
But if you should drop on Nowlett in the far an' distant west—
An' if Jimmy uses doubleyou instead of ar or vee,
An' if he drops his aitches, then you're sure to know it's he.
An' you won't forgit to arsk him if he still remembers Joe.
As knowed him up the country in the days o' long ago.

Then it's yoke up the bullicks and tramp beside
    'em slow,
An' saddle up yer horses an' a-ridin' we will go,
To the bullick-drivin', cattle-drovin'
Nigger, digger, roarin', rovin'
Days o' long ago.

HERE'S LUCK

OLD Time is tramping close today—you hear his bluchers fall,
A mighty change is on the way, an' God protect us all;
Some dust'll fly from beery coats—at least it's been declared.
I'm glad that women has the votes—but just a trifle scared.

I'm just a trifle scared—For why? The women mean to rule;
I feel just like in days gone by when I was caned at school.
The days of men is nearly dead—of double moons and stars—
They'll soon put out our pipes, 'tis said, an' close the public bars.

No more we'll take a glass of ale to banish care an' strife,
An' chuckle home with that old tale we used to tell the wife.
We'll laugh an' joke an' sing no more with jolly beery chums,
Or shout "Here's luck!" while waitin' for the luck that never comes.

Did we prohibit swillin' tea—clean out of commonsense!—
Or legislate 'gainst gossipin' across a backyard fence?
Did we prohibit bustles, or the hoops when they was here?
The women never think of this—yet want to stop our beer.

The track o' life is dry enough, an' crossed with many a rut,
But, oh! we'll find it rougher still when all the pubs is shut,
When all the pubs is shut, an' closed the doors we used to seek,
An' we go toilin', thirstin' on through Sundays all the week.

For since the days when pubs was "inns"—in years gone past 'n'
    far—
Poor sinful souls have drowned their sins an' sorrows at the bar;
An' though at times it led to crime, an' debt, and such complaints—
Will times be happier in the days when all mankind is saints?

'Twould make the bones of Bacchus leap an' bust his coffin lid;
And Burns' ghost would wail an' weep as Robbie never did;
But let the preachers preach in style, an' rave, and rant, 'n' buck,
I rather guess they'll hear awhile the old war-cry: "Here's Luck!"

The world may wobble round the sun, an' all the banks go bung,
But pipes'll smoke, an' liquor run, while *Auld Lang Syne* is sung.
While men are driven through the mill, an' flinty times is struck,
They'll find the private entrance still!
    Here's Luck, old man—Here's Luck!

WITH DICKENS

At Windsor Terrace, Number Four,
  I've taken my abode—
A little crescent off the street,
  A bight from City Road;
And, hard up and in exile, I
  To many fancies yield;
For it was here Micawber lived,
  And David Copperfield.

A bed, a table, and a chair,
  A bottle and a cup.
The landlord's waiting even now
  For something to turn up.
His better half is spiritless—
  They both seem tired of life;
They cannot fight the battle like
  Micawber and his wife.

Out in the little open space
  That lies back from the street,
The same poor, ancient, shabby clerk
  Is sitting on a seat.
The same sad characters go by,
  The ragged children play—
For things have very little changed
  Since Dickens passed away.

Some seek religion in their grief,
   And some for friendship yearn;
Some fly to liquor for relief,
   But I to Dickens turn.
I find him ever fresh and new,
   His lesson ever plain;
And every line that Dickens wrote
   I've read and read again.

The Tavern's just across the way,
   And frowsy women there
Are gossiping and drinking gin,
   And twisting up their hair.
And grubby girls go past at times,
   And furtive gentry lurk;
I don't think anyone has died
   Since Dickens did his work.

There's Jingle, Tigg, and Chevy Slyme,
   And Weevle—whom you will;
And hard-up virtue proudly slinks
   Into the pawnshop still.
Go east a bit from City Road,
   And all the rest are there;
A friendly whistle might produce
   A Chicken anywhere.

My favourite author's heroes I
   Should love, but somehow can't.
I don't like David Copperfield
   As much as David's aunt,
I don't like Richard Carstone, Pip,
   Or Martin Chuzzlewit,
And for the rich and fatherly
   I scarcely care a bit.

The "Charleys" and the haggard wives,
   Kind hearts in poverty,
And yes! the Lizzie Hexams, too,
   Are very near to me;
But men like Brothers Cheeryble,
   And Madeline Bray divine,
And Nell, and Little Dorrit live
   In better worlds than mine.

The Nicklebys and Copperfields,
   They do not stand the test;
And in my heart I don't believe
   That Dickens loved them best.
I can't admire their ways and talk,
   I do not like their looks—
Those selfish, injured sticks that stalk
   Through all the Master's books.

They're mostly selfish in their love,
   And selfish in their hate,
They marry Dora Spenlows, too,
   While Agnes Wickfields wait;
And back they come to poor Tom Pinch
   When hard-up for a friend;
They come to wrecks like Newman Noggs
   To help them in the end.

They get some rich old grandfather
   Or aunt to see them through,
And we can trace self-interest
   In nearly all they do.
But scoundrels like Ralph Nickleby,
   In spite of all their crimes,
And crawlers like Uriah Heep
   Tell bitter truths at times.

But—yes, I love the vagabonds
   And failures from the ranks,
The hard old files with hidden hearts
   Like Wemmick and like Pancks—
And Jaggers had his "poor dreams", too,
   And fond hopes like the rest—
But, somehow, somehow, all my life
   I've loved Dick Swiveller best!

But let us peep at Snagsby first
   As softly he puts down
Beside the bed of dying Joe
   Another half-a-crown.
And Nemo's wretched pauper grave—
   But we can let them be,
For Joe has said to Heaven: "They
   Wos werry good to me."

And Wemmick with his aged P—
　No doubt has his reward;
And Jaggers, hardest nut of all,
　Gets justice from the Lord.
And Pancks, the rent-collecting screw,
　With laurels on his brow,
Is loved by all the bleeding hearts
　In Bleeding Heart Yard now.

Tom Pinch is very happy now,
　And Magwitch is at rest,
And Newman Noggs again might hold
　His head up with the best;
Micawber, too, when all is said,
　Drank bravely Sorrow's cup—
Micawber worked to right them all,
　And something *did* turn up.

How do "John Edward Nandy, Sir"
　And Plornish get along?
Why! if the old man is in voice
　We'll hear him pipe a song.
We'll have a look at Baptiste, too,—
　While still the night is young—
With Mrs Plornish to explain
　In the Italian tongue.

We'll pass the little midshipman
　With heart that swells and fills,
Where Captain Ed'ard Cuttle waits
　For Wal'r and Sol Gills.
Jack Bunsby stands by what he says
　(Which isn't very clear),
And Toots with his own hopeless love—
　As true as any here.

And who that read has never felt
　The sorrow that it cost
When Captain Cuttle got the news
　The *Son and Heir* was lost?
And who that read has not rejoiced
　With him and "Heart's Delight",
And felt as Captin Cuttle felt
　When Wal'r came that night?

And yonder, with a broken heart
   That people thought was stone,
Deserted in his ruined home,
   Poor Dombey sits alone.
Who has not gulped a something down,
   Whose eyes have not grown dim,
While feeling glad for Dombey's sake
   When Florence came to him?

(A stately house in Lincolnshire—
   The scene is bleak and cold—
The footsteps on the terrace sound
   Tonight at Chesney Wold.
One who loved honour, wife, and truth,
   If nothing else besides,
Along the dreary avenue
   Sir Leicester Dedlock rides.)

We'll go round by Poll Sweedlepipe's
   The bird and barber shop;
If Sairey Gamp is so disposed
   We'll send her up a drop.
We'll cross High Holborn to the Bull,
   And, if he cares to roam,
By streets that are not closed to him
   We'll see Dick Swiveller home.

He's looking rather glum tonight,
   The why I will not ask—
No matter how we act the goat,
   We mostly wear a mask.
Some wear a mask to hide the false
   (And some the good and true)—
I wouldn't be surprised to know
   Mark Tapley wore one too.

We wear a mask of cheerfulness
   While feeling sad inside;
And men, like Dombey, who are shy,
   Oft wear a mask called pride.
A front of pure benevolence
   The grinding "Patriarch" bore;
And kind men often wear a mask
   Like that which Jaggers wore.

But never mind, Dick Swiveller!
  We'll see it out together
Beneath the wing of friendship, Dick,
  That never moults a feather.
We'll look upon the rosy yet
  Full many a night, old friend,
And tread the mazy ere we woo
  The balmy in the end.

Our palace walls are rather bare,
  The floor is somewhat damp,
But, while there's liquor, anywhere
  Is good enough to camp.
What ho, Mine Host! bring forth thine ale
  And let the board be spread!—
It is the hour when churchyards yawn
  And wine goes to the head.

'Twas you who saved poor Kit, old chap,
  When he was in a mess—
But what ho, Varlet! bring some wine!
  Here's to the Marchioness!
"We'll make a scholar of her yet,"
  She'll be a lady fair,
"And she shall go in silk attire
  And siller hae to spare."

From sport to sport they hurry her
  To banish her regrets,
And when we win a smile from her
  We cannot pay our debts!
Left orphans at a tender age,
  We're happiest in the land—
We're Glorious Apollos, Dick,
  And you're Perpetual Grand!

You're king of all philosophers,
  (So let the kill-joys rust)
Here's to the obscure citizen
  Who sent the beer on trust!
It sure would be a cheerless world
  If never man got tight;
You spent your money on your friends—
  Dick Swiveller! Good night!

    .   .   .   .

      And "which I meantersay is Pip"—
         The voices hurry past—
      "Not to deceive you, sir"—"Stand by!"
         "Awast, my lass, awast!"
      "Beware of widders, Samivel,"
         And shun strong drink, my friend;
      And, "not to put too fine a point
         Upon it," I must end.

PROFESSIONAL WANDERERS

When you've knocked about the country—been away from home for years;
When the past, by distance softened, nearly fills your eyes with tears—
You are haunted oft, wherever or however, you may roam,
By a fancy that you ought to go and see the folks at home,
You forget the ancient quarrels—little things that used to jar—
And you think of how they'll worry—how they wonder where you are;
You will think you served them badly, and your own part you'll condemn,
And it strikes you that you'll surely be a novelty to them,
For your voice has somewhat altered, and your face has somewhat changed,
And your views of men and matters over wider fields have ranged;
Then it's time to save your money, or to watch it (how it goes!);
Then it's time to get a Gladstone and a decent suit of clothes;
Then it's time to practise daily with a hair-brush and a comb,
Till you drop in unexpected on the folks and friends at home.

When you've been at home for some time, and the novelty's worn off,
And old chums no longer court you, and your friends begin to scoff;
When the girls no longer kiss you, crying "Jack! how you have changed!"
When you're stale to your relations, and their manner seems estranged;

When the old domestic quarrels round the table, thrice a day,
Make it too much like the old times—make you wish you'd stayed
    away;
When, in short, you've spent your money in the fullness of your
    heart,
And your clothes are getting shabby ... then it's high time to
    depart.

SAINT PETER

Now, I think there is a likeness
    Twixt St Peter's life and mine,
For he did a lot of trampin'
    Long ago in Palestine.
He was "union" when the workers
    First began to organize,
And—I'm glad that old St Peter
    Keeps the gate of Paradise.

When the ancient agitator
    And his brothers carried swags,
I've no doubt he very often
    Tramped with empty tucker-bags;
And I'm glad he's Heaven's picket,
    For I hate explainin' things,
And he'll think a union ticket
    Just as good as Whitely King's.

When I reach the great head-station—
    Which is somewhere "off the track"—
I won't want to talk with angels
    Who have never been Out Back;
They might bother me with offers
    Of a banjo—meanin' well—
And a pair of wings to fly with,
    When I only want a spell.

I'll just ask for old St Peter,
    And I think, when he appears,
I shall only have to tell him
    That I carried swag for years.

"I've been on the track," I'll tell him
"An' I done the best I could."
He will understand me better
Than the other angels would.

He won't try to get a chorus
Out of lungs that's worn to rags,
Or to graft the wings on shoulders
Stiff with humpin' tucker-bags;
But I'll rest about the station,
Where a work-bell never rings,
Till they blow the final trumpet
And the Great Judge sees to things.

A WORD TO TEXAS JACK

TEXAS JACK, you are amusin'. Great Lord Harry how I laughed
When I seen your rig and saddle with its bulwarks fore-and-aft;
Holy smoke! From such a saddle how the dickens can you fall?
Why, I've seen a gal ride bareback with no bridle on at all!

Gosh! so help me! strike me balmy! if a bit o' scenery
Like of you in all your rig-out on this earth I ever see!
How I'd like to see a bushman use your fixins, Texas Jack—
On the remnant of a saddle he could ride to hell and back.
Why, I've heerd a mother cheerin' when her kid went tossin' by,
Ridin' bareback on a bucker that had murder in his eye.

What? you've come to learn the natives how to sit a horse's back!
Learn the bloomin' cornstalk ridin'? W'at yer giv'n us, Texas Jack?
Learn the cornstalk! Flamin' jumptup! now where has my country
    gone?
Why, the cornstalk's mother often rides the day afore he's born!

You may talk about your ridin' in the city, bold an' free,
Talk o' ridin' in the city, Texas Jack; but where'd you be
When the stock-horse snorts an' bunches all 'is quarters in a hump,
And the saddle climbs a sapling, an' the horseshoes split a stump?

No, before you teach the native you must ride without a fall
Up a gum, or down a gully, nigh as steep as any wall—
You must swim the roarin' Darlin' when the flood is at its height
Bearin' down the stock an' stations to the great Australian Bight.

You can't count the bulls an' bisons that you copped with your
    lassoo—
But a stout old myall bullock p'raps ud learn you somethin' new;
You had better make your will an' leave your papers neat an' trim
Before you make arrangements for the lassooin' of *him*;
Ere your horse and you is cat's-meat—fittin' fate for sich galoots—
And your saddle's turned to laces like we put in blucher boots.

And you say you're death on Injins! We've got somethin' in your
    line—
If you think your fightin's ekal to the likes of Tommy Ryan.
Take your carcass up to Queensland where the alligators chew
And the carpet-snake is handy with his tail for a lasso,
Ride across the hazy regions where the lonely emus wail
An' ye'll find the black'll track you while you're lookin' for his trail;
He can track you without stoppin' for a thousand miles or more—
Come again, and he will show you where you spat the year before.
But you'd best be mighty careful—you'll be sorry you kem here
When you're skewered to the fakements of your saddle with a
    spear;
When the boomerang is sailin' in the air, then Heaven help you.
It will cut your head off goin', an' come back again to scalp you.

P.S.—As poet and as Yankee I will greet you, Texas Jack,
For it isn't no ill-feelin' that is gettin' up my back;
But I won't see this land crowded by each Yank and British cuss
Who takes it in his head to come a-civilizin' us.
Though on your own great continent there's misery in the towns,
An' not a few untitled lords, and kings without their crowns,
I will admit your countrymen is busted big, an' free,
An' great on ekal rites of men and great on liberty:
I will admit your fathers punched the gory tyrant's head—
But then we've got our heroes, too, the diggers that is dead,
The plucky men of Ballarat, who toed the scratch so well,
And broke the nose of Tyranny and made his peepers swell,
For yankin' Lib's gold tresses in the roarin' days gone by,
An' doublin' up his dirty fist to black her bonny eye;

So when it comes to ridin' mokes, or hoistin' out the Chow,
Or stickin' up for labour's rights, we don't want showin' how.
They came to learn us cricket in the days of long ago,
An' Hanlan came from Canada to learn us how to row,
An' "doctors" come from Frisco just to learn us how to skite,
An' pugs from all the lands on earth to learn us how to fight;
An' when they go, as like as not, we find we're taken in,
They've left behind no learnin'—but they've carried off our tin.

DOWN THE RIVER

I'VE done with joys an' misery,
    An' why should I repine?
There's no one knows the past but me
    An' that ol' dog o' mine.
We camp, an' walk, an' camp an' walk,
    An' find it fairly good;
He can do anything but talk—
    An' wouldn't, if he could.

We sits an' thinks beside the fire,
    With all the stars a-shine,
An' no one knows our thoughts but me
    An' that there dog o' mine.
We has our Johnny-cake an' scrag,
    An' finds 'em fairly good;
He can do anything but talk—
    An' wouldn't, if he could.

I has my smoke, he has his rest,
    When sunset's gettin' dim;
An' if I do get drunk at times,
    It's all the same to him.
So long's he's got my swag to mind,
    He thinks that times is good;
He can do anything but talk—
    An' wouldn't, if he could.

THE CITY BUSHMAN*

It was pleasant up the country, City Bushman, where you went,
For you sought the greener patches and you travelled like a gent;
And you curse the trams and buses and the turmoil and the push,
Though, you know, the squalid city needn't keep you from the bush;
But we lately heard you singing of the "plains where shade is not",
And you mentioned it was dusty—"all was dry and all was hot".

True, the bush "hath moods and changes"—and the bushman hath 'em, too.
For he's not a poet's dummy—he's a man, the same as you;
But his back is growing rounder—slaving for the absentee—
And his toiling wife is thinner than a country wife should be.
For I noticed that the faces of the folks I chanced to meet
Should have made a greater contrast to the faces in the street;
And, in short, I think the bushman's being driven to the wall,
And it's doubtful if his spirit will be "loyal through it all".

Though the bush has been romantic and is nice to sing about,
There's a lot of patriot fervour that the land could do without—
Sort of *British Workman* nonsense that shall perish in the scorn
Of the drover who is driven and the shearer who is shorn—
Of the struggling western farmers who have little time to rest,
Facing ruin on selections in the sheep-infested West;
Droving songs are very pretty, but they call for little thanks
From the people of a country in possession of the Banks.

No, the "rise and fall of seasons" suits the rise and fall of rhyme,
But we know that western seasons do not run on schedule time;
For the drought will go on drying while there's anything to dry,
Then it rains until you'd fancy it would bleach the sunny sky,
Then it pelters out of reason, till the downpour day and night
Nearly sweeps the population to the Great Australian Bight.
It is up in Northern Queensland that the seasons do their best;
But it's doubtful if you ever saw a season in the West—
There are years without an autumn or a winter or a spring,
There are broiling Junes, and summers when it rains like anything.

* A rejoinder to "Banjo" Paterson's "In Defence of the Bush". "Banjo" replied in his "Answer to Various Bards".

In the bush my ears were opened to the singing of the bird,
But the "carol of the magpie" was a thing I never heard.
Once the beggar roused my slumbers in a shanty, it is true,
But I only heard him asking, "Who the blanky blank are you?"
And the bell-bird in the ranges—well, his "silver chime" is harsh
When it's heard beside the solo of the curlew in the marsh.

No, the bushman isn't always "trapping brumbies in the night",
Nor is he for ever riding when "the morn is fresh and bright",
And he isn't always singing in the humpies on the run,
And the camp-fire's "cheery blazes" are a trifle over-done.
We have grumbled with the bushman round the fire on rainy days
When the smoke would blind a bullock, and there wasn't any blaze
Save the blazes of our language, for we cursed the fire in turn
Till the atmosphere was heated and the wood began to burn.
Then we had to wring our blueys, which were rotting in the swags,
And we saw the sugar leaking through the bottoms of the bags,
And we couldn't raise a chorus for the toothache and the cramp,
While we spent the hours of darkness draining puddles round the
    camp.

Would you like to change with Clancy—go a-droving? tell us true,
For we rather think that Clancy would be glad to change with you,
And be something in the city; but 'twould give your muse a shock
To be losing time and money through the foot-rot in the flock;
And you wouldn't mind the beauties underneath the starry dome
If you had a wife and children and a lot of bills at home.

Did you ever guard the cattle when the night was inky-black,
And it rained, and icy water trickled gently down your back,
Till your saddle-weary backbone started aching at the roots
And you almost felt the croaking of the bull-frog in your boots?
Did you shiver in the saddle, curse the restless stock and cough
Till a squatter's blanky dummy cantered up to warn you off?
Did you fight the drought and pleuro when the "seasons" were
    asleep,
Felling sheoaks all the morning for a flock of starving sheep,
Drinking mud instead of water—climbing trees and lopping boughs
For the broken-hearted bullocks and the dry and dusty cows?

Do you think the bush was better in the "good old droving days",
When the squatter ruled supremely as the king of western ways,
When you got a slip of paper for the little you could earn—
But were forced to take provisions from the station in return—

When you couldn't keep a chicken at your humpy on the run.
For the squatter wouldn't let you, and your work was never done;
When you had to leave the missus in a lonely hut forlorn
While you "rose up Willy Riley"—in the days ere you were born?

Ah! we read about the drovers and the shearers and the like
Till we wonder why such happy and romantic fellows strike.
Don't you fancy that the poets ought to give the bush a rest
Ere they raise a just rebellion in the over-written West?
There the simple-minded bushman gets a meal and bed and rum
Just by riding round reporting phantom flocks that never come;
There the scalper—never troubled by the "war-whoop of the push"—
Has a quiet little billet, breeding rabbits in the bush;

There the idle shantykeeper never fails to make a draw,
And the dummy gets his tucker through provisions in the law;
There the labour-agitator—when the shearers rise in might—
Makes his money sacrificing all his substance for The Right;
There the squatter makes his fortune, and "the seasons rise and fall",
But the poor and honest bushman has to suffer for it all,
While the drovers and the shearers and the bushmen and the rest
Never reach that Eldorado of the poets of the West.

So you think the bush is purer, and that life is better there,
But it doesn't seem to pay you like the "squalid street and square".
Pray inform us, City Bushman, where you read, in prose or verse,
Of the awful "city urchin who would greet you with a curse".
There are golden hearts in gutters, though their owners lack the fat,
And I'll back a teamster's offspring to outswear a city brat.

Do you think we're never jolly where the trams and buses rage?
Did you hear the gods in chorus when "Ri-tooral" held the stage?
Did you catch a ring of sorrow in the city urchin's voice
When he yelled for Billy Elton, when he thumped the floor for Royce?
Do the bushmen, down on pleasure, miss the everlasting stars
When they drink and flirt, and so on, in the glow of private bars?

You've a down on "trams and buses", or the "roar" of 'em, you said,
And the "filthy, dirty attic", where you never toiled for bread.
(And about that selfsame attic—Lord! wherever have you been?
For the struggling needlewoman mostly keeps her attic clean.)
But you'll find it very jolly with the cuff-and-collar push,
And the city seems to suit you, while you rave about the bush.

. . . .

You'll admit that Up-the-Country, more especially in drought,
Isn't quite the Eldorado that the poets rave about,
Yet at times we long to gallop where the reckless bushman rides,
In the wake of startled brumbies that are flying for their hides,
Long to feel the saddle tremble once again between our knees
And to hear the stockwhips rattle just like rifles in the trees,
Long to feel the bridle-leather tugging strongly in the hand—
Long to feel once more a little like a native of the land!
And the ring of bitter feeling in the jingling of our rhymes
Isn't suited to the country or the spirit of the times.
Let us go together droving, and returning, if we live,
Try to understand each other while we reckon up the div.

TROUBLE ON THE SELECTION

You lazy boy, you're here at last,
    You must be wooden-legged;
Now, are you sure the gate is fast
    And all the sliprails pegged?
Are all the milkers at the yard,
    The calves all in the pen?
We don't want Poley's calf to suck
    His mother dry again.

And did you mend the broken rail
    And make it firm and neat?
I s'pose you want that brindle steer
    All night among the wheat!
If he should find the lucerne patch,
    He'll stuff his belly full,
And eat till he gets "blown" on it
    And busts, like Ryan's bull.

Old Spot is lost? You'll drive me mad,
    You will, upon my soul!
She might be in the boggy swamps
    Or down a digger's hole.
You needn't talk, you never looked;
    You'd find her if you'd choose,
Instead of poking possum logs
    And hunting kangaroos.

How came your boots as wet as muck?
    You tried to drown the ants!
Why don't you take your bluchers off?
    Good Lord, he's tore his pants!
Your father's coming home tonight;
    You'll catch it hot, you'll see.
Now go and wash your filthy face
    And come and get your tea.

THE FOURTH COOK

He has notions of Australia from the tales that he's been told—
Land of leggings and revolvers, land of savages and gold;
So he begs old shirts, and someone patches up his worn-out duds,
And he ships as "general servant", scrubbing pots and peeling spuds
(In the steamer's grimy alley, hating man and peeling spuds).

There is little time for comfort, there is little time to cry—
(He will come back with a fortune—"We'll be happy by and by!")
Scarcely time to kiss his sweetheart, barely time to change his duds,
Ere they want him at the galley, and they set him peeling spuds
(With a butcher's knife, a bucket and, say, half a ton of spuds).

And he peels 'em hard to Plymouth, peels 'em fast to drown his grief,
Peels 'em while his stomach sickens on the road to Teneriffe;
Peels 'em while the donkey rattles, peels 'em while the engine thuds,
By the time they touch at Cape Town he's a don at peeling spuds
(There's no end of time for dreaming while he gets on with the
    spuds).

In the steamer's slushy alley, where the souls of men are dead,
And the adjectives are crimson and the substantives are red,
He's perhaps a college blacksheep and, maybe, of ancient blood—
Ah! his devil grips him sometimes as he reaches for a spud
(And he jerks his head and sadly gouges dry-rot from a spud).

But his brave heart hopes and sickens as the weary days go round;
There is lots o' time for blue-lights ere they reach King George's
    Sound.

He will get his best clothes ready—two white shirts and three bone
    studs!
He will face the new world bravely when he's finished with the
    spuds
(But next week, perhaps, he'll take another job at peeling spuds).

There were heroes in Australia, great explorers, long ago;
There are heroes in Australia that the world shall never know;
And the men who are our heroes in the land of droughts and floods
Often won their way to Sydney scrubbing pots and peeling spuds
(Plucky beggars; brave, poor devils! gouging dry-rot from their
    spuds).

THE OLD HEAD NURSE

I saw her first from a painful bed,
    Where I lay just after a fearful fall,
With a broken leg and a broken head,
    In the accident ward of the hospital.
Some women are hard as the road to grace
    That natural sinners are doomed to tread;
And beautiful some as a camel's face—
    But *our* head nurse was the limit, they said.

She walked like a trestle, with toes turned in,
    As gaunt she was as a drought-baked horse,
With big buck teeth and a downy chin,
    And a three-haired mole—and a nose, of course.
She had us there where we could not strike,
    And she could punish in many ways, too;
She was hated by nurses and patients alike—
    But she knew *much* more than the doctors knew.

With deep respect they would wait for her,
    In a desperate case where the chance was slim,
To take her place in the theatre
    Of the hospital with its secrets grim.
Of many a ghastly grapple with death,
    When doctors paled, she could tell, no doubt,
Of hours she fought for the fluttering breath—
    Yes!—she knew mankind, inside and out.

And, speaking of nurses, now's my chance
    To put in a word for the sisterhood,
Their life has little or no romance,
    The work is grand, and their hearts are good.
They take it, of course, "for better or worse";
    But, when the "Head" is a Tartar, I know
That between the patients and that head nurse
    The sisters have a hard row to hoe.

I lived at "Thelma" in Belgrave Street
    Off Belmore Park. 'Twas a good address
For the head of a memo short and sweet
    To the editors of the Sydney press.
'Twas a four-roomed shanty, built in a plain
    Colonial fashion—Australian quite;
The local pound was just down the lane,
    The Mongolian gardens were opposite.

We kept a servant, a stunted freak
    I caught at a Government Bureau;
She might have been seventeen last week—
    Or six-and-twenty, for aught I know,
She'd been trained backward (of immigrant stock—
    A midland county—I know no more).
She started each morning at six o'clock
    By scrubbing a hole in the kitchen floor.

Intentions excellent. Short of breath.
    Our troubles caused her acute distress.
By the wife she was called Elizabeth
    But known to me as "The Marchioness".
"Master's narrer" (she meant "The Boss")
    She'd say to the wife when I could not eat,
"He's nearly as narrer as father was;
    I wish the master would take his meat."

She never could understand at all
    That this was a Land of Democracy.
She'd bully the tradesmen great and small
    Till those sons of freedom appealed to me.
They had to "go round to the kitching door"—
    Butcher, and Baker, and Milk! no less,
A thing they never had done before;
    But they all were afraid of the Marchioness.

The sledgehammer force of simplicity
   And truth was hers by an innate right,
Hard practical kindness, and sympathy,
   And a great love somewhere—but out of sight
Kiddies obeyed her; what is more,
   They loved her and came to her early and late,
And she'd dole out alms at the "kitching" door
   With the air of a Dame at her castle gate.

They never come singly to palace or tent,
   Twins or troubles, or human ills;
And I think that wherever a man pays rent
   The same thing mostly applies to bills.
And so, one Monday, when all behind
   With the rent (or ahead of it—which you will)
And the Butcher and Baker had been unkind,
   And a story rejected—wee Joe fell ill.

The doctor came, but he shook his head
   As he looked at the child for a moment or two:
He listened and nodded to what we said,
   And told the wife what she *mustn't* do.
He said we must keep the child in bed—
   (It was bitter cold and 'twas raining too!)
And then he wrote a prescription and fled—
   A district doctor must earn his screw.

I looked in the kitchen—don't know for what—
   The Marchioness there, with an altered face,
Was hurriedly making water hot,
   In every kettle and pan in the place.
She plucked a rug from her skimpy bed,
   And dragged in a tub on the bedroom floor,
And, when I protested, she only said,
   "I know it, Master—I've seen it before."

Ten o'clock in the morning found
   Joe still doubtful, and in distress
I was bracing up for the second round;
   "Same time tonight" said the Marchioness.
I *felt* that my face was drawn and white—
   No doubt you'll think I'm a womanish one—
But have you ever been up all night
   Fighting with Death for your first-born son.

Or seen your child in convulsions, you chaps?
    I rose, and I went to the door at last
To look for the Unexpected, perhaps—
    And who should I see but the "Head" go past!
In mufti, too—but you'd know *her* walk
    If you saw her passing on Paradise Track.
'Twas a desperate case—I don't want to talk—
    I was clean knocked out, so I called her back.

She was having a holiday—first in her life—
    And resting, of course, on her restless feet;
She was staying a week with her brother's wife
    On the height overlooking Belgrave Street.
This much I gathered—my wits were slow,
    I was faint and ill, and as dull as a dunce;
But she took charge of the wife and Joe,
    The Marchioness, "Thelma", and me at once.

The Marchioness looked at the Head Nurse hard;
    And the Head Nurse looked at the Marchioness—
(So the wife whispered to me in the yard)
    Why they chummed up at once I never could guess.
We hadn't yet told the Head Nurse about
    How the Marchioness saved Joe from Paradise
And to this very hour I can never make out
    What those two saw in each other's eyes.

She packed the pair of us into a room
    To sleep for an hour by the Blessed Grace,
And she sent the priestess of our old broom
    For a lot of things from her brother's place.
By hidden signs that were known to me
    (And known, perhaps, to Elizabeth),
And her hardening eyes, I could see that she
    Was bracing herself for a scrap with Death.

In the grey of the morning I crept by stealth,
    To listen and peep in the passage gloom,
And the cleverest nurse in the Commonwealth
    Was sweeping and dusting the "dining room".
Eyes of a hawk! She caught me, and said
    "What do you here in the dead of night?
Get on with your writing, or go to bed—
    Your wife is asleep, and the boy's all right."

Eyes half-blinded with—well, 'tis a poor
  Unmanlike, unwriterlike thing to do.
I've had always a fancy (but couldn't be sure)
  That some of the tears were in her eyes too.
But she only muttered "Confound the man!"
  Giving her duster a vicious twirl—
"Go back as quietly as you can;
  Elizabeth is asleep, poor girl."

. . . . . .

Ten long years—and the Nurse is dead,
  Forgotten by hundreds she helped to live;
You gave her her uniform, and her bread,
  I gave her a headstone ('twas little to give).
But I want you to know that preachers and pugs,
  Doctors and editors (publishers, too),
Likewise spielers, and also mugs,
  And nurses, and poets, have hearts—like you.

JACK CORNSTALK

I MET with Jack Cornstalk in London today,
He saw me and coo-eed from over the way.
The solemn-faced Londoners stared at Long Jack,
At his hat, and his height, and the breadth of his back.
Then he coo-eed again (and his voice was not low)
And—there's not room to coo-ee in London, you know.

And I said to him, "Jack!" as he gripped my hand fast,
"Oh, I hear that our country's a Nation at last!
I hear that they *have* launched the new ship of State
(And with men at the wheel who are steering it straight)
By the vote, I am told, of your Bush-mates and you;
Oh tell me, Jack Cornstalk, if this can be true?

"—That the things we have fought for are coming in sight—
Oh tell me, Jack Cornstalk, if I have heard right?"
For a moment he dropped the old grin that he wore;
He'd a light in his eyes that was not there before
As he reached for my hand (which I gave, nothing loth)
And he replied in two words, and those words were *"My Oath!"*

1901

WRITE IT DOWN FOR ME

In the parlour of the shanty where the lives have all gone wrong,
When a singer or reciter gives a poem or a song,
Where the poet's heart is speaking to their hearts in every line,
Till the hardest curse and blubber at the thoughts of Auld Lang Syne;
Then a boozer lurches forward with an oath for all disguise—
With a soul where prayers and curses bring the liquor to his eyes—
Grasps the singer or reciter with a death-grip by the hand:
"That's the truth, bloke! Sling it at 'em! Oh! Gorbli'me, that was grand!
Don't mind me; I've got 'em. *You* know! What's your name, bloke! Don't you *see*?
Who's the bloke what wrote the po'try? *Will* you write it down for me?"

And the backblock bard goes through it, ever seeking as he goes
For the line of least resistance to the hearts of men he knows;
Yes, he tracks their hearts in mateship, and he tracks them out alone—
Seeking for the power to sway them, till he finds it in his own;
Feels what they feel, loves what they love, learns to hate what they condemn,
Takes his pen in tears and triumph, and he writes it down for them.

WHEN THE ARMY PRAYS FOR WATTY

When the kindly hours of darkness, save for light of moon and star,
Hide the picture on the signboard over Doughty's Horse Bazaar;
When the last rose-tint is fading on the distant mulga scrub,
Then the Army prays for Watty at the entrance of his pub.

Watty lounges in his arm-chair, in its old accustomed place,
With a fatherly expression on his round and passive face;
And his arms are clasped before him in a calm, contented way,
And he nods his head and dozes when he hears the Army pray.

And I wonder if he ponders on the distant years and dim,
Or his chances Over Yonder, when the Army prays for him.
Has he not a fear connected with the warm place down below,
Where, according to good Christians, all the publicans should go?

But his features give no token of a feeling in his breast,
Save of peace that is unbroken and a conscience well at rest;
And we guzzle as we guzzled long before the Army came,
And the loafers wait for "shouters", and they get there just the same.

It would take a lot of praying, lots of thumping on the drum,
To prepare our sinful, straying, erring souls for Kingdom Come;
But I love my fellow-sinners, and I hope, upon the whole,
That the Army gets a hearing when it prays for Watty's soul.

AFTER THE WAR

The big rough boys from the runs Out Back were first where the balls flew free,
And yelled in the slang of the Outside Track: "By God, it's a Christmas spree!"
"It's not too dusty"—and "Wool away!—stand clear o' the blazin' shoots!"
"Sheep O! Sheep O!"—"We'll cut out today"—"Look out for the boss's boots!"
"What price the tally in camp tonight!"—"What price the boys Out Back!"
"Go it, you tigers, for Right or Might and the pride of the Outside Track!"—
"Needle and thread!"—"I have broke my comb!"—"Now ride, you flour-bags, ride!"
"Fight for your mates and the folks at home!" "Here's one for the Lachlan-side!"
Those men of the West would sneer and scoff at the gates of hell ajar,
And often the sight of a head cut off was hailed by a yell for "Tar!"

. . . . . .

I heard the Push in the Red Redoubt, grown wild at a luckless shot:
"Look out for the bloomin' shell, look out!"—"Gor' bli'me, but that's red-hot!"

"It's Bill the Slogger—poor bloke—he's done. A chunk of that shell was his;
I wish the beggar that fired that gun could get within reach of Liz."
"Those foreign gunners will give us rats, but I wish it was Bill they'd missed.
I'd like to get at their bleedin' hats with a rock in my (something) fist."

"Hold up, Billy; I'll stick to you; they've hit you under the belt;
If we get the waddle I'll swag you through, if the blazin' mountains melt;
You remember the night I was held by the traps for stoushing a bleedin' Chow,
And you went for 'em proper and laid out three, and I won't forget it now."
And, groaning and swearing, the pug replied: "I'm done . . . . they've knocked me out!
I'd fight 'em all for a pound a side, from the boss to the rouseabout.
My nut is cracked and my legs is broke, and it gives me worse than hell;
I trained for a scrap with a twelve-stone bloke, and not with a bursting shell.
You needn't mag, for I knowed, old chum, I *knowed*, old pal, you'd stick;
But you can't hold out till the boys come up, and you'd best be nowhere quick.
They've got a force and a gun ashore, and both of our wings is broke;
They'll storm the ridge in a minute more, and the best you can do is 'smoke'."

And Jim exclaimed: "You can smoke, you chaps, but me—Gor' bli'me, no!
The Push that ran from the George-street traps won't run from a foreign foe.
I'll stick to the gun while she makes them sick, and I'll stick to what's left of Bill."
And they hiss through their blackened teeth: "We'll stick! by the blazin' flame, we will!"
And long years after the war was past, they told in the town and bush
How the ridge of death to the bloody last was held by a Sydney push;

How they fought to the end in a sheet of flame, how they fought
   with their rifle-stocks,
And earned, in a nobler sense, the name of their ancient weapons—
   rocks.

. . . . .

In the Western camps it was ever our boast, when 'twas bad for the
   Kangaroo,
"If the enemy's forces take the coast, they must take the mountains,
   too;
They may force their way by the Western line or round by a
   northern track,
But they won't run short of a decent spree with the men who are
   left Out Back!"
When we burst the enemy's ironclads and won by a run of luck,
We whooped as loudly as Nelson's lads when a French three-decker
   struck;
And when the enemy's troops prevailed the truth was never heard—
We lied like heroes, and never failed to explain how that occurred.

You Bushmen sneer in the old bush way at the new-chum jackeroo,
But cuffs-'n'-collars were out that day, and they stuck to their posts
   like glue;
I never believed that a dude could fight till a Johnny led us then;
We buried his bits in the rear that night for the honour of Pitt-
   street men.
And Jim the Ringer—he fought, he did. The regiment nicknamed
   Jim
"Old Heads-a-Caser" and "Heads-a-Quid", but it never was tails
   with him.
The way that he rode was a racing rhyme, and the way that he
   finished grand;
He backed the enemy every time, and died in a hand-to-hand!

. . . . .

I'll never forget when the Ringer and I were first in the Bush
   Brigade,
With Warrego Bill, from the Live-till-you-Die, in the last grand
   charge we made.
And Billy died—he was full of sand—he said, as I raised his head:
"I'm full of love for my native land, but a lot too full of lead.
Tell 'em," said Billy; "and tell old Dad to look after the cattle-pup;"
But his eyes grew bright, though his voice was sad, and he said, as
   I held him up:

"I have been happy on western farms. And once, when I first went wrong,
Around my neck were the trembling arms of the girl I'd loved so long.

"Far out on the southern seas I've sailed; I've ridden where brumbies roam,
And often when all on the station failed I've driven the outlaw home.
I've spent a cheque in a day and night, and I've made a cheque as quick;
I've struck a nugget when times were tight and the stores had stopped our tick.
I've led the field on the old bay mare, and I hear the cheering still,
When mother and sister and *she* were there, and the old man yelled for Bill;
But, save for *her*, could I live my time again in the old Bush way,
I'd give it all for the last half-mile in the race we rode today!"
And he passed away as the stars came out—he died as old heroes die—
I heard the sound of the distant rout, and the Southern Cross was high.

AS GOOD AS NEW

OH, this is a song of the old lights that came to my heart like a hymn;
And this is a song for the old lights—the lights that we thought grew dim.
They came to my heart to comfort me, and I pass it along to you;
And here is a hand to the dear old friend who turns up as good as new.

And this is a song for the camp-fire out west where the stars shine bright—
Oh, this is a song for the camp-fire where the old mates yarn tonight;
Where the old mates yarn of the old days, and their numbers are all too few,
And this is a song for the brave old times that will turn up as good as new.

Oh, this is a song for the old foe—we have both grown wiser now,
And this is a song for the old foe, and we're sorry we had that row;
And this is a song for the old love—the love that we thought untrue—
Oh, this is a song of the old true love that comes back as good as new.

Oh, this is a song for the blacksheep, for the blacksheep that fled from town,
And this is a song for the brave heart, for the brave heart that lived it down;
And this is a song for the battler, for the battler who sees it through—
And this is a song for the broken heart that turns up as good as new.

Ah, this is a song for the brave mate, be he Bushman, Scot, or Russ,
A song for the mates we will stick to—for the mates who have stuck to us;
And this is a song for the old creed, to do as a man should do,
Till the Lord takes us all to a wider world—where we'll turn up as good as new.

THE KING, THE QUEEN AND I

OH, Scotty, have you visited the Picture Gallery,
And did you see the portraits of the King and Queen and me?
The portraits made by Longstaff, all the pictures done by Jack,
Of the King and Queen and Lawson and the Lady all in Black?

The King is robed in royal state, with medals on his breast,
And like the mother Queen she is Her Majesty is dressed.
The Lady's dressed in simple black and sports no precious stones,
And I in simple reach-me-downs I bought from Davy Jones.

We're strangers two to two, and each unto the other three—
I do not know the Lady and I don't think she knows me.
We're strangers to each other here, and to the other two,
And they themselves are strangers now, if all we hear is true.

I s'pose we're just as satisfied as folks have ever been:
The Lady would much rather be her own self than the Queen;
And though I'm down, and precious stiff, and I admire King Ned,
I'd sooner just be Harry, with his follies on his head.

We four may meet together—stranger folk have met, I ween,
Than a rhymer and a monarch and a lady and a queen,
Ned and I might talk it over on the terrace, frank and free,
With cigars, while Alexandra and the Lady's having tea.

Anyway, we'll never quarrel while we're hanging on the wall—
Friends! we all have had our troubles—we are human, one and all!
If by chance we hang together—hang together on the line,
And the thing should shock the gentry—then it's Longstaff's fault,
    not mine.

THE SHEARER'S DREAM

Oh, I dreamt I shore in a shearin'-shed, and it was a dream of joy,
For every one of the rouseabouts was a girl dressed up as a boy—
Dressed up like a page in a pantomime, and the prettiest ever seen—
They had flaxen hair, they had coal-black hair—and every shade
    between.

There was short, plump girls, there was tall, slim girls, and the
    handsomest ever seen—
They was four-foot-five, they was six-foot high, and every height
    between.

The shed was cooled by electric fans that was over every shoot;
The pens was of polished ma-ho-gany, and everything else to suit;
The huts had springs to the mattresses, and the tucker was simply
    grand,
And every night by the billerbong we danced to a German band.

Our pay was the wool on the jumbucks' backs, so we shore till all
    was blue—
The sheep was washed afore they was shore (and the rams was
    scented too);
And we all of us wept when the shed cut out, in spite of the long,
    hot days,
For every hour them girls waltzed in with whisky and beer on
    tr-a-a-a-ys!

There was three of them girls to every chap, and as jealous as they
    could be—
There was three of them girls to every chap, and six of 'em picked
    on me;
We was draftin' them out for the homeward track and sharin' 'em
    round like steam,
When I woke with me head in the blazin' sun to find 'twas a
    shearer's dream.

FOREIGN ENGINEERS

Old Ivan McIvanovitch, with knitted brow of care,
Has climbed up from the engine-room to get a breath of air;
He slowly wipes the grease and sweat from hairy face and neck,
And beneath his bushy eyebrows glowers round the open deck.

The weirdest Russian in the fleet, whose words are strange to hear
He seems to run the battleship, though but an engineer.
He is not great, he has no rank, and he is far from rich—
'Tis strange the admiral defers to McIvanovitch.

He gives the order "Whusky!" ere he goes below once more—
And whusky is a Russian word I never heard before;
Perhaps some Tartar dialect, because, you know, you'll meet
Some very varied Muscovites aboard the Baltic fleet.

And on another battleship, that sailed out from Japan,
The boss of all the engineers you'll find another man
With flaming hair and eyes like steel, and he is six-foot three—
His name is Jock McNogo, and a fearsome Jap is he.

He wears a beard upon his chest, his face you won't forget,
His like was never found among the heathen idols yet;
His words are awesome words to hear, his lightest smile is grim,
And daily in the engine-room the heathen bow to him.

Now, if the fleets meet in the North and settle matters there,
Say, how will McIvanovitch and Jock McNogo fare?
If ye ken that bearded Russian and that Jap, you needn't fret,
They'll hae a drap, or maybe twa, some nicht in Glesca yet.

Those foreigners will ship again aboard some foreign boat,
And do their best to drive her through and keep the tub afloat.
They'll stir the foreign greasers up and prove from whence the
    came—
And all to win the bawbees for the wife and bairns at hame.

THE FREE-SELECTOR'S DAUGHTER

I MET her on the Lachlan-side—
  A darling girl I thought her,
And ere I left I swore I'd win
  The free-selector's daughter.

I milked her father's cows a month,
  I brought the wood and water,
I mended all the broken fence,
  Before I won the daughter.

I listened to her father's yarns,
  I did just what I "oughter",
And what *you'll* have to do to win
  A free-selector's daughter.

I broke my pipe and burnt my twist
  And washed my mouth with water;
I had to shave before I kissed
  The free-selector's daughter.

Then, rising in the frosty morn,
  I brought the cows for Mary,
And when I'd milked a bucketful
  I took it to the dairy.

I poured the milk into the dish
  While Mary held the strainer,
I summoned heart to speak my wish,
  And oh! her blush grew plainer

I told her I must leave the place,
  I said that I would miss her;
At first she turned away her face,
  And then she let me kiss her.

> I put the bucket on the ground,
>   And in my arms I caught her:
> I'd give the world to hold again
>   That free-selector's daughter!

THE SHANTY ON THE RISE

When the caravans of wool-teams climbed the ranges from the West,
On a spur among the mountains stood The Bullock-drivers' Rest;
It was built of bark and saplings, and was rather rough inside,
But 'twas good enough for bushmen in the careless days that died—
Just a quiet little shanty kept by "Something-in-Disguise",
As the bushmen called the landlord of the Shanty on the Rise.

City swells who "do the Royal" would have called the Shanty low,
But 'twas better far and cleaner than some toney pubs we know;
For the patrons of the Shanty had the principles of men,
And the spieler, if he struck it, wasn't welcome there again.
You could smoke and drink in quiet, yarn (or p'raps soliloquize)
With a decent lot of fellows in the Shanty on the Rise.

'Twas the bullock-driver's haven when his team was on the road,
And the waggon-wheels were groaning as they ploughed beneath the load;
I remember how the teamsters struggled on while it was light,
Just to camp within a cooee of the Shanty for the night;
And I think the very bullocks raised their heads and fixed their eyes
On the candle in the window of the Shanty on the Rise.

And the bullock-bells were clanking from the marshes on the flats
As we hurried to the Shanty, where we hung our dripping hats;
Then we took a drop of something that was brought at our desire,
As we stood with steaming moleskins in the kitchen by the fire.
Oh, it roared upon a fireplace of the good old-fashioned size,
When the rain came down the chimney of the Shanty on the Rise.

They got up a Christmas party in the Shanty long ago,
While we camped with Jimmy Nowlett on the river-bank below;
Poor old Jim was in his glory—they'd elected him M.C.,
For there wasn't such another raving lunatic as he.
"Mr Nowlett! Mr Swaller!" shouted Something-in-Disguise,
As we walked into the parlour of the Shanty on the Rise.

There is little real pleasure in the city where I am—
There's a "swarry" round the corner with its mockery and sham;
But a fellow can be happy when around the room he whirls
In a party Up-the-Country with the jolly country girls.
Why, at times I almost fancied I was dancing on the skies,
When I danced with Mary Carey in the Shanty on the Rise.

Jimmy came to me and whispered, and I muttered, "Go along!"
But he shouted "Mr Swaller will oblige us with a song!"
And at first I said I wouldn't, and I shammed a little too,
Till the girls began to whisper, "Mr Swallow, now, ah, do!"
So I sang a song of something 'bout the love that never dies,
And the chorus shook the rafters of the Shanty on the Rise.

Jimmy burst his concertina, and the bullock-drivers went
For the corpse of Joe the Fiddler, who was sleeping in his tent;
Joe was tired and had lumbago, and he wouldn't come, he said,
But the case was very urgent, so they pulled him out of bed;
And they fetched him, for the Bushmen knew that Something-in-
    Disguise
Had a cure for Joe's lumbago in the Shanty on the Rise.

Jim and I were rather quiet while escorting Mary home,
'Neath the stars that hung in clusters, near and distant, from the
    dome;
And we walked in such a silence, being lost in reverie,
That we heard the "settlers'-matches" softly rustle on the tree;
And I wondered who would win her, when she said her sweet
    good-byes—
But she died at one-and-twenty, and was buried on the Rise.

I suppose the Shanty vanished from the ranges long ago,
And the girls are mostly married to the chaps I used to know.
My old chums are in the distance—some have crossed the border-
    line,
But in fancy still their glasses chink against the rim of mine;
And, upon the very centre of the greenest spot that lies
In my fondest recollection, stands the Shanty on the Rise.

POETS OF THE TOMB

The world has had enough of bards who wish that they were dead.
'Tis time the people passed a law to knock 'em on the head,
For 'twould be lovely if their friends could grant the rest they crave—
Those bards of "tears" and "vanished hopes", those poets of the grave.
They say that life's an awful thing, and full of care and gloom,
They talk of peace and restfulness connected with the tomb.

They say that man is made of dirt, and die, of course, he must;
But, all the same, a man is made of pretty solid dust.
There is a thing that they forget, so let it here be writ,
That some are made of common mud, and some are made of grit;
Some try to help the world along, while others fret and fume
And wish that they were slumbering in the silence of the tomb.

'Twixt mother's arms and coffin-gear a man has work to do,
And if he does his very best he mostly worries through,
And while there is a wrong to right, and while the world goes round,
An honest man alive is worth a million underground.
And yet, so long as sheoaks sigh and wattle-blossoms bloom
The world shall hear the drivel of the poets of the tomb.

Still, though the graveyard bards may long to vanish from the scene,
I notice that they mostly wish their resting-place kept green.
While, were I rotting underground, I do not think I'd care
If wombats rooted on the mound or if the cows camped there;
And should I have some feelings left when I have "gone before",
I think a ton of solid stone would hurt my feelings more.

Such wormy songs of mouldy joys can give me no delight;
I'll take my chances with the world—I'd rather live and fight.
Fortune may laugh along my track, or wear her blackest frown—
I'll try to do the world some good before I tumble down.
Let's fight for things that ought to be, and try to make 'em boom;
Mankind gets small assistance from our ashes in the tomb.

GROG-AN'-GRUMBLE STEEPLECHASE

'Twixt the coastline and the border lay the town of Grog-an'-Grumble
  (Just two pubs beside a racecourse in a wilderness of sludge)
An' they say the local meeting was a drunken rough-and-tumble,
  Which was ended pretty often by an inquest on the judge.
Yes, 'tis said the city talent very often caught a tartar
  In the Grog-an'-Grumble sportsman, 'n' retired with broken heads,
For the fortune, life, and safety of the Grog-an'-Grumble starter
  Mostly hung upon the finish of the local thoroughbreds.

Pat M'Durmer was the owner of a horse they called The Screamer,
  Which he called the "quickest shtepper 'twixt the Darling and the sea",
But I think it's very doubtful if a Banshee-haunted dreamer
  Ever saw a more outrageous piece of equine scenery;
For his points were most decided, from his end to his beginning;
  He had eyes of different colour, and his legs they wasn't mates.
Pat M'Durmer said he always came "widin a flip av winnin'",
  An' his sire had come from England, 'n' his dam was from the States.

Friends would argue with M'Durmer, and they said he was in error
  To put up his horse The Screamer, for he'd lose in any case,
And they said a city racer by the name of Holy Terror
  Was regarded as the winner of the coming steeplechase;
Pat declared he had the knowledge to come in when it was raining,
  And irrelevantly mentioned that he knew the time of day,
So he rose in their opinion. It was noticed that the training
  Of The Screamer was conducted in a dark, mysterious way.

Well, the day arrived in glory; 'twas a day of jubilation
  For the careless-hearted bushmen quite a hundred miles around,
An' the rum 'n' beer 'n' whisky came in waggons from the station,
  An' the Holy Terror talent were the first upon the ground.
Judge M'Ard—with whose opinion it was scarcely safe to wrestle—
  Took his dangerous position on the bark-and-sapling stand:
He was what the local Stiggins used to speak of as a "wessel
  Of wrath", and he'd a bludgeon that he carried in his hand.

"Off ye go!" the starter shouted, as down fell a stupid jockey;
  Off they started in disorder—left the jockey where he lay—
And they fell and rolled and galloped down the crooked course and rocky,
  Till the pumping of The Screamer could be heard a mile away,
But he kept his legs and galloped; he was used to rugged courses,
  And he lumbered down the gully till the ridge began to quake:
And he ploughed along the sidling, raising earth till other horses
  An' their riders, too, were blinded by the dust-cloud in his wake.

From the ruck he'd struggle slowly—they were much surprised to find him
  Close abeam of Holy Terror as along the flat they tore—
Even higher still and denser rose the cloud of dust behind him,
  While in more divided splinters flew the shattered rails before.
"Terror!" "Dead heat!" they were shouting—"Terror!" but The Screamer hung out
  Nose to nose with Holy Terror as across the creek they swung,
An' M'Durmer shouted loudly, "Put yer tongue out, put yer tongue out!"
  An' The Screamer put his tongue out, and he won by half-a-tongue.*

* This "take-off" of Banjo Paterson appeared in 1892, while the Bush v. Town controversy was raging.

HAWKERS

Dust, dust, dust and a dog—
  Oh, the sheep-dog won't be last,
Where the long, long shadow of the old bay horse
  With the shadow of his mate is cast.
A brick-brown woman, with her brick-brown kids,
  And a man with his head half-mast,
The feed-bags hung, and the bedding slung,
  And the blackened bucket made fast
Where the tailboard clings to the tucker and things—
  So the hawker's van goes past.

BURSTING OF THE BOOM

The shipping-office clerks are "short", the manager is gruff—
"They cannot make reductions", and "the fares are low enough".
They ship you West with cattle, and you go like cattle too;
And fight like dogs three times a day for what you get to chew....
But you'll have the pick of empty bunks and lots of stretching-room,
And go for next to nothing at the Bursting of the Boom.

So wait till the Boom bursts!—we'll all get a show;
Then when the Boom bursts will be our time to go.
We'll meet 'em coming back in shoals, with looks of deepest gloom,
But we're the sort to battle through at the Bursting of the Boom.

The captain's easygoing when Fremantle comes in sight;
He can't say when you'll get ashore—"perhaps tomorrow night";
Your coins are few, the charges high; you must not linger here—
You'll get your boxes from the hold "when she's 'longside the pier".
The launch will foul the gangway, and the trembling bulwarks loom
Above a fleet of harbour craft—at the Bursting of the Boom.

So wait till the Boom bursts!—we'll all get a show;
He'll "take you for a bob, sir," and "Where d'you want to go?"
"I'll take the big portmanteau, sir, if I might so presume"—
You needn't hump your luggage at the Bursting of the Boom.

The loafers—Customs-loafers—that you pay and pay again,
They hinder you and cheat you from the gangway to the train;
The pubs and restaurants are full—they haven't room for more;
They charge you each three shillings for a shakedown on the floor;
But, "Show this gentleman upstairs—the first front parlour room.
We'll see about your luggage, sir"—at the Bursting of the Boom.

So wait till the Boom bursts!—we'll all get a show;
And wait till the Boom bursts, and swear mighty low.
"We mostly charge a pound a week. How do you like the room?"
And "Show this gentleman the bath"—at the Bursting of the Boom.

You go down to the timber-yard (you cannot face the rent)
To get some strips of oregon to frame a hessian tent,
To buy some scraps of lumber for a table or a shelf:
The boss comes up and says you might just look round for yourself;
The foreman grunts and turns away, as silent as the tomb—
The boss himself will wait on us at the Bursting of the Boom!

So wait till the Boom bursts!—we'll all get a load.
"You'd better take those scraps, sir, they're only in the road."
"Now, where the hell's the carter?" you'll hear the foreman fume;
And, "Take that timber round at once!" at the Bursting of the Boom.

Each one-a-penny grocer, in his box of board and tin,
Thinks it is condescension to consent to "take you in";
And not content with twice as much as what is just and right,
They charge and cheat you doubly, for the Boom is at its height.
It's "Take it now or leave it now"; "Your money or your room";—
But "Who's attending Mr Brown?" at the Bursting of the Boom.

So wait till the Boom bursts!—and take what you can get,
"There's not the slightest hurry, and your bill ain't ready yet."
They'll call to get your orders until the crack o' doom,
And "send them round directly", at the Bursting of the Boom.

THE GREENHAND ROUSEABOUT

CALL this hot? I beg your pardon. Hot!—you don't know what it means.
(What's that, waiter? lamb or mutton! Thank you—mine is beef and greens.
Bread and butter while I'm waiting. Milk? Oh, yes—a bucketful.)
I'm just in from west the Darling, "picking-up" and "rolling wool".

Mutton (stewed) or chops for breakfast, dry and tasteless, boiled in fat;
Bread or brownie, tea or coffee—two hours' graft in front of that;
Legs of mutton boiled for dinner—mutton greasy-warm for tea—
Mutton curried (gave my order, beef and plenty greens for me).
Breakfast, curried rice and mutton till your innards sacrifice,
And you sicken at the colour and the very look of rice.
All day long with living mutton—bits and belly-wool and fleece;
Blinded by the yolk of wool, and shirt and trousers stiff with grease,
Till you long for sight of verdure, cabbage-plots and water clear,
And you crave for beef and butter as a boozer craves for beer.

.   .   .   .   .

Dusty patch in baking mulga—glaring iron hut and shed—
Feel and scent of rain forgotten—water scarce, and feed-grass dead.
Hot and suffocating sunrise—all-pervading, sheepyard smell—
Stiff and aching, Greenhand stretches—"Slushy" rings the bullock-bell—
Pint of tea and hunk of brownie—sinners string towards the shed—
Great, black, greasy crows round carcass—screen behind of dust-cloud red.

Engine whistles. "Go it, tigers!" and the agony begins,
Picking up for seven shearers—rushing, sweating for my sins;
Picking up for seven demons, seven devils out of Hell!
Sell their souls to get the bell-sheep—half-a-dozen Christs they'd sell!
Day grows hot as where they come from—too damned hot for men or brutes;
Roof of corrugated iron, six-foot-six above the shoots!

Whiz and rattle and vibration, like an endless chain of trams;
Blasphemy of five-and-forty—prickly heat—and stink of rams!
Barcoo leaves his pen-door open and the sheep come bucking out;
When the rouser goes to pen them, Barcoo blasts the rouseabout.
Injury with insult added—trial of our cursing powers—
Cursed and cursing back enough to damn a dozen worlds like ours.
"Take my combs down to the grinder!" "Seen my (something) cattle-pup?"
"There's a crawler down in my shoot—just slip through and pick it up."

"Give the office when the boss comes." "Catch that gory ram, old man."
"Count the sheep in my pen, will you?" "Fetch my combs back when you can."
"When you get a chance, old fellow, will you pop down to the hut?
Fetch my pipe—the cook'll show you—and I'll let you have a cut."
Shearer yells for tar and needle. Ringer's roaring like a bull:
"Wool away, you (son of angels). Where the hell's the (foundling)?
Wool!"

. . . .

Pound a week and station prices—mustn't kick against the pricks—
Seven weeks of lurid mateship—ruined soul and four pounds six.

. . . . .

What's that? Waiter! *Me?* Stuffed Mutton! Look here, waiter, to be
    brief,
I said beef! you blood-stained villain! Beef—moo-cow—Roast
    Bullock—BEEF!

HIS MAJESTY'S GARDEN SPADE

It was the old King of Virland,
    The monarch of all the land,
Who toiled away through a sunny day
    With a garden spade in his hand.
There was peace in his wide dominions
    For arts and tillage and trade—
He'd won it with something sharper
    Than ever a garden spade.

The old king wiped his forehead,
    And he blew a long breath—so,
As he'd done when the fight was over
    In the warlike long ago.
And he sat close under the ivy,
    And spelled in the dark green shade,
And thought of nought but potatoes
    As he scraped his garden spade.

There stood a knave in the shadow,
    Unsuspecting and unafraid,
With his head through the buttery window
    And his arms round a buttery maid.
He tempted and she resisted—
    To tempt and resist was their trade;
They were all unaware of his majesty
    And his majesty's garden spade.

The old king stood by the ivy
    And listened to every word;
The oath, and the yielding murmur,
    And the plan for the night he heard.
And, were it a boor and a serving wench,
    Or were it a lady and knight,
He wanted his maids to be mated,
    But he wanted them mated right.

So a sudden smack smote the silence,
    And startled both knave and maid:—
'Twas the mighty monarch of Virland,
    And the back of his kingly spade!
The knave swung round with a bad word—
    Then bowed with a knavish mien,
His head bent low to the gravel
    And a hand where the spade had been.

The old king pondered a moment,
    And leaned on his garden spade,
While the other maids ran affrighted
    At the screams of the buttery maid.
The old king paused for a moment,
    Then said with a kingly frown:
"I command you twain to get wedded
    The moment the sun goes down.

"For, be it a boor and a besom,
    Or a lady and knight love-hot,
Though I want strong sons in my kingdom,
    I'll have them honestly got;
That the son on the eve of battle,
    As he lies on the starlit sward,
May think without shame of his mother's name,
    And be proud of his father's sword!"

SIGN OF THE OLD BLACK EYE

When your rifle is lost, and your bayonet too,
    And your mates have all turned tail,
And captain and country are done with you,
    And the prospect is death or gaol—
When the treacherous knife to your throat is raised
    Or the handcuffs held for your wrists—
Then put up a fight with your fists, old man!
    Oh, put up a fight with your fists!

For the sign of a Man since strife began
    (Which nobody can deny),
Of the Man who Won, and the Beaten Man,
    Is the sign of the Old Black Eye.

Oh, the signs of a man, since a man had foes
   To show him the reason why,
Are ever the brand of the Broken Nose
   And the badge of the Blue-Black Eye.

When you're down in the world where you once were up
   (When weather and friends were fair),
And the coat you wear is a lonesome coat,
   And your pants are a lonesome pair,
When the friends who borrowed when luck was good
   All leave you severely alone,
Then put up a fight on your own, Old Man!
   Oh, put up a fight on your own!

You'll need to stand, where the down-track ends,
   With your drink-dulled senses clear,
For you'll get no help from your fine new friends,
   And you'll get no help from beer.
They'll call you a boozer, those Pharisees all,
   And triumph in your disgrace;
But put your back to the nearest wall,
   And strike at the nearest face.

There are friends you helped, when your star was high,
   Who pass you as something strange—
     they drank your beer in the days gone by,
     And they borrowed your careless change!
Though you pass 'em blind, and you pass 'em dumb,
   They'll borrow your cash again,
And they'll drink your wine in the days to come—
   For of such is the world of men.

There were friends that you lost by your own neglect
   In the days of your sinful pride;
There were friends that you lost, with your self-respect,
   Who'd have fought for you side by side.
You'd never have thought it would come to this
   That you battle the world alone—
But swallow the lump in your throat, old man,
   And put up a fight on your own.

There were friends who came with help and advice,
   Ere the days of your folly were spent—
Oh, you wish you had answered the letters they wrote
   And paid back the money they lent!

Think not of the grey-black haze behind,
    Nor the future's lurid mists,
But put up a fight with your fists (so to speak),
    Oh, put up a fight with your fists.

You'll know, when it's done, and the fight you've won—
    And won on your lonesome own—
That a man climbs up with a host of friends,
    But always goes down alone.
But you'll laugh at it all when they chair you in,
    As they did in the days gone by,
And they'll chuckle and grin, and drink to your win,
    At the Sign of the Old Black Eye.

AUSTRALIAN BARDS AND BUSH REVIEWERS

WHILE you use your best endeavour to immortalize in verse
The gambling and the drink which are your country's greatest curse,
While you glorify the bully and you take the spieler's part—
You're a clever southern writer, scarce inferior to Bret Harte.

If you sing of waving grasses when the plains are dry as bricks,
And discover shining rivers where there's only mud and sticks;
If you picture mighty forests where the mulga spoils the view—
You're superior to Kendall, and ahead of Gordon too.

If you swear there's not a country like the land that gave you birth,
And its sons are just the noblest and most glorious chaps on earth;
If in every girl a Venus your poetic eye discerns—
You are gracefully referred to as the "Young Australian Burns".

But should you find that Bushmen—spite of all the poets say—
Are just common brother-sinners, and you're quite as good as they—
You're a drunkard, and a liar, and a cynic, and a sneak,
Your grammar's simply awful, and your intellect is weak.

SONG OF THE BACK TO FRONT

The Finn stokes well in the hot Red Sea, where the fireman cooks his soul;
And the played-out sons of a warm country went farthest towards the Pole.
The grief is oft to the topside pup—and the dux drops out of the hunt—
And—this is the song of the downside up, and a song of the back to front.

Oh! this is the way that it all began since first on one end we trod.
The short girl yearns for the six-foot man, and the long for the four-foot-odd;
Yet this is the way that it all began (or my point is misunderstood),
The good girl loveth the bad, bad man, and the bad girl loves the good.

The thin girl seeketh the stout boy oft when the slight boy's there to win;
And often the man who is fat and soft gets roped by the hard and thin.
The slave-wife loveth her "boss" and house, and everything seems to suit,
And the pampered wife leaves a generous spouse and sticks to a drunken brute.

The woman says "Yes" when she meaneth "No", and "No" when she meaneth "Yes";
But the blithering fool who would take her so is about to fall in, I guess.
The mother sticks fast to the worthless one who treateth her with contempt,
And often she hateth the good old son of whose fondness she never dreamt.

The low comedian's glum off-stage, and the heavy tragedian's gay;
With the artist or poet, in print or page, 'tis ever the selfsame way.
The fool looks wise, and the wise a fool, and the candid soul looks sly;
The smart and the cunning is oft the tool that the plain and the simple ply.

S

The weeds go through where the strong men fail—be it office, desert
   or trench,
And the fattest coward in England's tale brought tucker slap
   through the French!
The coward dies for his king and gods, and he throws his men away,
But the brave man runs from the doubtful odds—that his foe may
   run next day.

The pig is clean, and the bulldog kind, but the man is a brute or
   hog.
'Tis starve, sty, or bludgeon, you'll mostly find, that spoileth man,
   pig, and dog.
The poet is generous, noble and clean, and singeth by day and
   night,
But the Edit—or Publisher—Woddidimean?—well, I didn't mean
   that way quite.
***——!——!——!!—— —— all right —!!—— But I didn't—mean
   —thatwayquite.

FROM THE FOOT OF THE STAIRS:
The Low is Up, and the Great is Down—and——
   (*Now-I'm-goin'-quietly-don't-you-lay-a-hand-on-me*)

OUTSIDE:
——and the scissoring fool is wise—
   (*All right, Constable!*)

BY TELEPHONE:
The cur must run, but the hound can wait, and——
   (*cut off*)

BY POST:
——and the *Bulletin*'s mostly lies.

BECAUSE OF HER FATHER'S BLOOD

SIR William was gone to the Wars again,
   That went through the world at large,
And he left the Keep with some forty men,
   And his aunt, Dame Ruth, in charge.
The soldiers swore, and each knave looked grave,
   And the maids shed tears in a flood,
For a fearsome mistress she was to serve,
   Because of her father's blood.

There was never a smile on her grim old mouth,
    Nor a tear in her hard old eye,
For her mincing days and her simpering days
    And her tearful days were by.
There was never a siege-starved horse so gaunt,
    Nor a camel's face less fair;
But no court lady could gaze her down
    And never a knight out-swear.

Sir William had been but a year away,
    And the land was a land of woe,
When the outlaw Marr came down from afar
    With a hundred men or so.
He cooped us up with the country folk,
    And he was a cur in truth;
He knew that the knight was not there to fight—
    But he had not met Dame Ruth.

He gathered the cattle and gathered the grain,
    And he promised to let us be,
But he'd heard of gold in the oak-chest old,
    So he sent for his outlaw's fee.
We gathered like sheep in the castle keep,
    And an angry old dame was there:
Oh, we feared Dame Ruth with a tenfold fear
    On the days when she did not swear.

When she felt too much. "Outnumbered?" she cried;
    "Ye slime, and the spawn of slime!—
Would a Marr for a day in the Westland bide
    In my father's father's time?
There are forked things left that can stand upright,
    But no *men* left in the land—
Must I carry you forth? hold your blades in the fight
    Like a spoon in a baby's hand?"

So we got us out through the eastern gate,
    And down through the old oak-trees,
Till, backward borne in the wintry morn,
    We fought them by twos and threes.
We'd gathered to win to the gate again—
    The gate of our grim despair—
When Gurth, who fought on my right hand, cried,
    With a backward glance, "Look there!"

Heels first in retreat—for they pressed us close—
    Just time to glance back through the trees—
And she sat on her horse on the top of the knoll
    With her ragged grey hair in the breeze.
Her old house-gown was the armour she wore,
    And her old grey hair the crest,
And a long, tough whip on the pommel she bore,
    And—we did not look for the rest.

Her screech was heard in the startled land,
    And the outlaws paused in affright
As she spurred her down to her gallant band,
    Crying "Fight! ye scullions! Fight!"
Then Gurth drew sword when his shaft was sped
    (And he was a mettlesome youth),
"I'll face them one to a dozen," he said,
    "But I will not face Dame Ruth."

The outlaws halted like stricken men
    Who stand ere they strike the sod—
They believed in warlocks and witches then
    Far more than they did in God.
We drove them clear and we chased them far,
    And we left a few in the mud,
And she hanged a few in the old oak-trees
    Because of her father's blood.

There was never a tear in her hard old eyes,
    On her grim face never a smile;
But she bound our wounds with her claw-like hands
    And swore at the maids the while,
But all of us knew, of her battered crew,
    As we grinned and winked aside,
That her bony old fingers trembled at times,
    And the oaths were to hide her pride.

WHEN THERE'S TROUBLE ON YOUR MIND

Now I do not want to bore you, or to take up too much time
When your nose is on the grindstone and to lift it seems a crime;
But in spite of all your wisdom you will nearly always find
That there's one you like to talk to when there's trouble on your mind.
            Never mind.
If it's Gaol, or Corns, or Toothache that's the trouble on your mind.

And he'll grip your hand a moment, and he'll beckon silently
To the waiter or the barmaid, as the case may chance to be;
And he'll signal you to light up—and you'll mostly always find
At this early stage the trouble seems much lighter on your mind.
            Why, you'll find
That 'twill cost you quite an effort for to keep it on your mind!

"I've been there!" he says, and fills up—or he only says "Same here",
And the humour of it strikes you as your head begins to clear.
And you say no more about it, for you see that you've been blind:
It was Nothing! Have another! Damn the trouble on your mind!
            Weren't you blind!
Why, there wasn't any trouble—it was just your silly mind!

And he grins the grin of sorrow as he sees you home to bed,
And you even cease to wonder what was bothering your head.
Let the godly cant and snuffle, and the shallow cynic scoff,
But the grandest thing in this world is the grin that won't come off—
            Won't wash off;
It may fade at times a little, but (in public) won't come off.

No, it won't come off in public when the world is there to see,
And it won't come off in private when there's only you and me.
You may shift it for a moment when you're sure you're quite alone,
Just to clasp your head in trouble, and to shed a tear and groan—
            Just one groan,
For you cannot always wear it when you're sure you're quite alone.

Man was always, for his comfort, just a worry-making brute;
When you've just escaped the gallows, then your corns begin to shoot.
When you're clear of debt or doctors, and the wolf has left your throat,

Then you find the time to worry at the fit of your new coat.
                (That damned tailor!)
Why is man for ever haunted by the fit of his new coat?

When the future's fair before him and when things are all serene,
Then he'll think of years he wasted and the man he might have been.
Why! we might have all been married, and been living with our wives,
With a world of things to worry and to irritate our lives—
                Just like knives,
And our grown-up children at us, backed up blindly by our wives.

Or he thinks about his boyhood, and he mourns his vanished Youth—
Now, who would live his life again, or face it? Tell the truth.
I am mighty glad *my* boyhood and *my* youth are far away—
I am in the straight for Fifty—and grow younger every day;
                Drink and play,
And I grow more interested in a woman every day.

Death is nothing! We're immortal—that's the blessing—or the curse:
But whate'er the further future, I am sure it can't be worse.
We shall live again in this world through the centuries to come,
And, should I return a woman, oh, I'll make it warm for some!
                Make things hum—
Breach o' Promise—Alimony—Oh, *I'll* score in times to come.

But the main thing for the present is just only to be kind—
You can always hear the scandal, but you don't know what's behind.
Take what friends can give in friendship, and pass on what you can get;
And, while jokes or kindly words can cheer, your life's not wasted yet—
                Never fret!
While a friend's in need of cheering, life is full of interest yet.

MY LITERARY FRIEND

Once I wrote a little poem that I thought was very fine,
And I showed the printer's copy to a critic friend of mine,
First he praised the thing a little, then he found a little fault;
"The ideas are good," he muttered, "but the rhythm seems to halt."

So I straightened up the rhythm where he marked it with his pen,
And I copied it and showed it to my clever friend again,
"You've improved the metre greatly, but the rhymes are bad," he said
As he read it slowly, scratching surplus wisdom from his head.

So I worked as he suggested (I believe in taking time),
And I burnt the midnight paper while I straightened up the rhyme.
"It is better now," he muttered, "you go on and you'll succeed,
It has got a ring about it—the ideas are what you need."

So I worked for hours upon it (I go on when I commence)
And I kept in view the rhythm and the jingle and the sense,
And I copied it and took it to my solemn friend once more—
It reminded him of something he had somewhere read before!

Now the people say I'd never put such horrors into print
If I wasn't too conceited to accept a friendly hint,
And my dearest friends are certain that I'd profit in the end
If I'd always show my copy to a literary friend.

DOGS OF WAR

Comes the British bulldog first—solid as a log—
He's so ugly in repose that he's a handsome dog;
Full of mild benevolence as his years increase;
Silent as a china dog on the mantelpiece.
    Rub his sides and point his nose,
    Click your tongue and in he goes,
    To the thick of Britain's foes—
    Enemies behind him close—
    (Silence for a while).

Comes a very different dog—tell him at a glance.
Clipped and trimmed and frilled all round, dandy
    dog of France
(Always was a dandy dog, no matter what his age);
Now his every hair and frill is stiff as wire with rage.
    Rub his sides and point his nose,
    Click your tongue and in he goes,
    While behind him France's foes
    Reel and surge and pack and close.

Next comes Belgium's market-dog—hard to realize—
Go-cart dog and barrow dog; he's a great surprise.
Dog that never hurt a cat, did no person harm;
Friendly, kindly, round, and fat as a Johnny Darm.
    Rub his sides and point his nose,
    Click your tongue and in he goes,
    At the flank of Belgium's foes
    Who could *not* behind him close.

Next comes Servia's mongrel pup—mongrel dogs can fight;
Up or down, or down or up, whether wrong or right.
He was mad the other day—he is mad today,
Hustling round and raising dust in his backyard way.
    Rub his sides and point his nose,
    Click your tongue and in he goes,
    'Twixt the legs of Servia's foes,
    Biting tails and rearmost toes.

There are various terrier dogs mixed up in the scrap,
Much too small for us to see, much too mad to yap.
Each one, on his frantic own, heard the row commence,
Tore with tooth and claw a hole in the backyard fence.
    No one called, but in they go,
    Dogs with many a nameless woe,
    Tripping up their common foe—
    (Uproar for a while).

From the snows of Canada, dragging box and bale,
Comes the sledge-dog toiling on, sore-foot from the trail.
He'll be useful in the trench, when the nose is blue—
Winter dog that knows the French and the English too.
    Rub his sides and point his nose,
    Click your tongue and in he goes,
    At his father's country's foes,
    And his mother's country's foes.

See, there comes to sunny France a dog that runs by sight,
Lean and yellow, sharp of nose, long of leg and light,
Silent and bloodthirsty, too; Distance in his eyes,
Leaping high to gain his view, the kangaroo-dog flies!

Rub his sides and point his nose,
Click your tongue and up he goes,
Lands amongst his country's foes—
And his country's country's foes;
While they sway and while they close—
(Silence for a while).

BUT WHAT'S THE USE

But what's the use of writing "bush",
   Though editors demand it?—
For city folk, and farming folk,
   Can never understand it.
They're blind to what the bushman sees
   The best with eyes shut tightest,
Out where the sun is hottest and
   The stars are at their brightest.

The crows at sunrise flopping round
   Where some poor life has run down;
The pair of emus trotting from
   The lonely tank at sundown,
Their snaky heads well up, and eyes
   Alert to man's manoeuvres,
And feathers bobbing round behind
   Like fringes round "improvers".

The swagman tramping o'er the plain—
   Good Lord, there's nothing sadder,
Except the dog that lopes behind
   His master like a shadder!
The turkey-tail to scare the flies,
   The water-bag and billy;
The nose-bag getting cruel light,
   The traveller getting silly.

The joy and hope the swagman feels
   Returning, after shearing,
Or when, from six months' tramp Out Back,
   He strikes the final clearing.
His weary spirit breathes again,
   His aching legs seem limber
When to the East across the plain
   He spots the Darling Timber!

But what's the use of writing bush,
    They do not understand it.
For city folk, and cockatoos,
    Though editors demand it?—
They're blind to what the bushman sees
    The best with eyes shut tightest,
Out where Australia's widest, and
    The stars are at their brightest.

SONG OF
GENERAL SICK-AND-TIREDNESS

I'm tired of raving at wrong things which must still to the end endure;
I'm sick and tired of the selfish rich, and I'm tired of the selfish poor.
Of the awful wrongs of the Social Plan (both sides, and in between)—
I'm tired of the *Bulletin*'s own Fat Man, and I'm also tired of the Lean.

Tis a weariness born of twenty years of wrestling with truth and lies,
And of writing on rum and in blood-stained tears, that the People might wake and arise!
I am wild, damned wild, at the wages paid for fighting with Freedom's Foes,
And the awful blunders the people made when at last they awoke and rose.

The motor-car is the Car of Greed, and I've often written it down
(With little effect, I fear, indeed, for I notice it still in town);
But now I'm tired of the Goggled Hog, and his veiled, contemptuous "tart".
I am also weary of Boko Bill and his fruit and bottle-oh! cart.

I'm weary of Clara Vere de Vere, and her bloque at the Grand Hotel,
And the Orphan Girl and the Orphan Boy—and their mother and father as well.
I'm tired of the languid Potts Point dames, and their lovers give me a pain—
I'm also disgusted with One-eyed Kate and her bloke in Red Rock Lane.

My soul is sad for the young bards here who rave of a Wrong
    Red-hot,
And care not a curse, so they get their beer, if the people starve
    or not.
With a fine contempt for the grave and tomb and the old books on
    the shelves,
They gibe and sneer at an old bard's gloom—and proceed to shed
    tears themselves.

I'm tired of the cruel, bleeding welt on the Young Heart tempest-
    tost;
Likewise of the love that we never felt, and the friend that we
    never lost.
I'm tired of long white limbs, small head, and eyes of unearthly hue;
Of the Bride, rose-red in her bridal bed—and I'm sick of the
    Bridegroom, too.

I'm tired—oh, I'm tired—of the Bleeding Heart of the bride who
    never was wed;
Of the girls that rave o'er the blood-stained grave of a lover who
    never was dead;
Of the wronged young wife, and her Blighted Life; not to mention
    the locket worn
With the Golden Curl from the head of the girl or the babe that
    never was born.

To resume:
I'm scared of the great Strong Arms and the Breast, and the Brute
    Force under control;
Of the Gloomy Eyes, and the head, and the rest—and the Hidden
    Heart and Soul—
Of the Muscle and Tan of the awful Man that our girl-bards rave
    about,
The first of his kind since the world began (but why don't they
    trot him out?)

Of the Swooning Love, 'neath the stars above, and the Slumbrous
    Burning Eyes;
Of the blast of scorn from our Bards of Morn, and our girl-bards'
    "Damn" likewise
(And let it be said, ere I go to bed, lest you curse me needlessly,
That I do not moan for these things alone—for I'm also tired of
    Me).

To proceed:

I'm sick of the sight of the One Lone White in the islands far away,
Who is jabbed with a poisoned spear by night, and pots the whole tribe next day;
Of the Clubman dead to the world he knew, and long by his love forgot,
And the innocent swims with the Lithe Brown Limbs, and—the rest of the Thomas Rot.

He's mostly a thin brown man in drill and specs—for his sight is dim—
And a score of niggers to work his will, and Ah Soon to cook for him,
With a steamer in sight—and a drunken white—and the rest of the world within hail,
A wife—or the pick of the native girls—and his fairly regular mail.)

And now to conclude:

I'm tired of the Love of a Bygone Day, of women and dice and wine—
You'll find, when his Washup has had his say, it's the Missus that pays the fine.
I'm tired of the sneering at friendship, too—for you'll find in the end, no doubt,
When you get run in, and the world looks blue there'll be *one* to bail you out.

You may shriek to high heaven of Love and Death, and howl of a Soul in Pain.
You may curse the Gods with your Latest Breath till the cows come home again;
But Dad plods home from his work at night, in his bosom a peace profound,
To his bustling wife and her kitchen bright—and *they* help the world go round.

You may rant and rave of your Fancy Loves that go by your fancy names,
But the bread you eat and the bills you meet are fixed by Lizzie and James.
You may ode your Gladyses, Enids, Pearls in a high Parnassian style—
But Lucy, and Mary, and Jack, and Fred—'tis they that make life worth while.

INDEX TO FIRST LINES

A cloud of dust on the long, white road,	49
A day of seeming innocence,	65
A dusty clearing in the scrubs	150
A lonely young wife	110
A long farewell to Genoa,	117
A public parlour in the slums,	123
A rouseabout of rouseabouts, from any land—or none—	43
A son of elder sons am I	81
A tall, slight, English gentleman	42
Above the ashes straight and tall,	17
Across the stony ridges,	62
Ah, well! but the case seems hopeless, and the pen might write in vain;	177
All is well—in a prison—tonight, and the warders are crying, "All's well!"	140
An hour before the sun goes down	57
As the night was falling slowly down on city, town, and bush,	202
At suburban railway stations—you may see them as you pass—	126
At Windsor Terrace, Number Four	215
Bill and Jim are mates no longer—they would scorn the name of mate—	196
But what's the use of writing "bush",	265
By homestead, hut, and shearing-shed,	86
By our place in the midst of the farthest seas we are fated to stand alone—	128
Call this hot? I beg your pardon. Hot!—you don't know what it means.	251
Comes the British bulldog first—solid as a log—	263
Day of ending for beginnings!	139
Did you hear the children singing, O my brothers?	81
Down here, where the ships loom large in	25
Down the street as I was drifting with the city's human tide,	180
Dust and smoke against the sunrise out where grim disaster lurks	161
Dust, dust, dust and a dog—	249
Far back in the days when the blacks used to ramble	95
Fight through ignorance, want, and care—	149
Fire lighted; on the table a meal for sleepy men;	30
Grown tired of mourning for my sins—	189
Have you seen the Bush by moonlight, from the train, go running by,	37
He comes from out the ages dim—	99
He had offices in Sydney, not so many years ago,	73
He has notions of Australia from the tales that he's been told—	230
He may not ride as you can ride,	105
He never drew a sword to fight a dozen foes alone,	191
He shall live to the end of this mad old world as he's lived since the world began;	45
His old clay pipe stuck in his mouth,	204
I am back from up the country—very sorry that I went	207
I gaze upon my son once more	28

I listened through the music and the sounds of revelry,	104
I met her on the Lachlan-side—	244
I met him in Bourke in the Union days—with which we have nought to do	200
I met Jack Ellis in town today—	14
I met with Jack Cornstalk in London today,	235
I saw her first from a painful bed,	231
If I ever be worthy or famous—	87
If you fancy that your people came of better stock than mine,	163
I'm lyin' on the barren ground that's baked and cracked with drought,	85
I'm tired of raving at wrong things which must still to the end endure;	266
In the parlour of the shanty where the lives have all gone wrong,	236
It chanced upon the very day we'd got the shearing done,	23
It is stuffy in the steerage where the second-classers sleep,	90
It was a week from Christmas-time,	185
It was built of bark and poles, and the roof was full of holes	184
It was pleasant up the country, City Bushman, where you went,	226
It was somewhere in September, and the sun was going down,	16
It was the old King of Virland,	253
I've done with joys an' misery,	225
I've followed all my tracks and ways, from old bark school to Leicester Square;	134
I've not seen a picnic for many a day,	89
Jack Denver died on Talbragar when Christmas Eve began,	70
James Patrick O'Hara, the Justice of Peace,	193
Long Bill, the captain of the push, was tired of his estate,	187
My army, O my army! The time I dreamed of comes!	68
No church-bell rings them from the Track,	103
Now I do not want to bore you, or to take up too much time	261
Now, I think there is a likeness	222
Now this is not a dismal song, like some I've sung of late	111
Now up and down the sidling brown	18
Oh, I dreamt I shore in a shearin'-shed, and it was a dream of joy,	242
Oh, my ways are strange ways and new ways and old ways,	8
Oh, Scotty, have you visited the Picture Gallery,	241
Oh, this is a song of the old lights that came to my heart like a hymn;	240
Old Ivan McIvanovitch, with knitted brow of care,	243
Old Mate! In the gusty old weather,	92
Old Time is tramping close today—you hear his bluchers fall,	214
On the runs to the west of the Dingo Scrub there was drought, and ruin, and death,	121
On western plain and eastern hill,	114
Once I wrote a little poem that I thought was very fine,	262
Once more I write a line to you,	159
One day old Trooper Campbell	77
Only one old post is standing—	133
Our Andy's gone with cattle now—	44
Out there by the rocks, at the end of the bank,	53
Out West, where the stars are brightest,	53
Rise ye! rise ye! noble toilers! claim your rights with fire and steel	211
Roll up, Eureka's heroes, on that Grand Old Rush afar,	118

Set me back for twenty summers,	72
She says she's "very sorry", as she sees you to the gate;	192
She's England yet! The nations never knew her;	61
Sir William was gone to the Wars again,	258
So, sit you down in a straight-backed chair, with your pipe and your wife content,	153
So the days of my riding are over,	60
So you rode from the range where your brothers "select",	172
So you're writing for a paper? Well, it's nothing very new	106
Some born of homely parents	170
Some carry their swags in the Great North-west,	158
Spirit girl, to whom 'twas given	102
Tall and freckled and sandy,	31
Tall, and stout, and solid-looking,	21
Ten miles down Reedy River	40
Texas Jack, you are amusin'. Great Lord Harry, how I laughed	223
The big rough boys from the runs Out Back were first where the balls flew free,	237
The boy cleared out to the city from his home at the harvest time—	55
The breezes waved the silver grass,	208
The brooding ghosts of Australian night have gone from the bush and town;	64
The Captains sailed from Portugal, from England, France, and Spain;	113
The channel fog has lifted	164
The colours of the setting sun	1
The cool breeze ripples the river below,	112
The creek went down with a broken song,	77
The diggings were just in their glory when Alister Cameron came,	115
The Eagle screams at the beck of Trade; so Spain, as the world goes round,	124
The East is dead and the West is done, and again our course lies thus:—	169
The Finn stokes well in the hot Red Sea, where the fireman cooks his soul;	257
"The ladies are coming," the super says	38
The mighty King of Virland	97
The night too quickly passes	9
The old Jimmy Woodser comes into the bar	175
The old year went, and the new returned, in the withering weeks of drought:	55
The plains lay bare on the homeward route,	125
The rafters are open to sun, moon, and star	166
The shipping-office clerks are "short", the manager is gruff—	250
The skies are brass and the plains are bare,	98
The squatter saw his pastures wide	154
The valley's full of misty clouds,	70
The world has had enough of bards who wish that they were dead,	247
The world is narrow and ways are short, and our lives are dull and slow,	50
There are scenes in the distance where beauty is not,	178
There was a young woman, as I've heard tell	209
There were ten of us there on the moonlit quay,	127
There's a class of men (and women) who are always on their guard—	160

There's a thing that sends a lump to my throat,	136
There's a wind that blows out of the South in the drought,	59
They can't hear in West o' London, where the worst dine with the best—	137
They lie, the men who tell us, for reasons of their own,	5
They say, in all kindness, I'm out of the hunt—	68
They say that I never have written of love,	179
They stood by the door of the Inn on the Rise;	27
They were ratty—they were hooted by the meanest and the least,	121
They'd parted just a year ago—she thought he'd ne'er come back;	206
Though poor and in trouble I wander alone,	176
Three bushmen one morning rode up to an inn,	39
'Tis a wonderful time when these hours begin	112
Turn the light down, nurse, and leave me, while I hold my last review,	181
'Twixt the coastline and the border lay the town of Grog-an'-Grumble	248
We boast no more of our bloodless flag that rose from a nation's slime;	2
We knew too little of the world,	165
We throw ourselves down on the dusty plain	168
We tried to get over the Bar today,	47
Weary old wife, with the bucket and cow,	120
When God's wrath-cloud is o'er me,	130
When I was up the country in the rough and early days,	212
When in charge of a rough and unpopular shed,	188
When the caravans of wool-teams climbed the ranges from the West,	245
When the heavy sand is yielding backward from your blistered feet,	93
When the kindly hours of darkness, save for light of moon and star,	236
When you wear a cloudy collar and a shirt that isn't white,	48
When your rifle is lost, and your bayonet too,	254
When you've come to make a fortune and you haven't made your salt,	157
When you've knocked about the country—been away from home for years;	221
Where's the steward?—Bar-room steward! Berth? Oh, any berth will do—	20
While you use your best endeavour to immortalize in verse	256
White handkerchiefs wave from the short black pier	11
Wide, solemn eyes that question me,	36
With eyes that are narrowed to pierce	162
With pannikins all rusty,	94
With the frame of a man and the face of a boy, and a manner strangely wild,	32
Ye children of the Land of Gold,	197
You almost heard the surface bake, and saw the gum-leaves turn—	173
You lazy boy, you're here at last,	229
You love me, you say, and I think you do	158
You may roam the wide seas over, follow, meet, and cross the sun,	166